THE
OCTOBER TWELVE

THE OCTOBER TWELVE

FIVE YEARS OF YANKEE GLORY 1949–1953

PHIL RIZZUTO

WITH TOM HORTON

A TOM DOHERTY ASSOCIATES BOOK
NEW YORK

THE OCTOBER TWELVE

Copyright © 1994, 1999 by Phil Rizzuto and Tom Horton

This book is printed on acid-free paper.

A Forge Book
Published by Tom Doherty Associates, LLC
175 Fifth Avenue
New York, N.Y. 10010

Forge® is a registered trademark of Tom Doherty Associates, LLC

Design by Michael Mendelsohn, MM Design 2000, Inc.

Library of Congress Cataloging-in-Publication Data

Rizzuto, Phil.
    The October twelve : five years of Yankee glory—1949–1953 / Phil Rizzuto and Tom Horton.
        p.   cm.
    "A Tom Doherty Associates Book."
    ISBN 0–312–86991–6
    1. New York Yankees (Baseball team)—History.   I. Horton, Tom, 1938–   .   II. Title.   III. Title: October 12.
GV875.N4R49   1994
796.357'64'097471—dc20   94–1576
                                                            CIP

First edition: May 1994
First mass market edition: March 1995
First trade paperback edition: September 1999

Printed in the United States of America

0 9 8 7 6 5 4 3 2 1

CONTENTS

ACKNOWLEDGMENTS

After you read this you should know why I must thank the other eleven men. So many people helped me along the way that to list them would put you to sleep and tax my memory, but I know in my heart they know I cared and am grateful.

—PFR

Ann was her usual sainted self. Marcia Jane, so tough but fair the last time, was busy with far more important issues, her firstborn and executive editorial duties with Prentice Hall, so I was spared her red pencil. Karen delivered Elena Christensen Ruiz in May of 1992 and became a baseball fan while giving guidance to her father like a midwife. Lee Ann, the best baseball fan in my family believed in me from the time she first played catch with me in the backyard. She was eight when she said, "Maybe you should write about baseball and not throw one."

Tom Quinn, who worked with me on my last book, and, how nice to write the words, is now a valued friend.

Bob Gleason, my shepherd on this journey, a serious Yankee fan from Gary, Indiana. A special man involved in a labor of re-

9

spect, affection, and awe. Bill Bryden's name might well be on the cover. Joe Jordan demanded that his appear, but we worked it out on the courthouse steps.

Daniel and Peter are not sure what I do when I am lucky enough to get an assignment like this, but they want one when they grow up. Which will be soon enough. So as well Patrick, Grace, Elena, Natalie and Jacob.

Don Zimmer and Phil Garner didn't have a thing to do with this book but they are both on my short hero list, so I include them with joy. Ed Robson's understanding of *schadenfreude* is only the first indication of his wisdom. Being blessed with three daughters made it possible for me to treasure the care and concern of Anna Magee and Camille Cline of Tor. Marge Wiley, another great lady, helped me understand the infield fly rule.

Buster, Shirley, and Melissa, your pleasure in all this means a whole lot. Matthew Taylor, please read this to your mom.

—TNH

THE
OCTOBER TWELVE

INTRODUCTION

BY YOGI BERRA

On December 7, 1993, Phil Rizzuto and I were driving up the New Jersey Turnpike talking, looking out for the eighteen-wheel trucks speeding by us, chatting the way grandfathers do when they get together. When I was catching for the New York Yankees and he was playing short, Phil always, I mean every time, let me know if he was going to cover second base. The last thing a player in the field wants is a surprise. The attack on Pearl Harbor on that same day in 1941 was an awful event made even worse because it came as a surprise. We talked about where we had been and of the changes it had made in our lives, all of our lives.

Gramps Rizzuto and I didn't spring any surprises that day in December on the New Jersey Turnpike. Not even pictures of a grandchild. I had some but was going to let Phil go first. We talked about his kids, and mine: I have three sons and he has three daughters and a son. We spoke about how our son-in-law and daughter-in-law setups are different. Like we pitched Ted Williams one way in Boston's Fenway Park and another way in Yankee Stadium. I am not going to go into the details of the conversation about our families for two reasons. First, I don't want to bore anyone, and if you are a grandparent or an in-law you will know what I am talking about.

Rolling along faster than the trains we used to ride on when we first played for the Yankees, we talked, not as much as you might expect, about what it was like "back then." We did touch on a few things that may interest the reader of this book, and I was asked to put them down. The value of the train trips we took cannot be overrated. Baseball teams were closer then than now, and the trains were an important reason. We would talk about the series we just played and the one coming up. Most of the time we got together in Joe DiMaggio's roomette. It was not an official meeting, or even the official place to meet. It just worked out that way. If you were on the team, you were welcome, and if you didn't feel welcome, it was your fault. We learned more baseball on the train than we did in the dugout. Lasting friendships still going today were started on those trains. Phil and I even started a business, a bowling alley we owned together, while on a train trip from Chicago. We had beaten the White Sox four straight and were feeling like a pair of tycoons.

After we paid a toll and wondered if the toll collector was one of the collectors making $70,000 a year, we got to talking about readers of *The October Twelve* who never saw anyone on that team play. If you never saw Joe DiMaggio track down a ball in center field, you missed a thrill—maybe forever. I saw some good men in center field; maybe some that were even better at catching a ball than Joe. Terry Moore of the Cards may have been one and Willie Mays and Jimmy Piersall might have been two more, but no one looked as good as Joe doing it. Joe was the best ballplayer I ever saw, and Ted Williams was the best hitter. If I have one memory of Joe it is of him running after he hit a ball to center and taking an extra base if the other team's outfielder did not make a perfect catch and throw. Just let someone like Vic Wertz of the Tigers or Wally Moses of the Philadelphia A's or Gil Coan of the Washington Senators bobble the ball. Not an error, maybe just a hitch. Such a tiny miscue, it would have to be looked at in a replay, which we didn't have in those days. When you looked up, Joe D took a base on you. The other teams got to know that and quickly. Once they knew it, and word spread around the league like wildfire, Joe could take the extra base while they were thinking about what had happened the last time.

Allie Reynolds said he pitched to "the whole string of them," meaning the other team's lineup. Joe did the same thing in his way to the other twenty-five outfielders in the American League—we had eight teams at the time, so the other seven teams had about that many men playing in the outfield. As the catcher, I had a good spot to watch Joe. I am sorry I can't show you the pictures in my mind. The pictures and the memories of the eleven other men lucky enough to be on that team and of all the other Yankees who shared in the special time will be with me always. Always is a long time.

I didn't play with Babe Ruth, but Frank Crosetti did. Then he coached third base long enough to see Joe D leave and Mickey come on like something shot out of some kind of ray gun. Frank helped make Bobby Brown and Jerry Coleman as good as they were and he had the good sense not to fool with Gene Woodling's batting stance. He did everything he did, all the while in the shadow of Casey Stengel. Frank Crosetti. Now there is a man with some pictures in his head. Something else as well. He wore number 2 on his back but he had integrity inscribed on him like a tattoo.

I don't want to go back to 1949. Maybe because as different as some people think I am, I know I can't. But I do treasure the time spent. It sure beat working in the shoe factory in St. Louis. I made good shoes, but it was a job. Baseball was never work. Never.

Way too much is said about what I said or didn't say. Somebody sent me a page from *The New Yorker* (July 1991) with this statement underlined, "Hardly anybody would quarrel . . . that Winston Churchill has been replaced by Yogi Berra as the . . . favorite source of quotations." I can't think of a better reason to question what you read, anything you read. In the first place, how would you go about proving it? I was in a boat off the French Coast on D day. Thousands of men died that day and Winston Churchill was one of the important leaders of the free world. To tell the truth I am not only sorry *The New Yorker* printed the comment, but that someone sent it to me. I am pleased to have a chance to say what I just did here.

When Bob Gleason, this book's editor, asked me to do this he didn't count on my ending it on a heavy note, so I won't. Someone sent me a videotape of Harry Smith of CBS interviewing Mickey Mantle and me on the CBS morning show. Harry asked me if I had said several things. "It ain't over 'til it's over" was one. I explained and then Mickey chimed in, even though I have been interviewed enough to know that Harry Smith thought the interview was over. Mickey was in a good mood because I don't like to be around people that are not in good moods. It rubs off. Besides, Mickey, Whitey Ford and a lot of those guys, guys like the twelve guys in this book, have a lot of fun at my expense. I don't mind and by now I have come to expect it from almost all those old guys. Better them than someone I just met at a cocktail party. One time, and I have wished I could remember who and where, one of the NY Met players stuck the needle in pretty good, and because I had just finished a cat food commercial, I said, "I may not be as bright as you but I got a nice check for talking to a cat." To get back to Harry Smith and Mantle, Harry was having a good time, so he figured the people watching were and he let the interview play out even though, as I said, a young woman was looking at Harry and putting her hand up to her throat, like you might if you wanted to show up an umpire. A sure way to get run out of the game. Mickey said, "The best thing Yogi ever said he said in my restaurant when his book came out. When the press started asking questions the first one was, 'What's your book about, Yogi?' Yogi said, 'I don't know, I haven't read it.' " We all laughed and I suppose people watching laughed too. But Mickey was wrong—it didn't happen in his place, it happened in Sardi's on 53rd Street. Arlene Francis was doing a radio interview show and was nice enough to ask me to be her guest. My wife Carmen and I both know Arlene. Not really know her, but we have been with her enough to know how sharp she is.

She greeted me warmly and I felt like I was in her home and not on a tiny stage in a restaurant in midtown Manhattan. She asked me some questions about the book *Yogi It Ain't Over*, and I thought I did a pretty good job of giving more than a yes or no answer. Interviewers hate them. I remember one question was something about Jerry Coleman and I thought I did OK with it. The first time she broke for a commercial, and I said she was sharp, she looked right at me and asked in a very pleasant voice, "Yogi, have you read this?" Wanting to stick to my full-swing answers, I said, "No. Why should I? I was there." It brought the house down, and *USA Today* wrote about it and maybe some other papers. But it was true. I spent a lot of time working with the guy who wrote the book. I trusted him or else he wouldn't have gotten the job. I knew what I had told him about what I said to Allie Reynolds after I dropped Ted Williams's pop-up in the last inning of his second no-hitter in 1951. Why would I want to read about it? I would rather read about a new Ping driver, or who was going to coach third base for the Yankees next year. Phil's book about twelve guys and the joy of that run, and I knew it at the time even more than some of the others, now that's a different kettle of fish. It's like doing it all over again, without having to take a shower. They say I said, "Nobody goes there anymore, it's too crowded," and I did. It was a place in St. Louis we used to go to before it got too busy. Nobody can go back as well as Phil to those five World Series championships. He was the only one to play in every game of the twenty-eight that made it possible, and he likes to talk. In fact, he never shuts up. Little guys are like that.

—Yogi Berra
Montclair, New Jersey
March 1994

THE TWELVE

"A diamond is forever." Ad people tell me those four words are the best advertising copy ever written. The diamond I played on as a kid in Brooklyn and the one in Bassett, Virginia, and the ones in Kansas City and Norfolk and Pearl Harbor, and the crown jewel of all the diamonds, Yankee Stadium in the Bronx, are forever for me.

Forever in my mind, for sure.

If you counted the games I played in Yankee Stadium and the games I broadcast from Yankee Stadium, they would add up to a lot. A great big bunch that you could tie up with a bright ribbon and put on a shelf along with me. Except that I am not ready for that yet, thank you. "Bonding" and "maven" are George Will words (I read his column) and as far as the New York Yankees are concerned, the Scooter is bonded. As for maven, if I am not a Yankee maven after all these years, you are not likely to come across one. My great old friend, Yogi Berra (he is old, and a great friend), would not use bonded or maven, but he would put his own stamp on my Yankee tenure: "Rizzuto's been going to Yankee Stadium for fifty-three years. And he is still trying to find a way to beat the toll on the George Washington Bridge."

19

This book is about five of those years and eleven other players. THE OCTOBER TWELVE: Yogi Berra, Charlie Silvera, Bobby Brown, Jerry Coleman, Johnny Mize, Joe Collins, Vic Raschi, Allie Reynolds, Eddie Lopat, Gene Woodling, and Hank Bauer. It is about the tolls paid, on both the bridge and the field. It is not going to read like Jim Bouton's *Ball Four*, but I hope it will not come across as "Stengel of Sunnybrook Farm."

We won five straight World Series in a row. The feat is unthinkable, and given today's baseball, unrepeatable. The twelve players won more than five World Series rings. What they won is not worn on a finger, it is carried in the heart.

But I was not alone. We will get to that later.

It was a great joy and good fortune to be included in the limited partnership that won five straight American League pennants and then beat the National League five times, again in a row. The National League sent the Dodgers three times, and the Phillies and Giants once each. The American League sent us five times and we came back with all the marbles each time: 1949, 1950, 1951, 1952, 1953. Old Blue Eyes would call them very good years, and they were.

My pal, Larry Ritter, the fine writer and baseball historian, is not alone in thinking that if George Weiss, our tough General Manager, had not sold Vic Raschi to the Cardinals during spring training in 1954 because of a contract flap, we might have won again. Sally Raschi, Vic's widow, told me it's a waste of time to think about it. The Indians won 111 games in '54, is the way she remembers it, and she is right on both counts. They did, and "what if?" is not a good game. It gets played a lot. Let me say this much: It hurt at the time. Vic and Reynolds and Lopat and our pitching coach, Jim Turner, and Turner's black book (he knew if one of them changed a blade in their razors) were a team on the team, and Mr. Weiss broke the spell. The magic was gone. So was the Springfield Rifle, Vic Raschi, who that year (1954), won eight games for a second-division team, the St. Louis Cardinals.

Sadly, Vic Raschi, Ed Lopat, Joe Collins, and Johnny Mize all died while this project developed. All of them left wives and families, and without sounding pretentious, it is our hope this volume will serve as their legacy. The passing of former teammates is always a chilling event because your memory of them is so removed from the reduced gait of old age, but when one of the twelve men who shared such a special time in baseball dies, it is an even more emotionally charged experience. At least it is for me. Maybe you will understand if you think of it this way: Only twelve of us were lucky enough to be included in the group, so each passing diminishes the rest of us.

In a few pages I would like to tell you about the first game of the 1949 World Series. It was more important than just being the first game. It was at the time. It still is, over forty years later. First you need to get to know our starting pitcher for that game—the Super Chief, Allie Reynolds.

Along with Allie, some other players, coaches, and officials will be introduced. Only twelve Yankees were given the World Series ring with the number five in the center. More than twelve made it possible and I will mention a few of them also.

Allie Reynolds was born in Oklahoma, and really never left there. He loved the competition of baseball, or of any contest, including golf, bridge, football, track, or basketball, but not time away from his family. To many rugged individuals from out West, New York was back East. The East was to be avoided. Mistrusted, at least. Part Creek Indian, Allie Pierce (his friends always used his middle name), was the son of a minister and was not allowed to play baseball on Sunday, which may, in part, explain his advanced age when he arrived in the big leagues. He was twenty-eight when he won 11 and lost 12 for the Cleveland Indians in 1943.

Tommy Henrich described Reynolds in one word: winner. He was built like Jim Thorpe, but he threw like Bobby Feller. He knew what it took to win and the price he had to pay to win. Allie didn't need to learn how to throw a baseball, but he had to learn the game of baseball, and he will tell you that is why he spent so long in the minor leagues. Once he got to the majors, he never looked back, and he quit when he was on top. Not many of us are smart enough to do that.

Reynolds became a New York Yankee because Larry McPhail, one of the Yankee owners, asked Joe DiMaggio and Tommy Henrich about Reynolds, who was with the Indians at the time.

Had Olympic great Jim Thorpe become a major league pitcher, Thorpe and Reynolds would have shared one asset: remarkable physical ability. Reynolds's scholarship at Oklahoma State was charged to the track and field budget, and he was, like Thorpe, a sprinter. His ability to throw a baseball was discovered while wearing street shoes. He was asked by the legendary Hank Iba of Oklahoma State in Stillwater to fill in during a fraternity game the spring of his junior year. "I heard you can throw," Iba said to Reynolds. After he'd pitched half an inning, the baseball coach called time and issued him a uniform and cleats along with instructions to report to practice the next day. It was good news for Reynolds but bad news for the University of Oklahoma in Norman. They lost to Oklahoma State the first time Allie faced them, breaking their interstate rival's ten-year dominance of this game. ⚾

—*Philip Francis Rizzuto*

Both said, "If you can get him, get him. Reynolds will win big for this team."

Allie felt good about the trade. Today, he says, "The Yankees gave up Joe Gordon and Eddie Bockman to get me. At the time, it was controversial, but when Joe and Tommy went to bat for me, that was really all the Yanks needed to know to make it happen. I made sure that Joe and Tommy knew I was grateful, but I slipped a needle in when I did. 'Guess you two guys didn't want to go to bat against me anymore, so you went to bat for me.'

"My box [locker] was right next to DiMaggio's, and I don't ever remember a response from him, but Tommy told me he felt sorry for me and wanted me to find out what it was like to play on a real team. Tommy was kidding, but he was right. Playing in New York after playing in Cleveland, at least in those days, was like going from the minors to the majors. Joe and Tommy changed my life before I ever met either one of them. Then I had the pleasure of pitching in front of them. I could throw a bad pitch to Bobby Doerr and think, base hit, then turn to see DiMaggio, with that easy grace, track the ball down as if it was a routine fly. Nobody ever played center field like Joe. Henrich was no slouch either, but playing next to Joe could make a great player look merely real good." A pensive Reynolds sighs just a bit. "Too bad it didn't last a little longer, but Hank Bauer and Mickey Mantle could make a pitcher's day, too. All of the Yankees could make a good pitcher even better."

The Yankees were different. I had been in the major leagues five seasons, but when I was traded to the Yankees, it was going from a church supper to the Stork Club. ⚾

—*Allie Reynolds*

Reynolds adjusted to living in Ridgewood, New Jersey, during the season but he was more at home on the range. His late wife, Earlene, played golf to a low handicap, and once beat Yogi in a match at the Ridgewood Country Club.

"Earlene never forgot it, and Yogi never remembers it," Reynolds says, his eyes misty as he recalls his wife. Reynolds's emotion makes one think of Jerry Coleman's statement about the biggest asset required for success in the major leagues: "A stable home life," was the comment of decorated Marine pilot Coleman.

Allie continues, "She always loved to see me pitch. Early in the season she would wear white gloves. All the wives did, and every man and boy removed his hat when they played the National Anthem. The wives sat together. I wondered why George Weiss arranged this, but you can count on this: It did not just happen. George knew about it, and approved the allocation.

"As smart as he was, the seating arrangements may have been an error. It would be fun to see that in a baseball book: Error, General Manager. Here is my point. Suppose Earlene is sitting next to Carmen Berra, and the balls gets by Yogi. If it's a passed ball, it's his fault. If it's a wild pitch, it's mine. Either way, it can make for an awkward inning (or lifetime) for some ladies, if the runner on third scores. If it was an error on Weiss to put the wives and families together, here is the other side. From Weiss's perspective perhaps it was the way we were and we were close. For instance, Gene Woodling's wife, Betty, used to baby-sit for my family when Gene played the outfield and I pitched in Wilkes-Barre. Betty and Earlene would not let a passed ball get in the way of their friendship. In Wilkes-Barre, Pennsylvania—hot plates and Campbell's soup—we were young and poor. Luckily, none of us is old and poor." Allie Reynolds smiles. "Gene played right field. We used to call Gene, Rock. He was as hard as one. Harder, maybe."

"I was offered a front-office job with the Yankees after I retired. They knew when to give me a job pitching, and I knew when to leave. You leave before they tell you to," Allie said, still pleased he had made the decision not only to retire but to say no to a job in the front office. He had been a player rep for the team and enjoyed the job, but Oklahoma was home, and now it was time to go home. He returned to Oklahoma City and was even more successful in business than he had been in baseball. But he is well beyond the need to posture. As sure of himself as ever, he keeps up. His bridge group not only respects him as a Yankee great but as a mean competitor as well. Reynolds is the major force behind an annual Indian celebration in Oklahoma called "Red Earth." "Jim Turner, at age ninety, still comes over from Nashville," Reynolds says proudly. "The last time he was here we talked about the golf coach at one of the local colleges. The men's coach was making x dollars, so the women's coach wanted the same thing. Something will happen. It always does. I hope it doesn't mess up college sports. Just because something has been around a long time does not mean it will always be. Baseball, to my way of thinking, has gone sour. College football and basketball are not immune. Turner goes to a game almost every night. Nashville has two teams in two leagues. He pays his way every time he goes. After his years in baseball, he has a lifetime gold pass, but he pays at the gate. He was different back then and still is." ⓧ

—*Allie Pierce Reynolds*

A survey of 645 former major league players ranked Reynolds number 13 under the heading "All Time Best Right-Handed Pitchers." Allie is pleased, but most of all he is pleased to be on the list. "If 654 players were surveyed, I am sure some of them saw me pitch, and I worked at it," said Reynolds. "I was sort of a dart thrower."

Al Rosen, an outstanding third baseman for the Indians and one-time New York Yankee President, used two words to comment on Reynolds's description: "Poison darts." ⓧ

Reynolds leans back on the couch of his photo-covered den and indicates without remorse, "I can't name all the folks in the pictures but I can remember the events. That is what stays with you, that and what it took to get you there." Reynolds's den is filled with photos, from Ali to Ike.

One item hangs alone. It is a bronze plaque purchased by Jim Turner and given to Reynolds, Raschi, and Lopat. It cites the three pitchers who won 240 games in five years. Raschi died three days before Turner planned to present the trio of pitchers his gift.

Reynolds: "When the Yankees, or any team for that matter, retires a number or puts a plaque on the fence, tickets are sold. There is nothing wrong with that. Turner was not selling tickets. In fact, he sent all three of us first-class tickets to pick up the plaques and meet in Nashville, so it is special.

"Before a game, in the bull pen while I was warming up, Jim Turner would watch me like a hawk. He acted as though he was thinking about dinner, but he was really wondering whether I was getting ready for a big game. For me, it always seemed that way. Stengel sometimes even gave me a day off. He would tell the writers it was a little extra rest for the Chief. That way I could face Bobby Feller and the second-place Cleveland team and not the struggling Washington Senators. I knew, and anyone who followed the team knew. It was a polite fiction.

"Then at home, you would hear the lineups and Jim would say five more pitches and I might take four or six pitches just to show him, and we would start walking in. On the road it was a little different because the other pitcher had to start and I came in at the half inning.

"At home or on the road, no matter how many times I started, the mound always seemed off-kilter when I faced the first hitter. If you pawed the ground too much with your feet, trying to smooth it so it was comfortable, the hitter would get on you and then the other bench and then the umpire. You had to get used to the mound and you better do it quickly. If you didn't, and the hitters started sending some shots to the wall or off the wall, someone else would be doing the pawing for you. Stengel would futz around with the dirt as he waited for Page to come in so I could go out. Any sign that you were not comfortable was picked up and the next day the writers would write about it.

"Getting used to the mound was a simple problem, really. Given the choice between having no trouble with the mound and a weak arm, I will take the mound problem any day. Life is learning to cope, and so is pitching. Lopat seldom threw a strike and he won. I tried to throw a lot of them and I won. My delivery was smooth, Lopat was like a windup doll that needed WD 40 and new cogs. The hitters' mouths used to water while they waited to hit. When they came back, they were foaming at the mouth. Lopat drove hitters nuts. I used to laugh, but I never had to face him. Raschi either, for that matter. Vic was stronger than I was, but we were all strong in our own way. Even Silvera. He only played in one game during the five World Series. That takes a different kind of strength. Think about it; he was one of the first guys chosen on the playground in school and most everywhere he played, and was a star in the minors, and now he watches Yogi. We all knew he was important and I guess he knew it too.

In 1949, my rookie year, I batted .315. Joe and I were the only ones to hit .300 that year. Yogi broke his thumb and missed six weeks. I took his place. On the next-to-the last Sunday I pulled a groin muscle, and Yogi was forced back into action. We ended up winning the pennant by one game. I haven't been given much credit for the role I played in 1949. I'm going to blow my own horn a little here. I didn't hang around all those years because I was Casey's illegitimate son. Without me I don't know whether the Yankees would have taken that '49 pennant. Ⓗ

—*Charlie Silvera*

"All twelve of us were important. And it sure helped to have guys like Joe DiMaggio and Mantle, Billy Martin and McDougald on those teams. You don't win with twelve guys or even with twenty-five. You win with everyone knowing it's their job to win.

"George Weiss wanted to win as much as anyone. That is why he always, and I mean every time, asked for a throw-in after a trade. That's the way he got some very good people, Jim Turner, for example.

"Lots of teams never learn what it takes and how it feels. They used to say we knew how to win. We knew what it was like to win, what it felt like, and what was the price of winning.

"We were also a self-confident bunch. Some people say the line between self-confidence and arrogance is a thin one, and you pay a price when you cross it. Self-confidence seldom backfires, arrogance often does. I am sure we crossed that line, but we also knew how to win."

Getting back to Allie's start on October 5, 1949, I don't know why Stengel decided to start Reynolds instead of Vic Raschi or Ed Lopat. I am sure that Casey consulted with Jim Turner. Casey and the pitching staff knew they had a gem in Turner and when Casey asked Turner what he thought, Casey listened.

More important to a reader's understanding of Yankee baseball in that period, it would never have occurred to me, or any of us, to ask. Especially one of the other pitchers, Raschi and Lopat for sure. Today's baseball people have an especially hard time believing this. If a player starts game one and wins, he can come back and maybe win two games, maybe even three. Great stats—words we never used—to take to a contract table, today or fifty years ago.

Some baseball people, even at this late date, will say the selection of the pitcher is simple. It is a left-hand, right-hand thing. You can always find an expert on any subject. Frank (Cro) Crosetti, who participated in twenty-three World Series—more than anyone and the closest to him is Yogi, who participated in twenty-one—would say, "Who's to say? Who's to say?" Bright people often talk that way, because a really smart person knows how little he or she knows.

It may have been a left-right thing, and I am sure when this books comes out, someone will have something to say about the subject. At any rate, I always thought that part of the game was overrated. If you make it to the big leagues, you ought to be able to hit right-handers and the crazy ones also. Left-handers are supposed to be a little nuts, like Danish people are supposed to be stubborn, the Scots tightwads.

But as Cro always says: "Who's to say? Who's to say?"

The Yankees played the Dodgers in our home park, Yankee Stadium. The stadium, the old one and the new one, has been a sort of home for me for over fifty years.

Some of the players you are going to read about will smile when they see I used the words "sort of." I took a lot of kidding when I played for the Yanks. The kidding started when I started playing. I played 133 regular-season games in 1941, and 5 more in the World Series against the Dodgers. We won the series in five games. My birthday is in late September, so most of the season I was twenty-three. Really, twenty-three.

Most of the kidding was good-natured, not as mean-spirited as some of the college hazing in vogue at the time. Some of it is hardly worth repeating. One joke played on me several times is, though, because it shows how some everyday things about the game of baseball have changed over the years.

Next time you see a major league game, watch the players after the third out. As the first baseman starts to enter his dugout, someone in there will throw him a ball. He will put it in his glove and use it, when his team retakes the field, to throw grounders to the infielders. The first baseman is the only player who needs his glove as he returns to the bench. The other players do not, but they bring theirs along into the dugout.

It used to be different. It stopped some time in the early fifties, but for years every player except the catcher threw his glove on the field. The first and third basemen threw theirs right near the coaching box. The shortstop and second baseman would fling their gloves into the outfield and the outfielders would drop them in the outfield. Let me say a bit more about throwing my glove. After an inning-ending double play, when my keystone buddy and later broadcasting partner, Coleman, and I would pull off a particularly fancy one, it was a huge thrill to add to the drama of the event by adding a little extra to the fling.

Now we get to the kidding part. Sometimes, after flinging my glove, I would return and put it back on only to find a mouse, snake, or worm in the fingers. I do not ever remember this being done to me when the game was close. But let the game get out of hand and there they were.

Yogi said he never remembered seeing a loose glove on the field come into play—in other words, end up getting hit by a ball in play. I do not know of a keener observer of baseball than Lawrence Peter Berra, so you can bet it didn't happen. You can also make book on this: Mr. Berra had nothing to do with worms in my glove.

So, I was twenty-three during most of my first major league season. At the time, a lot of ball players said they were younger than they were. It made the brass think you could play better and longer. Tommy Henrich, Yankee right fielder in 1941, was one. Later on, when it came time for his baseball pension, he added the years back. Others did the same. As far as I know, the other two guys playing the outfield in 1941, Charley Keller and Joe DiMaggio, did not fudge on their age. Keller came to the Yankees after playing for the University of Maryland, so perhaps his age was more a matter of record. As for DiMaggio, who would ask? The Yankee outfield had some guys in those days. Also, as far as I remember, Keller, Joe, and Tommy did not bother to get on me or join in the kidding when it started. Joe kept to himself, and so pretty much did Charley and Heinie, as Henrich was called.

One year Phil won an Austin-Healey sports car for being the most popular Yankee. It was real small and Phil drove it down to St. Pete. A couple of veterans grabbed a hold of the car with their bare hands and wedged it sideways between two palm trees. Phil couldn't get it out. ⓧ

—*Mickey Mantle*

Later, in what some people would call my salad days, 1946 until 1953–54, when I was starting almost every game, I got a lot of needles from teammates. At the end, as I was on the way down, it may have lessened a little bit. To tell the truth, the last days were tough. You are still a young man, and a younger man, who is quicker (and, in my case, bigger) comes along, and you know it is only a matter of time.

Then, since I was lucky enough to broadcast the Yankee games, I saw it happen to the guy who replaced me. I saw Gil McDougald, Billy Hunter, and then Tony Kubek start at short-stop. All three are friends. Even better friends now. Incidentally, guys breathing down your neck seldom kid you. They know better.

Yankee Stadium may have been my "sort of home," but I was born in Brooklyn and the Dodgers were "my team." My tryout with the Dodgers, managed by Casey Stengel, was awful. The best thing about the tryout is that it was over quick. Short and painful. Stengel told me I was too small, which I knew. He also told me to get a shoe shine box, which was unnecessary. At seventeen, I was going to give baseball a chance, if baseball would give me a chance.

The New York Giants also said I was too small and might get hurt during the tryout, so I was told to sit in the stands and watch. Bill Terry, their manager, didn't give me a tumble, but he didn't tell me to get a shoe shine box.

Since the story of my Dodger and Giant tryouts took all of two paragraphs, you can see why I was delighted to end up playing for the New York Yankees, but when the job was done I wanted to punch out and go home, to my real home. I was almost always the first one to leave the park after the game. They used to say Bill Dickey every so often beat me out the club-house door because he didn't use soap in the shower. What other players, guys like John Lindell and Dr. Brown, would say is Dickey, a Yankee coach, got wet and left thinking if he ran to his car he would dry off. Not too much bothered Dickey. He had been a great catcher for the team and at six feet plus he did not worry about what guys might say about his departure. I might have wondered too about Dickey or others on the team, but my goal then and today is to spend as much time with my family as possible. The Yankees didn't hire me to do anything in the clubhouse except get ready.

You hear a lot about guys who are the first at the park and the last to leave. The old New York Giants had a catcher named Clyde Kluttz. He was a good one, but all I ever heard about him was that he opened the clubhouse door, played nine innings, did the laundry and mopped up. I was there on time, played hard, and then it was time to go home. On the road (and we spent half our time on the road) it was different, and I might hang around a little, but by then my reputation was set.

Well, by now Allie may be nodding off in Oklahoma City, waiting for me to get to his start and the reason this book began with the Super Chief facing the Brooklyns, as old writers used to call them.

Yankee Stadium was not full for the first game of the 1949 World Series. Only 66,224 paid. Game 2 in our park drew 70,053 paid. General Manager George Weiss was probably fussing, wondering what happened to the 3,829 fans who should have been sitting in those seats, drinking beer and eating hot dogs. Allie was not. Allie Pierce Reynolds, the son of a minister, part Indian and loaded with self-confidence, did something that first game fifty years ago.

We took the field, and in the first inning he faced Pee Wee Reese, Spider Jorgensen, Duke Snider, and Jackie Robinson. He did something you don't see today; you don't see it because someone or some group in baseball put a stop to it. What Allie did to Reese, Jorgensen, Snider, and Robinson was to challenge them with a fast ball right under their chin. We called it busting a fast ball; some announcers called it "chin music." If you ever encountered it on your high school team, you would call it a mixture of fear, nausea, and the shakes. Every pitch, of course, was not calculated to strike fear in mere mortals, and I used to wonder about Snider and Jackie when they had a bat in their hands. During this half inning, Reynolds may have moved each of them back once. Maybe only two of them one time. The number is not important. The weapon is. Reynolds's fast ball was lethal. As his shortstop, I was only feet away from Allie, and you could see what his fast ball did. Campy, a great bear of a man and a great classy guy, used to call it "Jelly Leg." (He would get his taste in the second inning.) In the first inning, Allie took their breath away, weakened their resolve, and if they did hit the ball, he made them feel they hit it in self-defense, not as offense. I played behind Allie in both his no-hitters—July 12, 1951, in Cleveland against the Indians, and his second that year, September 28 at home against the league-leading Red Sox. He was great, as he almost always was. In the first inning when he faced the Dodgers, he showed them why he was called the Super Chief. He feels it was the best he ever was and that, fans, is very good.

As a self-proclaimed Yankee maven, I should be able to tell you the date and time chin-music pitchers were banned. If we were the best team in baseball during that time, it would stand to reason the time and day would be right here in my maven file. I am sorry, I only know matters have changed. I am going to leave it to Bobby Brown, our third baseman and the sixth President of the American League, to make that information available.

The twelve guys, the ones in the title—Silvera, Yogi, Dr. Brown (most people call him Bobby, but my wife Cora feels, considering the years he spent in medical school, Bobby earned the Dr., and I think she is right), Jerry Coleman, Gene Woodling, Hank Bauer, Allie, and, until they died, Vic Raschi, Johnny Mize, Joe Collins, and Eddie Lopat, are, and were, close.

Let me explain close. Some people you see every day but seldom think about, and others you seldom see but find them in your mind often. The twelve men (and their wives) were the kind that were often in your mind. Some more than others, but they were all on a front burner, not cooling on the back of the stove.

Consider this: All of us were married, and none of us were divorced. That should help you understand.

I am also honest enough to tell you this—if we had not all been ball players good enough to play for the New York Yankees, the chance of us ending up as close as we were is slim or none. But it's also true, if you have the ability, and get along, you have a better chance of winning.

So, we keep in touch, and this book, in its way, forces us to stay in touch a bit more.

After that game in 1949, I went straight home, as usual, and have no memory of speaking to Allie. His locker was on the other side of the clubhouse, and after a Series game, the room looked like the floor of the stock exchange. Our usual beat writers were joined by dozens of others, and what was usually a comfortable room turned into a zoo. If I did say anything, it would have been something like "nice game."

You might think what I had to say about that game would not mean much, if anything, to Allie today. You would be wrong. In a strange way, he felt it meant even more to learn at this late date how his first inning is burned into my memory. I do not mean to suggest that Reynolds needs my blessing, or my approval; any of the Yankee players could have made my comment. It might just as well have been the guy I replaced, Frank Crosetti, who was our third base coach, making the observations and comments about Reynolds. Several things were at work to make the information Reynolds received out there in Oklahoma special. His age and my age, our ages—the combined ages of the October Twelve is like the national debt—had a lot to do with it. So as well did the nature of my memory. Vivid. The memory is vivid and I tried to make it that way when I spoke with Allie. Lawyers have a saying: Justice delayed is justice denied. Recognition delayed is that much sweeter, and that is all I have to say about Mr. Allie Pierce Reynolds's first game in the 1949 World Series, except this—he won. It was his second of seven wins, putting him second behind Whitey Ford for the most World Series victories.

The following is a list of catchers who at one time played behind Yogi, or were in the Yankee organization and traded to other clubs.

- Charlie Silvera
- Aaron Robinson
- Gus Niarhos
- Sherm Lollar
- Ralph Houk
- Clint Courtney
- John Blanchard
- Elston Howard

- Darrell Johnson
- Cal Neeman
- Moe Thacker
- Hank Foiles
- Jake Gibbs
- Elvin Tappe
- Harry Chiti
- Jim Robertson

- Jesse Gonder
- Gus Triandos
- Lou Berberet
- Ken Silvestri
- Hal Smith
- Billy Shantz

Reynolds had quite a game. He got a hit and gave up only two hits to Dodgers Reese and Jorgensen. He also showed tremendous poise. When Jerry Coleman opened the fifth inning with an error, putting Carl Furillo on first, Allie showed no emotion. He didn't look at Jerry, or speak to one of his infielders. Yogi was not an infielder. Even when Gil Hodges sacrificed Furillo to second and Campy walked, Reynolds did not show he was flustered. He struck out Newcombe, and Reese forced Furillo at third. The score was still 0 to 0. Allie's composure when Coleman made an error might be the reason Jerry doubled in the last of the eighth. Tommy Henrich won the game with a home run in the ninth. It came off Don Newcombe, on a 2 and 0 count. Sadly for his team, Don never won a World Series game. Had the game been played in Ebbets Field, the Dodgers' home, the Henrich home run might have been caught, given the dimensions of their park and the stadium. Considering the way Newcombe and Reynolds were pitching that day, the game could have gone on forever.

Allie and Gene Woodling knew each other when they were both in the Cleveland chain, as we called the farm system at the time. Both of them were and are strong-willed. Hard-headed would be a fair description. Great guys to have on a team, and I know that sounds sappy, but it was true.

Let me connect Woodling and Reynolds to give some insight into both personalities. Allie did not like to pitch batting practice and Woodling did not like to take batting practice. Gene had one of the most unusual batting stances any of us had ever seen, and he was one of the few players I ever knew who didn't love to take BP. As for pitching BP, Allie was like most pitchers—it was OK when he needed to loosen up or work on something, say, his change. He may still be working on it, as I never saw him throw a good one. When you throw 200 miles an hour, who needs one? Allie knew he didn't have a change. Jim Turner felt his delivery was so smooth it was even harder to throw a change-up. I am not sure I understand that, but I am also not sure I understand pitchers. One time when we were playing Cleveland and had a 10-run lead, Reynolds told Yogi he was going to throw a change to the Cleveland catcher Aaron Robinson. Robinson was one of the catchers who had been the property of the Yankees and had been sold because of Yogi. You can guess that Aaron Robinson hit the change out. He did the same thing the next time. Allie stopped throwing it.

Woodling had two good reasons to avoid BP. Gene felt if you were hitting, it didn't help. If you were not hitting, or in a slump, it could hurt. At least that's what he used to say, and still does. The players on the bench were the only ones who needed the practice, not the ones on the lineup for 154 games a season. Lots of people feel that way. Americans who played in Japan say that the teams there hit too much. A .250 hitter will always be a .250 hitter. Gene didn't even want to be called a hitting coach when he went to work for Hank Bauer when Bauer managed Baltimore.

According to Gene, only God could make a hitter. ⑂

—*Philip Francis Rizzuto*

So here is the scene: Allie pitching BP, Woodling taking it. Allie lets Woodling know he is going to throw a curve, Woodling suggests he does not wish a curve; he would prefer a fast ball. Allie had the ball and was going to throw a curve. He did and Woodling showed his displeasure by hitting the pitch back up the middle. Batting practice screens were not in use at the time, and Allie had to jump, which, of course, he could, as Woodling knew.

Reynolds said, "Rock, I need to get my work in, too," and that was that.

I think it is a useful story for several reasons. One is that the two men remember the event. Both of them brought it up. Today, given the egos, media coverage, and perhaps the number of dollars involved, the same exchange might have become ugly or turned up on TV, the newspapers, or both. Back then, beat writers made about as much money as most of the rest of us, it was just different. We were different and they were different.

The twelve players, Stengel, coaches Turner, Cro, Dickey, and Ralph Houk, and our trainer, Gus Mauch, are all on a plaque. The Yankees had them made up. They didn't order them when we won in 1953 because everyone on the team and in the front office thought we would win again in 1954. We were a sure thing. When Billy Martin drove in Hank Bauer with the winning run in 1953, no one said, "This is a red-letter day; we won five in a row." A lot was said and written about that game: Martin's hit was his twelfth, a record. Reynolds won, in relief of Whitey Ford. Clem Labine lost. Jackie Robinson, Carl Furillo, Yogi, and Billy all had doubles, and Carl hit a home run. All this and more was covered, but if someone said the winning streak is over, I missed it.

I would guess the plaque idea came after Cleveland won 111 games in 1954 and we didn't. The plaque has photographs of Stengel, Frank Crosetti, Jim Turner, Ralph Houk, Bill Dickey, Gus Mauch, and the players, as I said. At this stage it is hard to know who came up with the idea for it. The best guess is Red Patterson, the Yankee PR man at the time.

Most people feel it was his brainchild and some baseball people feel he was the first PR director for any big league team. This much is certain, Patterson came up with the idea to call Mickey Mantle's long home run in Washington "a tape measure job." It was in the early fifties, and while Mickey didn't need anyone to showcase his ability, it helped focus media attention on Mickey, so Patterson is remembered.

> Speaking of Mantle, I was there the day he hit that ball out of Griffith Stadium. He hit one farther the next year at Sportsman's Park in St. Louis. But he got so much publicity the year before that they couldn't surpass it. No one, including Babe Ruth, hit them consistently as far as Mantle did. Mantle was unbelievable. I don't think he ever realized the talent he had. He was just a small-town boy who came to New York to swing a bat. ⚾
>
> —*Gene Woodling*

He was an early PR director, that is for sure, and gets my vote for the individual most responsible for the plaque. Plaque may be too fancy a word to describe a fading plastic sepia wall hanging, 3 feet by 2 feet, commemorating (the words come from the plaque) the twelve players and others members of the team that won five in a row. This much is certain, the twelve players lucky enough to appear on the plaque know it is one of a kind. It is also a good bet that Patterson, or whoever came up with the idea, had to clear the expense with George Weiss, because, considering the event (five World Series wins in a row), it is a cheap plaque.

When I say cheap, I also need to tell you not everyone on it agrees with me. One of the nice things about playing the A's in Oakland is that when the Yanks play a day game, Frank Crosetti drives in from Stockton. I love to see him and hear that raspy voice tell me or someone else to "go fry your ass." It takes me back, as it does anyone who heard him say it when he coached third base for the team. He coached for about ninety years. When I told him I thought they might have spent a little more on the plaque, he didn't agree at all. You can guess what he said.

Cro thinks the plaque is great, and I may be wrong about others. Jerry Coleman, for example. Jerry told me that on one trip to New York, Barry Halper, a limited partner in the New York Yankee group, as well as an important collector, had purchased one of the plaques. I'm told the plaque belonged to the late Bob Fishel, who used to work in Public Relations for the Yankees. Bob worked with Bill Veeck before his Yankee days, and for the American League with Lee McPhail after, so he had a lot of things collectors like. Someone brought that particular plaque to a game and asked Jerry to sign it, so at least that one was worth something to someone.

I want to say how I think this book is different from the several dozen others about Yankee teams and Yankee players. Most of these have been written by an individual interested in the subject and with a certain level of cooperation from players and with personnel on the team. No matter what its level, the book was written and published without the people covered seeing what had been written. I am talking about a book here, and a book should be factually accurate. Some of the stuff the twelve of us have seen in these is flat-out wrong and I will give some examples later on.

During the last few years it has become fashionable for "serious journalists" to write baseball books. I don't know how closely they stick to the facts when they write about "serious subjects," but when they write about baseball they sure play fast and loose.

Take David Halberstam's *The Summer of '49*. I have nothing against Mr. Halberstam personally, and I understand his book sold a lot of copies, but I don't have the vaguest idea where he got his material. In fact, in those cases where I or my teammates were there, I can tell you that a number of his anecdotes are just plain untrue.

In one scene, for instance, Mr. Halberstam has Allie Reynolds threatening to cross Yogi up, that is, to hit Yogi in the chest with a fastball, and then later he has Allie threatening to punch Yogi out in the clubhouse. I played right behind Allie at short and never heard Allie say it. I've talked to both Allie and Yogi about it and they say it never happened. And I can tell you one thing, if the three of us say it didn't happen, it didn't.

As I said, I have nothing against Mr. Halberstam and don't mean to single him out. Many writers of baseball books do the same thing. In fact, I hope Mr. Halberstam's books continue to sell countless millions of copies and he grows even richer than he already is. ⓧ

—*Philip Francis Rizzuto*

Another genre is books about a player or manager. Yogi had a few written about him and I had one myself. The author may have talked with the guy named on the cover, but that is it. The books typically give a distorted picture of people and events. They are a sort of false advertising in my mind and an exercise of free speech in the mind of the other guy.

If you are a public figure, say an actor or even a mayor, you live under a different set of conditions. Things can be written or said about you that would be grounds for a lawsuit if you worked in a bank. The bank teller can sue for libel or slander. Now what I am saying is not defensive. I'm merely trying to explain how this book came to be written. If the words are here, one of the twelve players or our wives or teammates saw it, and had something to say about its being here. No one can ever check every source, and even if it was done you would still find disagreement. But if we do slip up, we can always count on Frank Crosetti to tell the whole bunch, "Go fry your ass."

Living in New Jersey has made it easy to keep in touch with players like Yogi and, when they were alive, Joe Collins and Ed Lopat. I know all of them have a plaque like the one in my den. At one time they may have hung one in Yankee Stadium, but if so, it is gone. I am not suggesting one should be there. I am just making an observation.

When I got involved with this book I remembered a photograph I had heard was hanging in Allie's den. It is a photo of the second no-hitter. The batter is Ted Williams. The pitching rubber under

Allie's foot is in the Hall of Fame. Allie signed it. Ted did not. I don't know why, but someone does. This pitch ended the game. The one just before this one. The same kind of pitch. Fast ball high and tight. Williams fouled it off. A high foul between first and the mound—the sort of pop-up Yogi catches in his sleep in 1951. The kind that gave him fits when he first came up, until Bill Dickey worked with him after games. Yogi drops that ball. Carmen, Mrs. Berra, is in a hospital in New Jersey waiting to deliver Dale, the third of the Berra boys. I am Larry Jr.'s godfather, and Ed Lopat was Tim's, the middle son's, godfather (I told you we were close).

When Yogi dropped the ball, Carmen was listening to the game and she screamed. The nurse ran down the hall and wanted to know if she should call the doctor.

Carmen said, "My husband dropped the ball."

If I knew what the nurse said, I have forgotten. I was not listening to the game; I was the shortstop, and I wanted to scream too. If I had been in the broadcast booth I would have said "HOLY COW." As the shortstop, all I could think was, "Poor Yogi" and "What if he hits the next one out?" Perhaps not in that order. It is OK to think it; but the one thing you cannot do (at least if you ever played for Joe McCarthy, the best manager I ever had, who just happened to be in the Boston dugout as the Sox manager) is let them know you are thinking it. You've got to act the part of the hostess who sees one of her guests spill his wineglass on her new tablecloth. She smiles sweetly. The infielders do the same thing. We don't cover it up with a smile, but we do cover it up so that you don't know how it hurts. If you know, Ted knows. He was tough enough for Allie, or any of our guys, without giving him the advantage of knowing the ball Yogi dropped was a big deal. To-morrow, it's a big deal in the papers. Now it is what we would call a bump in the road to the American League flag.

Yogi and Allie may have a different version, but this is my story and I am sticking to it. Allie throws the same pitch, I guess Yogi called for it, and the same thing happens except this time he catches the ball.

I remember Del Webb, one of the co-owners, coming down to the clubhouse. He had been a pitcher in the high minors and knew baseball. He was surprised that Allie would throw the same pitch. Really surprised. I am told he talked about it for years—maybe because it involved Reynolds, Williams, and Yogi—a nice parley of names to drop at a cocktail party.

THE MINORS

Bassett, Virginia, made the short list of diamonds I mentioned in the first chapter. It was on my list because it was the first place the Yankees sent me to find out if signing me had been an error or if I might develop into a big league ball player or a player who could play a week, a month, part of a season or, if your arm has Nolan Ryan on the other end, a lifetime.

Baseball fans know the longevity references are not exaggerations. Pick a page, any page, in *The Baseball Encyclopedia*, and you will find players who lasted a few games, sometimes over a few years. Walter Alston, the Dodger manager, is often mentioned when talking about longevity. His total league record: one at bat, one strike-out. The thing about Walter Alston, and a host of others who had what is called a "cup of coffee" in the big leagues, is that they were all, every one, a hotshot at one time. They were not the last picked when they chose sides at recess.

The Yankees, and the other fifteen teams in the major leagues at the time, knew they could place a thousand kids under contract in order to find one who could play in the majors. So, while they were saying nice things when I was signing the contract, as soon as I signed, their actions told me, "Go down there and see if you can make it back here."

I can barely remember some of the names on that team, and here is a hard fact of baseball life; only a few baseball people can remember any. None of them made it to the majors. Not for a day, not a week, not a month. Disappointment, broken dreams, the destruction of hope.

Jerry Coleman, on his way up to the Yankees, spent some time in the Eastern League. It was a higher-classification league than the Pony League, where he started, which was D, like Bassett. Say it was an A league, and I am sure it was, only one other guy in the whole league made it to the majors. His name was Frankie Zak and he played 123 games for Pittsburgh over three years, 1944, '45, and '46. It's a good bet he spent five or six years in the minors to spend three years in the majors. For him, kind of sad. I was not thinking sad thoughts at the time and I am sorry I brought some into this story.

Bassett is about 15 miles from the North Carolina line, and most of the towns on the Virginia side of the line were small, like Bassett. In those days, I called the state line, the border. I also called the Civil War, the Civil War. I still do. The local people, and they were all wonderful to me, called it the War Between the States. I bet some of them still refer to the conflict that way. I got the map out and it did not appear that around Bassett things have changed that much. Bassett's population is under three thousand today. It's nice that some things stay as they were.

Making a comment about wishing things were like they used to be—a good-old-days, we-walked-26-miles-to-school sort of thing—is a sure sign of getting older. I try to avoid such statements. I also try to avoid that big word "if." I try not to dwell on what might have been.

On the other hand, some changes I might not have minded. If only I had been as tall as Marty Marion, the great Cardinal shortstop, six-feet-two, I could have been called Slats instead of Scooter.

Scooter is fine, if people don't say it too often. Some Yankees play-ers of today call me Scoots. I don't know any of them well enough to use a nickname, unless it's Money Bags and it seems they would all answer if you called that out in the clubhouse. Any clubhouse.

I also wouldn't have minded the nickname Duke—it would have been a hard name to shorten. Duke Rizzuto has a nice ring, don't you think?

Suggesting I do not know any of the current Yankee players well prompts me to tell you what I do for the Yankees. I am a broadcaster and when I am on the road and tell the parking atten-dant, I am Phil Rizzuto, the Yankee broadcaster, that statement and a few bucks gets me a place to park. Along with Tom Seaver and Bobby Murcer I do the games on WPIX. WPIX does sixty or seventy games a year. We work for WPIX, but if Yankee principal owner George Steinbrenner did not want one of us to do his games, I think it's a fair bet we would not be asked back.

My normal routine does not include going down on the field or going into the clubhouse to talk to the players. That's why the nicknames used by the players, often not the same ones used by the announcers, would be a surprise to me.

True love came my way because Joe DiMaggio asked me to pinch-hit for him in 1942 and I am sure he remembers the event, and it's the reason he came to Yankee Stadium when George Steinbrenner ar-ranged to fete my wife, Cora, and me on our golden wedding anniversary.

Joe was in great demand after breaking Wee Wil-lie Keeler's record in 1941 by hitting in 56 straight games, and in the early forties players were more likely to make group appearances than today. I might add they did so for the most part without a fee.

Newark, New Jersey, had a large Italian population and many of them held Joe in high esteem. Our Lady of Sorrow Church in Newark asked Joe to attend a communion breakfast and he agreed to do so. Early in the morning that he was to go to Newark, he called me from the hospital. It was the middle of the night really and his wife, Dorothy Arnold, an actress, was giving birth to Joe, Jr.

To Joe's credit, he was not only thinking about his wife but also about his obligation to the church. I might add he was not thinking about what it would mean to the church to have Philip Francis Rizzuto take his place at the communion breakfast. When he asked me to take his place I said yes immediately with no thought of how would I do it. How could you say anything but yes when Joe asked you for a favor? I had no idea what was going to happen and didn't really have time to think until I arrived, was introduced, and heard the moans. One priest told me it was the first time he had ever seen someone booed at a communion breakfast, or in church, for that matter. I have no idea what I said when called on to speak.

One of the men in charge of the breakfast was Emil Elenborg. He was what was called in those days a first-generation German and he was a fire chief in Newark and a pillar of the church. Most people went on about their business when the moaning stopped. Emil was a man of action and compassion; he took me by the arm and said, "Come along with me, Mr. Rizzuto."

I still remember some of the details. His car was only a few feet from the front door and soon we were making the short trip to his home for coffee and cake. Putting the scene of the crime behind us was his way of solving the problem.

Emil was not a baseball fan, but he made me feel welcome in his home and his wife was just as gracious. He told me how little it would all matter the next day and that in a week it would be a faint memory, and here I am writing about the details fifty years later.

I heard some activity on the second floor—you could see the top of the stairs from my chair in the living room or parlor. I suddenly noticed two feet moving down the stairs. Then, dancing two steps at a time, appeared a vision in a red sweater and blue skirt. Their daughter, Cora.

I didn't think about my reception at the church, Joe, Dorothy Arnold, Jo, Jr., or my cake and coffee. All I could think about was I was in love. It has been that way for over fifty years. ⚾

—*Philip Francis Rizzuto*

There are several reasons I do not hang out on the field or in the clubhouse. The first is, as a player, I was never crazy about strangers in the clubhouse. It is a little like working in a factory and having a tour go through. The workers are saying, "Why don't you leave us alone." It is just sort of uncomfortable. The second reason is that getting to know someone can make it harder to comment on an error you might see that night.

Now, about George. Not only has he been very nice to me and my family, he has been generous to an extreme. Cora and I celebrated our golden wedding anniversary in 1993 and George honored us at home plate. It was really a thrill. They had a day for me as a player and I can still get chills thinking about that, but to have Cora, our kids and grandkids all on the field, the fans cheering, well, it was tears of joy for me. Cora is not the most important thing in my life, she is the reason for life itself. So standing at home plate with her was very special.

George Steinbrenner made that night happen, and so while I know about the fights with Billy Martin and Reggie Jackson and his firing of Yogi, for that matter, I have to feel as I do. I have the right to do so, and so does anyone else. I had hoped Yogi would come to the affair at the stadium, be he didn't. I respect him for his convictions. He won't go back to Yankee Stadium as long as George owns the team. End of subject. (Steinbrenner and Berra have since had a meeting of the minds. In fact, Yogi threw out the first pitch at Yankee Stadium for the home opener on April 9th, 1999, and was honored at Yogi Berra Day at the Stadium on July 18, 1999.)

But getting back to playing baseball in the southwest corner of Virginia, prior to World War II. It was, as Sidney Greenstreet said in the movie *Maltese Falcon*, describing the prize, "the stuff dreams are made of." It was my first time away from home and, at age seventeen, I missed my family and my high school coach, Al Kunitz, but the New York Yankees had enough confidence in me to send me to one of their farm clubs to play baseball for money.

It seems to me, if the kids you knew in high school think you are doing well, you are doing well. I was getting paid to do what I would have done for nothing. On the days I got four hits and played well in the field I would have paid them. Baseball knew the supply of young kids like me that wanted to play was well beyond the demand. Given that situation, I wonder, looking back, why some baseball mogul like Branch Rickey didn't come up with an indentured player plan. The players would pay the teams to let them play and learn the game. If you were good, you would turn the tables and later on they would pay you. Just a thought, but it seems the tables are turned anyway. They took advantage of us back then, and now it is the players' turn.

I didn't know it at the time, but we wore uniforms used by real Yankees, after they were shipped to the minors as hand-me-downs. In 1937, some player on one of the Yankee minor league teams was wearing Babe Ruth's shirt and pants.

Frank, the last Yankee to play on the same team with Ruth, can get on his soap box and lecture as follows: "Every major league baseball team should retire Babe Ruth's number 3. After the Black Sox scandal in 1919, baseball was dead. Babe Ruth, all by himself, put baseball back where it had been, and then made it better. Anyone who made a living in baseball, and I did for over forty years, should thank Babe, and I do. I am sorry that at the time I played with him on the Yankees that I really did not know, and fully understand what I know now, so I didn't thank him at the time. But I wish I had."

Cro is not alone in failing to understand something too late in the game to do something about it. A whole list of things begin to surface, like thanking your parents, but I am not going to get sidetracked from telling you about Babe Ruth's uniform. If you could find it, and maybe someone can, it is worth at least $100,000.

Charlie Silvera, who played in upstate New York on a Yankee team in Wellsville in 1942, wore Lou Gehrig's pants and Red Rolfe's shirt. I like to kid Charlie, by saying he played so little he had time to see whose pants he was wearing and that Jerry Coleman (who was on that team in the Pony League with Silvera) and I were too busy playing to have time to look to see what Yankee great's uniform ended up on our back.

Silvera, as you can imagine, was a regular in the minors and, as he points out, he was second-string on our team. Ralph Houk was third-string when they both played behind Yogi all those years.

If you are wondering why anyone, including the brilliant Mr. Silvera, knew just whose pants he wore, it is because, at that time, every regular Yankee player had his name stitched in a seam. It was done with red thread and no one took the time to rip it out when the uniform was sent down. Today, the player's name is written on a seam with an indelible pen and the old ones are sold in baseball-card shops. I don't spend much time in the Yankee clubhouse, as I explained, but the *New York Times* did a piece on the Yankees that said they were the only team that had a full-time tailor. I saw it in the *Times*, meaning it's true.

Even my family is not much interested in what happened in the third inning of the game when Bassett played Figsboro or even Sydorsville for that matter, so let me wrap it up by saying that the shortstop hit every pitch and made every play. Most every game, he was carried off the field on the shoulders of his teammates and fans. If Ozzie Smith had played on the Bassett nine before Rizzuto, they would have forgotten how to spell his name.

One thing that happened is worth mentioning because it ties in with what I said about things staying the same. Baseball is not the same as it used to be, but compared to some other institutions in this country, baseball has been in a deep freeze. Well, perhaps not frozen, but at least on ice. Take medicine. They are doing things now no one dreamed of fifty years ago.

Let me give you a minor example and if you are my age, you may have an even better story. Several days after I hurt my leg playing in Virginia, I went to a doctor. We played hurt more in those days. Today the DL, or the disabled list, needs a thumb index, at least in the majors it does, though I guess that's not so true, even today, in the minors. I did not want to sit out a game so I didn't go to the doctor as quickly as I should have. By the time I did, I had a serious infection—gangrene and other bad things were going on in my thigh.

Good things, like penicillin, had not been invented and I ended up in Roanoke, Virginia, in a hospital. My leg was bad and my folks flew right down. The doctors never thought I would lose my leg, but they did say I was finished playing ball. Part of my thigh still looks like a cheap golf ball that's been hit with an expensive five iron. I had surgery to connect the big muscle in the thigh because it was not all in one piece. Attention paid to the marvels of modern medicine.

I am told that if the same thing happened today and the patient was slow seeing a doctor, the problem could be solved with outpatient surgery.

So let me complete the visit to Bassett with some words that could apply today. When I recovered enough to walk, I limped over to see a doctor. I don't recall if it was a team doctor or if it was the same one or a new one. The point is, I was a seventeen- or eighteen-year-old kid, making a living playing baseball, and my leg was a problem. He examined me, and this is the part I have a hard time believing, and it happened to me.

After looking at my leg and talking with me, this doctor took me outside and said "See that mail box?" It was about thirty yards away. Then he told me to run as hard as I could to the box and run back the same way. How I did so, I will never know. Why I did so and why I was asked to do so is another question. Sometimes I think about it, like when you must think back, to work on a book. I think about the kid in Bassett who was told to do something foolish.

But I did it, and when I made it back he said I was fit to play. He may have seen the cold sweat on my brow, because he did not say, tonight. "Give it a few days," he told me.

When I tell that story to modern medical people, orthopedic surgeons, for example, they wince and shake their heads.

The comments run along the lines, "You might have permanently injured the leg and never walked, much less played again. A lame horse would have gotten better treatment. At the very least you should have run slowly a few weeks before going all-out.''

No one comes right out and says the guy I saw was a quack and I do not think he was. He did the best thing he could with the knowledge he had at the time. That is my view anyway.

Modern medical people look at the leg, and say I was lucky. I think I knew that all along. Holy Cow. I don't think I was lucky, I know I was. So long, Bassett. I wonder whose pants I was wearing? Miller Huggins's?

TALK

Casey Stengel was one of the great talkers of all time. He used a lot of words when he talked and when he finished talking, usually to take a breath, most people understood them. The words were fine and held people's attention, but don't forget the individual doing the talking also held a coveted position—he was the manager of the New York Yankees. Not someone standing behind you in the checkout line at a supermarket.

The more people in the room holding paper and pencil, the better he was at holding their interest. Every so often, Stengel would stop in mid-rant to give "his" writers a chance to finish a line in their notebooks. When a major league manager holds his usual postgame interview, players don't hang around to listen. The British would say, "It just isn't done." The other place Casey held court was on the road. He received his subjects in the hotel bar, which was off limits to players, so I am not a student of what was called "Stengelese." My feeling was he used ordinary words in extraordinary ways.

Joe Durso, a *New York Times* writer, was one of the people with a notebook and pencil. Later, when he wrote a book about

Stengel, he said, "Part of the anatomy of Stengelese consisted of certain understated adjectives like 'fairly' as in 'fairly amazing,' and certain rich or mid-Victorian words or usage, that he dropped neatly among the 'ain'ts' and 'fellas' such as 'commence' and 'numerous' and 'splendid.' " I am going to take Joe's word for it. Durso earned a Phi Beta Kappa key from NYU.

Whatever Casey did, he was good at it. It seems certain to me that he was "doing" it. Stengel knew the value of the reporter's notebook and he responded. Nothing wrong with that.

If we were playing the Philadelphia A's, and Connie Mack, their manager, didn't have his third baseman, Hank Majeski, playing in, I would respond and lay down a bunt. I did it once in 1945, then Mr. Mack and Hank responded. The response: to play in. This, by the way of showing you I have nothing against reacting to the ground rules of a situation, and telling you I was pretty good at laying down a bunt.

> You can't learn speed or power, but you can learn to bunt. One reason you should be pleased if you become good at doing so. ⒣
>
> —Philip Francis Rizzuto

When Joe DiMaggio talked, he only used a few words and when he finished, if you didn't understand what he said, it was not Joe's fault. Joe and Casey were very different when it came to talking and I think I am being fair-minded in that assessment.

Given the pleasure I receive from trying to balance events, let me come clean and tell you Mr. Stengel was not my cup of tea. If I were marooned on the proverbial South Sea island, Stengel would not be on a list of people I would want to help me build signal fires, or wave at ships. Since Joe's father made a living as a fisherman in Martinez, California, Joe might be a good bet. My wife Cora better head my list, and if you are married, I suggest you do the same.

One of the best talkers in baseball was also one of the best hitters. Ted Williams, a great hitter, loved to talk about hitting. But not in the batter's box. Ted did not want to be distracted. You might be asking yourself, Who would? The answer was a surprise to me. Bobby Doerr, the Hall of Fame second baseman on that Red Sox team, not only welcomed Yogi's line of chatter, he encouraged it. Not so much that Yogi would catch on and stop chatting, but enough to keep the conversation going.

Bobby told me years later, "When we played you guys, it was always a big game with a big crowd and Yogi's banter relaxed me. I know if Lopat made me look bad on a pitch and I could feel my neck getting hot and Yogi would tell me to step into the ball, make the fans think you know what the hell you are doing, you just had to smile to yourself. He was trying to make you madder and in my case it not only didn't work, it did just the opposite."

Bobby, another fishing nut, lives on a river in Oregon and still catches dinner. When he told me about Yogi, his face looked like he just landed a huge trout or whatever they catch out there. "It gave me as much pleasure to tell that damn Berra his chatter didn't work as getting a double off Raschi," Doerr said.

Yogi, in character until the last out, smiled and told me, "It didn't work with everybody. Nothing does."

For sure, it used to drive Ted crazy. Yogi could be in a room with you for an hour and feel no need to say anything. He is happy with himself. He is sure you are happy with him, and if you are not, it is your problem. Yogi Berra is one of the most secure individuals I have ever known. As our catcher, he was great at talking. I somehow think he thought it was part of his job, like putting on the shin guards.

Williams hated a blabbermouth catcher, which Yogi was, but he could not hate Yogi. "Have a good dinner last night?" Yogi would ask. "Didn't eat, wanted to stay quick for today's game."

Or "The food is all bad here in New York." Or: "Maybe just shut up, you ugly bastard," Ted would respond.

"If you leave a tip, the food gets better," Yogi would say and even Reynolds might wish the two guys at home plate would shut up and the little one would give him a sign.

As you can see from the nature of those conversations, despite Ted's skill with a fly rod, he would not be my choice for a maroon-mate either. Since I brought Ted into this, I would like to make some comments about him.

He is like Yogi, hard not to like. He always had nice things to say about me and that is a good thing to admit when you are saying nice things about someone. Shows I may have a reason. When Boston played the Yankees, they brought along a slew of writers. Several things were at work to swell the number of reporters from New England.

Berra could move the runner, and move him late in the game like no one else I ever saw play the game. A lot of people said their shortstop Rizzuto was too small, but, damn, those two guys knew how to beat you. Makes me sick to think about it. ⓧ

—*Ted Williams*

The Red Sox and the Yankees were longtime rivals. I think the fans in Boston hated us more than our fans hated them. This maybe was because we won, but some people who see a lot more in baseball than I ever have feel the sale of Babe Ruth to us and the Red Sox losing to us are symbols of something way beyond eighteen guys, some bats, and one ball.

As long as it is harmless and to my way of thinking it is, then it's fine. It may be like the designated hitter, it gives people something to talk about. We liked to beat them and they wanted to beat us because we were good. I think they felt if they beat us, they would win the American League. Say the Red Sox were beating the St. Louis Browns—instead of saying to themselves, this is good—they thought to themselves, the Yankees will win all their games in St. Louis, so if we don't beat New York we are still in second place. Maybe they had an attitude problem, but if you think of how many times we won and they lost, you should be able to understand why even if they did they would not admit it today.

A great many ingredients went into the mix making up the Sox' and Yanks' chowder. My point is that to some people it still seems important, and it is.

They had a great park, Fenway, bright, knowing fans, and we had a storied ballyard, Yankee Stadium, and fans from guys that looked and sounded like William Bendix to Marianne Moore, the poet, and John Simon, the songwriter. That's about the way I saw it and I will leave the smoke and mirrors to others.

Another reason so many writers came down from Boston is because there were so many papers in and around Boston. It was also a cheap trip. As long as I am giving reasons, the cost of the story to the New England paper should be mentioned. You can bet the herd of Red Sox writers going to Cleveland was smaller than the one that came to the Bronx.

One of the writers, Ed Rumill, wrote for the *Christian Science Monitor* for over forty years. He became, as some writers did in those days, close to some of the players. In Rumill's case, the player was Ted Williams. I am told he was one of a few. I do know that Ted said in his book, *My Turn at Bat,* "Rumill was one of three writers I confided in."

He wrote on a picture he gave to Ed Rumill, "The one I trusted, fair with me, most of the time—Ted Williams." As you can see, Ted had a sense of humor when signing that photograph. Most of the pitchers in the American League would say it was the only time.

I have fun even thinking about this next scene, so let me try to paint the picture. Ted lived in the Florida Keys, down below Key

Largo, in a very small town, Islamorada. Ted's passion for fishing is something I have never understood, but his concern for his privacy should be obvious to anyone taking the time to think about what it was like to be Ted Williams.

Most everyone wanted a piece of Ted, so when his phone rang, at least in those days, a friend of his who ran a photo store would answer. Then, if he was home, he would pick up and listen in to see what was going on. If he was interested, he would chime in and if not, he might get the boat out. Or for all I know he might take a nap. To my way of thinking, he earned the right to do what makes him happy, and the trouble I have seen with a lot of older people is that they have not yet figured out just what that is.

Ted Williams has, at least I think he has. I know this may sound self-centered as hell, but try to see his point of view. He was a great baseball player during a time when doing what he did somehow seemed more important than it may have been. He was well paid and all he wants now is to, as Yogi describes it, "Tie a string to a pole and put it in the water."

His love of fishing is kin to the devotion some people feel for golf. (Now golf, I can understand that passion.) One very hot, humid, sticky Florida Keys day, three sixty-eight-year-old men went out in Ted's 18-foot flat-bottomed boat. The six-foot-three Williams, six-foot-four Rumill, and the huge ex-Cleveland Indians pitcher Early Wynn. The hitter, Williams, in the bow, Rumill without bait, pole, or fishing line—or interest in the sport—in the center. As Rumill explained it, "When you visit Ted and he says let's go fishing, you go fishing, relieved he isn't hooked on bull fighting, or skydiving."

The pitcher, Gus Wynn, not nearly as schooled in the art of fishing as his fellow Hall of Famer, Williams, was in the stern. He is also unwilling to admit to this lack of knowledge just as he was unwilling to confide in Williams how he planned to retire him when they were adversaries on the diamond.

Starting with remembered brushback pitches of yesteryear, and towering home runs hit in retaliation, Williams and Wynn shouted insults over the crouching Rumill. Teddy brought the rancor up-to-date by saying, "Don't stand up in the boat like that, or the fish will be feeding on us. Damn pitchers. Are you all dumb? Or just the ones from Cleveland? Watch me cast, I don't even have to stand up. See, I don't even make the boat rock. It's all in the wrist. Just like hitting your fastball."

Gus Wynn, still shouting: "With all the money you made, why didn't you buy a real boat? Come down to my place and we can go out in a real boat. Just the two of us. No writers."

"I am not a writer," Rumill said ruefully. "I'm retired."

Williams: "How the hell can you retire as a writer? You didn't do anything in the first place. What kind of child would want to become a writer?"

Rumill was Williams's guest, but fair game for Gus Wynn, who answered the question, "Guys that struck out all the time became writers, didn't you know that, you dumb bastard? Lucky you had good eyes or you would be lugging a typewriter around instead of a bat."

The fish did not bite, but the fishermen, even the one without a line in the water, did, and when the sun set they went back to the Williams home and went on into the night. Wish I could have been there, for the dry-land part at least.

Since I raised the fair-minded flag, let me wave it by saying, Stengel made his living by talking. Never forget, a baseball manager's job description would include what would now be called media relations. Getting the team's name in the papers is what they probably called it when Casey was in the ink business.

Branch Rickey said, "Casey was the best link or bridge between the team and the fans in the history of baseball."

It was different for a player like DiMaggio. Joe knew his paycheck didn't depend on what he told reporters. His physical ability and mental skills put bread on his table.

Since it may surprise some to see the reference to Joe's mental skills, let me explain. Running the bases is more of a mental skill than a physical skill. Even a slow player can become an excellent runner. Joe was a Grand Master, so was Yogi. ⊕

—*Philip Francis Rizzuto*

With Casey, however, ink was crucial.

When he arrived—and you can bet he would like the use of that term—to manage the Yankees, the National League had two teams in New York City. The New York Giants and the Brooklyn Dodgers. Every day, each team would have a contest: which one would be the lead story in the paper of record, the *New York Times*. The other papers were important, but the *Times* was crucial.

In the early spring, when it was still cold, we needed something to attract fans to our park. Opening Day was not a problem. The next Thursday was. If Whitey had a scoreless inning string going or Mickey hit two in one game, it would bring the fans out in the cold. ⊕

—*Del Webb, co-owner, New York Yankees*

From 1949 until 1953 the Dodgers had Burt Shotten and Chuck Dressen and the Giants had Leo Durocher competing with Stengel.

It seems to me that even a casual fan—we used to call them "World Series fans"—would say, "Advantage, Stengel." Casey wore well with the press, and later on, when Washington pols wanted to make some headlines of their own by looking into baseball and the antitrust issue, the then Senator Kefauver called Stengel to Washington.

Casey's testimony on July 9, 1958, was widely noted, as was the laughter of Mickey Mantle and Ted Williams seated behind him. So widely noted I will only repeat a few lines. Senator Joseph C. O'Mahoney asked Stengel, "How many minor leagues were there in baseball when you began?"

If Casey had answered twenty-five, chances are you would not see his response here. Stengel: "Well, there were not so many at that time because of this fact: For anybody to go into baseball at that time with the educational schools that we had were small, while you were probably thoroughly educated at school, you had to be—we only had only small cities that you could put a team in and they would go defunct." He went on for about twice that long, without giving an answer.

His induction speech at the Hall of Fame was the same sort of thing. You had to say he was a master. So was Joe, and while he was playing center field for the Yankees, the Dodgers and Giants had some pretty fair center fielders as well. Whitey Lockman, Carl Furillo, Bobby Thompson, Duke Snider and Willie Mays. It would seem to me if Senator Kefauver wanted to question a center fielder his choice of someone to represent that position would have been as easy as his selection of a manager.

Meeting famous people came with playing for the Yankees. Some of them were in the showers, every day. My first year, 1941, on Opening Day I stood ten feet from President Franklin D. Roosevelt. He threw out the first ball, in the old Washington ball park, Griffith Stadium. Only a few months back he had been a picture in my Civics textbook.

Now that I have dropped FDR's name, let me tell you about

another well-known man I knew who used to testify before Congress a lot. I don't want to use his name because he might not like it. When you tell someone something the way he told me, it may not please you to see it in print. He said that testifying before Congress was largely a waste of time. Yours and theirs, since for the most part nothing happened. You went down, they put you up, you answered the questions and it was over. He also said that he never knew anyone to tell the people who asked you to come down to Washington, no. When they asked, you went even when you knew it was a waste.

I said, "Next time they ask you, why don't you say no?"

I often wonder if he did. You can bet if they had asked Stengel back, he would have run as fast as those gimpy legs would have carried him.

Let me get on with the way I viewed Stengel, then, and now. No matter what you do for a living, you have a boss. Even if it is your own business you have a boss, a lot of them, they are called customers. My life centered around discipline. I didn't resent it. We all need to work to make a living. I worked for, or played for, Joe McCarthy and as I've said here and elsewhere, he was the best manager I ever saw. I played for Bucky Harris and he was a good manager as well. He just didn't have the chance to put in as many years with the Yankees as Joe and Casey, but he was good. You could trust him and he had an ego, but he was not full of himself.

I know, in my heart, I was better off that the Dodgers sent me packing, but my feelings about Casey are connected to that experience. I will tell you why I feel that way, as soon as I finish telling you about the experience. It's not that I was rejected—rejection is part of living—it was that I was made to feel like a fool for showing up. Have you ever looked for something in a department store and asked for help finding it and the clerk tells you, we do not carry the item, never did, have no plans to do so, and anyone asking for that item in the future will be requested to turn in their charge card and leave the store forever? That is the way my tryout was handled.

Let me anticipate several reactions. "So Casey said, 'Get lost.' That was years ago, forget it." Trust me, I have but I am trying to explain what it was like. A second reaction might be, "You should thank Stengel, he may have given you just the right dose of 'I will show you.' " Give that reaction first prize. I am sure it did me more good than harm. Carrying on this way about my tryout, as they would call it in Bassett (as in, my, that young'un does carry on), makes me wonder, what might have happened if one day during the early years I played for Stengel, if I had sat down in his office or in his room on the road and said, "Case, would it be OK if we have a little talk about us, the two of us? A little bonding, Skip, if you can spare the time."

The thought of doing so even today is so foreign to me I am "fairly amazed" I came up with the speculation.

> As it turned out, Pee Wee Reese and I were lucky the Dodgers rejected me. We could then compete but not for the same job. (X)
>
> —*Philip Francis Rizzuto*

I suppose another reason for not feeling warm and fuzzy about the "Ole Perfesser" is that almost anyone might have managed those teams and won. He had great players, great coaches, and it seemed, at least to me, that he took it for granted. I am sure he would not agree with my reading of that situation and I am not asking you either. Stengel might well remind me or anyone within earshot of the many days he spent learning his craft, ending with, "I paid my dues."

He did that for sure. The press called him a push-button manager and that irritated him something fierce, but it was true. When he first started in 1949 he gave a great speech in St. Pete. "I know little about this league and I am just going to watch and learn."

We won that year, as you know, and somewhere along the line, from '49 to '53, it went from the players won, to *I* won. What I am saying may be a little overstated, but I am not alone when I suggest that because Casey lived more of his life as a second-division manager, than as a manager of a World Series winner, the losing took a toll.

So when he did win with the great Yankee teams, it was a little hard for him to think he didn't have a lot to do with it. Maybe this will help explain, that when you lose, it is normal to explain it away or blame it away. It's natural, and because it is, you have to fight it. When you win, you did it all by yourself. In his mind, he was just as gifted when he managed the Toledo, Ohio, Mud Hens in 1926 as when he managed the New York Yankees in 1954. The Hens finished fourth, winning 87, losing 77, for a .530 percentage. In 1954, the Yankees finished second behind the Cleveland, Ohio, Indians who won a record 111 games. We won 103 and lost 51, making Casey's percentage .669. He may just have been right.

Ted Williams thought [Casey] was a big deal, and I did, too. Talking about Casey will take a little explaining. To start with, I liked him, respected him, and owed a lot to his confidence in me. I could also understand why some people, like Phil Rizzuto and even Joe D., did not feel the same way. You would never hear anybody say Casey was not interested in himself. ⚾

—*Yogi Berra*

Ty Cobb said, "Stengel deserves credit as the greatest manager of all time." No one could argue the fact that he had a huge impact on baseball and anyone who played for him would never forget the experience. That alone should make him happy. I hope he is.

CHAPTER FOUR

MIZE, THE BAT, AND THE MVP

When I read something, I want to be changed by what I read. Sometimes when I am on the road with the Yankees, in a strange hotel, I would like the change to be from sleepy to sleep. Even a dull book can be useful at such a time. I feel the same about listening and watching.

Let me make that point a little stronger, convinced as I am that we should try to learn from what is going on around us. I am still at a loss to understand what happened to me after I was voted MVP in the American League in 1950. If I were a mystery writer, I would call it "The Case of the Big Cat's Bat."

Late in the 1949 season, the Yankees acquired Johnny Mize from the New York Giants. It was a cash transaction, $40,000, on August 22. The date is important because a player changing teams that late in the season has to be sold by a certain date to be eligible for the World Series. The assumption when they make the rules in this sort of deal is simple. Only teams in contention would want to add a player. If you are in last place, they figure you can finish with the same guys. The "they" was the same then as now—the owners.

Mize was eligible to compete. The date then, and now, is August 31. Once you were eligible, another "they" came into play, the Stengel Brain Trust. How are we going to use the new player? Since Mize spent most of his playing time in the National League, Casey knew what he was getting. George Weiss made the deal to add Mize to our roster. He didn't do it in a vacuum, but it was his deal.

A good general manager looks on his field manager as a carpenter with an empty tool box and tries to give him the best tools available to do the job. The good general manager does not tell the field manager which hammer to use or, even while sitting up in his office, that he thinks a hammer is not the tool, a saw should be the tool of choice.

If you know even a little bit about the way organizations work, you know what I have just said is a textbook description. In real life or real baseball, it works out more like this. The General Manager makes it known, "Say, fellows, we paid a lot of money for this guy, doesn't it make sense that we use him?"

That Casey resisted using Mize I still find a mystery.

Even though I was a good long-ball hitter, I was a good contact hitter, too. I don't know, I was just good at getting the bat on the ball. Casey used to say, "He hits like a leadoff batter." Did you know I'm the only hitter to hit 50 or more home runs and strike out less than 50 times? I struck out 41 times in 1947. The next year I hit 40 homers and struck out 37 times. ⓧ

—*Johnny Mize*

Or the owner thinks a guy playing first base in the other league, or on another team in his league, is not playing enough. He is unhappy, but is a good guy and would be happy over here because everyone is happy over here. After all, I am the owner and I am a good guy to play for or even be around, for that matter. This player could be a useful addition. We ought to see about getting him. You can bring in the owner's wife, a golf pro, and some cab drivers, or a bartender in some cases, if you wish, because that is the way it happens.

So Johnny Mize is a Yankee in time to play in the 1949 World Series. After he came to the team and before we played the World Series, the players had a meeting to split up the pot of money. The pool of money relates to the first four games only. That is a Commissioner's rule, and as you would guess, it gives neither team an incentive to hope the series goes seven games.

If the players who won the opportunity to play in the World Series had any written rules covering the division of the cash pool, I was not aware of them. I do know this—we did it enough to get good at doing the job and my feeling is we were always generous. However, before you say to yourself, "as well you should be," think of that pool of money in 1949, '50, '51, '52, and '53 split up thirty ways as a major portion of our salary.

The player rep would call the meeting and my memory tells me that Joe McCarthy and Stengel would be sort of around. Not at the same time, Holy Cow, that would have been a great meeting and I would have no trouble remembering that one. When each had a pennant winner they arranged to be "around" at the divvy-up meeting. Joe and Casey may have said something, if they thought some player was not getting a fair shake, but I do not recall any specifics. It was our meeting run by the guy we wanted to run it in those years, Allie Reynolds.

> Winning the money was the hard part. The allocation chore was easy, RBI's, home runs, wins, even no-hit wins were not the factor. Perfect Attendance at Sunday school won a gold star. Perfect Attendance during the season won a full share. ⓧ
>
> —*Allie Pierce Reynolds*

Back to the mystery of the "The Case of the Big Cat's Bat." After we won the 1949 World Series, sometime during the off-season, the Yankees sent me, or I went on my own, to an ophthalmologist. Navy doctors and some other medical people had been telling me for a long time that my depth perception was not up to par. I think I knew what they were telling me, but I was also not concerned that sub-par depth perception was holding me back as a baseball player. If I had a problem, it would be my size and strength, and at age twenty-six, that was not about to change.

The idea of a weight room or strength coach was way down the road, as was the number of pulled hamstrings in major league baseball. The physician I went to see over the winter gave me a series of exercises. To tell the truth, I have forgotten if I did them in his office or if I had something I took home. I do know that I had to line up butterflies and other flying objects on a screen and then when I got it right, I did it again. The first few times it took a long time, but I got better at it. Like learning how to bunt, but you never got hit on the fingers. Just how long I did the butterfly dance I am not sure, probably a month or more. I do know this much, when I reported to spring training, I did not run into the clubhouse in St. Petersburg and say, "Hi, fellow Yankees. Who wants to be the first to hear what I did last winter?" While some players might tell you about a new car, no one would bring up butterflies—catching them, mounting them, or matching them up with bats and lady-bugs.

I went about the business of getting ready to play 154 games and being as good a shortstop or better as the rest of the American League players at that position. In case you have forgotten and I had, here are their names. Tigers: Johnny Lipon, Red Sox: Vern Stephens, Indians: Ray Boone, Washington Senators: Sam Dente, White Sox: Chico Carrasquel, St. Louis Browns: Tom Upton, and the Philadelphia A's: Ed Joost.

Spring training was not marked by any strong memories. When the bell rang, as the writers used to describe the first game of the season, my memory is vivid. I could not steal, buy, or lease a base hit. Had I been Joe D or Yogi, the writers would have been all over me, but since I was hitting down in the lineup, as I was for a few days, at least no one but me noticed. Except for Mize—he was not playing, which gave him time, but more important he was like Ted Williams, a student of hitting.

Fay Vincent, the Commissioner who took over when Bart Giamatti died, loved baseball as did Bart, and they both loved to talk about Mize. Johnny would talk about hitting a curve or a slider at the drop of a hat. He did so with as much passion at age seventy as he did at age thirty-three, about the age, plus a few, when he came by my locker, after I'd had another 0 for 4 afternoon.

Some of the players used to say that Mize sat in Stengel's lap. They were two National League rejects and so on. You can imagine some cheap shots. I would rather not take shots because they did little for the guy shooting them or the guy they were directed at. Mize convinced me, and it was a hard sell, since I was a tough prospect, that I should use his bat. Johnny Mize was 6 feet 2, over 200 pounds. He was the Big Cat and the bat he used looked and felt like something used on a wagon train on "Death Valley Days." He taped it up and said I could have it. He said he was not playing. So much for sitting in Stengel's lap. I may have tried it in BP or maybe I just tried it in a game when we were way behind or way ahead, I don't know which. I do know that the first time I swung it

I punched a hit over second and kept doing so the rest of the season. Not only did I do as well or better than the other shortstops, at the end of the season, I was voted the Most Valuable Player in the American League. Casey and the Dodgers had rejected the MVP of the American League. Holy Cow.

Someone in the musical *Mame* sings a song about a boy growing up and one line is, "Why did I buy you those damn long pants?" All during 1952 someone should have been asking me what the hell happened to the butterflies and that damn long bat? I don't even know what happened to the bat. My batting average dropped 50 points and my RBI's and runs scored also dropped off. We did not keep on-base percentage, a crucial stat in baseball, and it is funny George Weiss never came up with it, or perhaps he did and kept it to himself.

The sad thing for me and the good thing for the reader, at least I hope, is that my failure to do the things that had worked should be a lesson. Think about what it is, in any line of work, that makes you successful. Make sure you keep it up. They say, "If it isn't broken, don't fix it." In my case, if Johnny Mize and the eye doctor fixed it—don't break it.

PEARL HARBOR

"Money is the root of all evil, but it buys stuff." When I saw those words, it was hard not to smile. I wish I could remember where they were. Not a bumper sticker, because I can never remember seeing one of them. My best guess would be a college dormitory. The reason I started off with money is that whatever it is, it is important.

Edward R. Murrow, the CBS broadcaster, so important when I was playing and a faded footnote to today's players, said, "When they say it's not the money, it's the money." Casey Stengel liked to say that the last thing Yogi thought about before he went to sleep was money. Yogi was very good at pretending he didn't hear or at least didn't care about comments made about him, both in the clubhouse and from the stands. He was not simply very good, he was a master.

Yogi played in a golf tournament I help with in New Jersey and we had a chance to talk. He told me he has an answer if Casey gets on him in baseball heaven. Yogi is sure Stengel is already there and talking to "his writers" and will need a catcher. Here is Berra's comeback.

"Right, after thinking about how to pitch Williams and the rest of the Red Sox lineup and all the rest of my baseball responsibilities, then I think about the three boys and Carmen and the rest of my family, and then I have some time left I think about money, so it is the last thing."

In *The Summer of '49* David Halberstam writes, "Weiss firmly believed that a well-paid ball player was a lazy one. That gave him a philosophical justification to be penurious, but unbeknownst to the players he had a more basic motive. The lower the sum of all the players, salaries, the greater the additional bonus he received from the owners." Halberstam may know what took place in George Weiss's mind and I will not dispute his comments on Weiss's view of the level of energy exhibited by Yankee players. However, the allocation of funds and check disbursements from 1949 until the Yankees were sold to CBS in 1964 are another matter. George Weiss's income, and he was paid handsomely for that time, was in no way connected to the budget for player's salaries. ⚾

—*Joe Causin, Yankee accountant*

Edward R. Murrow hosted a show on CBS called, "Person to Person." It was a big show for CBS during the fifties, not as big as "Sixty Minutes," but mentioning that show will give you an idea.

I was nine years old and when the game was over I rushed down to the dugout and hung over with a scrap of paper and beseeched Phil Rizzuto to sign it. He did, gave it back, and smiled. I lost the paper, but still have the smile. ⓧ

—Pat Jordan, Sporting News *columnist*

Murrow was in the studio and he smoked a cigarette while the camera came into your living room and he said, "Good evening, this is Ed Murrow and tonight we are visiting the home of" . . . the home could have been anyone from Leonard Bernstein to Douglas MacArthur. It was an important show with big ratings and Murrow had what would now be called "presence." What it was called back then I don't know. "Good evening, tonight we are in New Jersey, paying a visit to the home of Phil and Cora Rizzuto. Hello Phil, hello, Mrs Rizzuto," and off they went—me showing Ed the den and Cora showing her china, for all I remember. You can bet I took some kidding the next day in the clubhouse and around the league for a while. Nothing new for him.

Murrow paid Yogi a visit too. CBS did not pay guests for letting them come into their homes and it cost Yogi because they messed up a flowerbed and he knows less about flowers than I do so he had to pay someone to fix what they messed up. I am sure he has forgotten all about that and will be surprised to see that I have not.

The subject of money and what effect I think it is having on baseball is something I want to get to a little later. Right now I want to tell you how money, big money, affected a baseball game the Army and Navy played during the height of World War II. The game was not money driven, as they like to characterize so much of what happens today. Put another way, the generals and admirals who got together and agreed to have a baseball game between the

Army and the Navy didn't share in the gate or have a piece of the action. In fact, I am sure they did not charge admission. If you happened to be in Hawaii in 1944 and you wanted to see a baseball game, you went.

The game was played on a field very near Pearl Harbor, in 1944. Everyone said, and I mean everyone—officers, enlisted men, the whole South Pacific theater—said more money was wagered on this game than on any other game in history. I was one of the people saying it but I don't mention that here to indicate that since I said it, it is true. As a matter of fact, I did not bet the game. I don't bet on professional sports. I am not against betting a few bob, as they say across the pond, and I lose some money on the golf course most every time I play. I just don't bet on professional games.

So take my word and a lot of words of others. This Army-Navy baseball game was covered by a lot of dollars. Take it the same way you take a road sign in a town you drive through in the Midwest, WELCOME TO CEDAR RAPIDS HOME OF THE BIGGEST CHICK HATCHERY UNDER ONE ROOF IN THE WORLD. If you are the kind of person who is going to stop and get out a tape measure, you are not going to believe a lot of money was risked at the same time people were risking their lives.

After the attack on Pearl Harbor, Sunday, December 7, 1941, baseball seemed, for a time, strangely unaffected. Some players, Bobby Feller, for example, went down Monday morning and signed up to join the service. If the attack had come on Monday the 8th of December, Bobby would have gone down the same day.

Others, and I was one, reacted to the war, but took more of a wait-and-see attitude. I don't know how else to explain how I felt, except to say that I loved my country but I was not going to run down and join the service. Looking back, I can now say something like, "They will get me soon enough," but I didn't then. We had draft-dodgers, and maybe some men went to Canada. I went to St. Petersburg, Florida, for spring training.

In 1942 we won the American League by 9 games and I played 144 games while our GI's were dying all over the world. Hard to write it, hard to think about it, but it happened. We played the St. Louis Cardinals in the Series and won the first game. They made four errors and didn't get a hit off Red Ruffing until the eighth inning. The series started in their park, Sportsman's Park, so we thought things were going our way.

Then they won four straight. Their outfield of Stan Musial, Terry Moore, and Enos Slaughter cooked our goose. They had good pitching. Mort Cooper for one and Johnny Beazley, Ernie White, and Max Lanier for three more, but what really killed us and remains in my mind are the plays made by their outfield in Game Three. Plays like Graig Nettles made against the Dodgers in 1978 for the Yankees or Ron Swoboda made for the Mets in 1969. In other words, heartbreaking for the other side.

Sportsman's Park has the distinction of being the home field for two major league teams for longer than any other stadium. The St. Louis Cardinals and St. Louis Browns shared the location bounded by Dodier Street, Grand Boulevard, Sullivan Avenue and Spring Avenue for thirty-three years. ⑂

—*Lawrence S. Ritter*, Lost Ball Parks

The broken Yankee hearts were DiMaggio's, Keller's, and Joe Gordon's. They were the ones robbed of hits but I guess we all had pain in the chest. I had a good series, hitting .381, best on our team, and if we had won the last game on October 5 in Yankee Stadium—and we had a real chance (Joe Gordon was picked off second base in the last of the ninth)—and the Series had gone to a sixth and seventh game, the .381-hitting Rizzuto would have been absent. I had joined the Navy and was asked to report at 0800 hours, October 6, 1942, Norfolk, Virginia. "Captain, sir, could I have some time, so I could finish up some work I am doing for a company, here in the city?" Answer, *"No."* As you can see, I was not asked to report at 0800 hours, I was told.

As I said, the Cards won in five games, I still can't believe it. What happened to me when I went into the Navy, *you* may not want to believe. If you paid income taxes in 1942 or spent time in the military, you will believe. Believe and perhaps shake your head a little as you do so.

When I began to think back and talk about my time in boot camp in Norfolk, Virginia, the word "coddled" came to mind. I used it and I don't use the word often so I looked it up and it means, "to treat tenderly, to pamper, to indulge." I would add this, from the Rizzuto dictionary, to coddle is to weaken.

Let me explain. I spent the required number of weeks in boot camp, I think it was three months. I did the time, time alone may work for monks, but the weeks I spent in boot did not make me into a sailor. Because I had the good fortune to play for the Yankees, in what was at the time last year's World Series, I did not learn anything. The Navy didn't scrimp on the shots, I got all of them and some extras, I also got the haircut. More than one. I was skinned several times. That way I at least looked like I fit in, but I knew I didn't, and they must have known it too. We all looked like peas in a pod, but when it came to training, I received zero.

Let me stop and try to explain something that may be hard to understand. I was proud to be making a living playing baseball for the Yankees. Doing something you like in front of 70,000 people and hearing them applaud when your name is announced is, well, it's a whole lot better than what happens to most people when they go to work. But I didn't try and make a big deal of it when I went to boot camp.

I went into the Navy like we all did, but when a chief looked at your file and saw under your occupation, Baseball Player, some-thing like this would ensue: "What team did you play for, kid, the Rocky Mountain Spotted Fevers?" When anyone heard Yankees, they responded with hate or affection, seldom with indifference.

I know it would have been wise on my part to refuse special treatment, but that is easy to say now. All I am saying is I did not seek the coddling. Now let me get to some examples. When they had knot tying 101, the chief would say, "Rizzuto, come up here." He would sit me down on a chair or a bench and the sailors would all practice tying knots on me. The class spent a lot of time talking about the Cardinal outfield of Musial, Moore, and Slaughter, so maybe some of them were shortchanged at the same time.

Knot tying comes back to me because it was an early class and you may be saying there is a lot more to being a sailor than tying knots. You are right and I missed some underwater drills and even bedmaking. I was coddled, recoddled, and while I left camp cer-tified as someone who could be in charge of a gun crew, the fact is I was not even in charge of my right arm. The one you use when saluting an officer.

If you think I am kidding, I am not. I remember one time one of the officers called me into his office. They didn't say, Sailor Coddle, report to the office, or anything like that, but that is the way I felt when I went in this captain's office. He greeted me and I greeted him and while I didn't sit down, I knew that from civilian life, I would not have been mistaken for Tom Cruise in *A Few Good Men*. We chatted for a few moments and perhaps I leaned a hand on his desk. Whatever I did, and it was not overtly out of character, like putting my feet on his desk or anything like that, it suddenly dawned on Captain Queeg that something was not right.

He said something like "Snap to." It wasn't straighten up and fly right, it was more of a command and it was given in a "What-the-hell-is-going-on-here" or "Just-who-do-you-think-you-are" tone of voice. I knew exactly who I was. I was a guy who had volunteered to serve my country. I respected our flag, and our institutions. They chose to coddle me and it would have taken a different person than I was to have said, "Don't coddle me and let me tie those knots, shoot those guns, and tote that barge."

The little incident in the captain's office was what they would now call a blip and they tied a few more knots and pretty soon I was graduated and told I was a sailor of quality, ready to shoot down enemy planes, or at enemy ships. The trouble was I knew better. When Casey Stengel told me I would never become a big league ball player I didn't know better, I hoped better, I prayed better, and I worked hard to get better. After boot camp I knew better.

The Navy in their own way knew better as well, because my first assignment along with some other major league ball players, who may not wish to see their names here, was playing baseball and selling war bonds. We played all the time, even traveled to play other teams. Most of our games that summer were played in the South, along the Eastern Seaboard. I am sure someone said it was good for morale. I am sure it was. It was good for the manager who got a chance to manage some major league players. Since other servicemen came to see the games, that had some value, but the net effect on me is that I looked like a sailor but I was really a hothouse flower and when I had to leave the greenhouse, it was a shock.

I was not thinking that way then. As I tried to say earlier, show me a twenty-two-year-old kid that doesn't take well to coddling, and I will say, "Nice to meet you, Mr. Vince Lombardi."

I began to think, this is not bad. I am getting a chance to work on my game and I always liked Virginia. Not long after, probably a few months, parents of kids fighting and dying, while other kids were playing baseball, started to complain about The Coddled. With good reason. The parents started to write letters to Congress and the press. I can just hear the call-in shows if it happened today.

Not long after the resentment started flowing, it seemed like days, the Navy (probably the Army as well) came out with a blanket order. It said in what we used to call "you will, and you will like it" language that all athletic personnel will on or before X date be shipped overseas.

They gave me a camouflage bag, some clothes to match, and a gun all in this canvas duffel. I knew right then they were going to send me—a guy who not only couldn't shoot straight, but couldn't shoot, along with a bunch of boot camp honor graduates, and maybe one other coddle—to someplace, say, an island where we would all blend in with the trees. The piece or gun was not in one piece. Some assembly required! How about all assembly required. How about carry me back to old Virginia.

I knew I had been coddled and I knew the party was over. I was going to be sent to someplace where I would blend into the scenery and we were not going on a snipe hunt. When someone said "Right shoulder arms," that someone expected me to know how to put that gun together. Forget about not knowing how to salute, I couldn't be worried about that now. If only the captain had taken a real interest in me and seen that what I needed was not special treatment but the same as all the rest, I would have been better off. Not pleased, mind you, but better off.

I was in a fog and when the fog lifted I was on my first island— Treasure Island, California. It occurs to me as I write this that if the reader hasn't been in the service some of what I am saying may not ring true. For example, getting to Treasure Island. This may help—you are told to "fall out," meaning you go from the place you sleep into an open space, and then they tell you what to do. Like go back to where you were sleeping and put all your stuff in that bag and fall out again, and then line up and get on these trucks. The trucks take you to the railroad and you fall out, again, are told to line up and get on the train. The train is not waiting, you may stand around for some time, but you do get on the train when it comes and they tell you to do so. They manage to feed you and the train moves, and you fall out in California. We got some more shots and a haircut, for all I remember, and in a few days we fell out and were told to get into a line to be ready to march, in my case walk or shuffle, down a line and up the steps to a ship for a long voyage. No one really said long voyage, because they never told you anything like that, but we knew this was not an outing, we somehow knew that.

As it turns out, it was thirty-three days and this sailor suffered from chronic sea sickness, perhaps as the result of too much coddling. But let me get back to the line. It, like most lines, moved slowly and I was in no hurry. I noted a phone booth and I slipped out of line, no one seemed to care, they were all thinking about that long voyage. I called Cora, my new young wife, and ranted about coddling, guns in pieces, and camouflage pants with matching shirts, ending with I am coming home. She said, and the words were the most important words of my life, "If you do, you will find an empty home." That was it—no lecture, nothing about I-understand-and-it-will-get-better, just the words as presented.

The reason I am comfortable in writing this is I did what I have written and I am proud of Cora for saying what she said. I am also making the assumption that anyone taking the time to read this is interested in what happened. Not just the hits and runs but the errors as well.

On the way to New Guinea, I got so sick they took me off the ship. Gamadodo had been a leper colony and while I was glad to get off the rolling ship for the moment, I thought I was having a nightmare. It turned out to be a mistake because on the ship, which was well stocked by the Navy, the food was fresh, and now I was getting powdered food. It was awful, but I had a great bed.

A bunch of the guys in Gamadodo were from New York, they were Seabees and had seen me play ball. It was coddle time. They made a bed for me out of two-by fours, inner tubes, and a mattress (where they found it I will never know) that was the best bed I ever had and ever will have. They put it under some trees and I slept for several days, got better, and pretty soon another ship picked me up and I went back to fruit and a bed of pain.

Next stop, Finch Haven. The Japanese controlled Northern New Guinea, but by the time we got there, the Allies had reconquered the area. Knowing what you know about my ability with a

20-millimeter gun you might well say, thank you lucky stars. I did and I do.

Not too long after we got to Finch Haven another blanket order came out. All major league ball players were to report to Hawaii. The two other guys in Finch Haven, perhaps in all of New Guinea, with big league experience were Dominick DiMaggio and Broadway Charlie Wagner.

Broadway was the right name for Wagner—even his dungarees were tailored. Joe's brother Dom played for the Red Sox but at the time had not been in a World Series, nor had Charlie, so I was the only one going from our sector with World Series stripes. It was important and they knew it, so I need to put it down.

They put the three of us on a plane for the flight to Hawaii. Now this is the truth, they had us sitting according to rank. We sat on a trunk in the back of the plane. In the front everyone had a lot of gold braid, one of the young Rockefellers was on the plane. I don't know which one it was and wouldn't know it if I heard his name today. I just know he was in front and they said he was a young Rockefeller. I remember him as pleasant, they all were, but we knew where to sit.

The trip, in what was called a Mars Seaplane, took forever. The noise when it took off—the noise and the shaking because it was in the water—was something awful. It seemed like they would go several hundred miles and then land with a crashing sound and they would pull up to an island to gas up. I am not sure which was worse, the crash landing and then the noise and the shaking when we took off again, or the fact that they were having a war on those islands. It may sound funny now and it does to me to think about it, but it was not at the time.

We made it to Hawaii and the Navy team was put on a floating barge, it was so big you did not know it was on water. The Army was right next door but for some reason I think they were on shore. Joe Gordon was one I remember on their team. None of us had any practice. We went on the field, threw the ball around, and played. We had baseball cleats, I am sure, because I would remember playing in something else, but what uniforms we wore, if any, is a blank. We had Johnny Mize at first base and our manager was Bill Dickey. Bill was a lieutenant commander and was already in Hawaii when I landed.

We played the next day and I have vivid memories of several things. One is that Bill—my Yankee teammate, Bill Dickey—told Pee Wee Reese to play short. The second is that the reason so many brass were on that plane was because so much money was bet on the game. —Here was this game played at the height of the war, in a war zone, and we were told more money was bet on this game than any game in history to that point. I don't know how true that was, don't forget I was sitting on a trunk in the back of the plane. The Navy had the better team, Mize, I mentioned, and Dom DiMaggio. We also had Schoolboy Rowe and Pee Wee.

Serious baseball fans are probably thinking right about now something like this. Reese is in the Baseball Hall of Fame and Rizzuto is not. Bill Dickey used Pee Wee at short and Rizzuto at third, that must tell you something. I can tell you this much. It never occurred to me to question a manager's decision about where I played or in what order I batted. Add to that normal Rizzuto rule, in Hawaii, during WWII, this: I was not about to make any waves. If Bill Dickey says, "I have always wanted to play the hot corner. I am at third, Pee Wee, you are at short, Scooter, get behind the plate," you can bet I would have put on the face mask. You can also bet that the odds on the game, if they were handicapping, would have changed.

We, the Navy, cleaned their clock and while I did not question Bill Dickey's decision to put me at third, I did implore, rather I begged him, to let me stay in Hawaii. I will run the clubhouse, rake the field, you name it, Bill, was just part of my pitch. All to no avail. The Army guys, the losing team, went out or back right after the series. I left the next day. Never saw any of Hawaii. As soon as it got dark that night, the lights were blacked out and a curfew enforced at night and every night.

It was a great break to participate in the series for several reasons. Almost every time I am on the road broadcasting a Yankee game, I run into someone who saw one or all nine of those games. We gave them a little time to savor America's pastime.

The competition was keen; the Navy roster had twenty-five players with major league experience and the Army had seven men with some time in the big leagues. Some of them, like Charlie Silvera of the Army, went on to make it in the big leagues. Ferris Fain was another.

Joe DiMaggio was on the Army team. Beating the Army seven out of eight games with Joe playing center field was another reason to be pleased to say I played in the games.

Johnny Mize played first base for the Navy and, until now, I did not realize three of the October Twelve were on the same diamond.

The third baseman playing for the Navy on the Kahului Fairgrounds in 1943 knew he was going to make a living playing baseball, and if it looked like he didn't belong on the same field with this level of play, you can be sure word would get around.

I know that some wondered about Manager Bill Dickey's decision to play me at third and Pee Wee Reese at short. I know because I was one of them. At the time, the rule was not to ask. However, if you have a chance to learn, even years later, what went into the decision, believe me, you do so.

A friend happened to be paired with Pee Wee on a golf outing last year. They talked about the games and Pee Wee, ever the gentleman, suggested that Bill Dickey, having played with me for several years, knew I was perhaps a little more versatile and could make the switch.

I will never know what was on Bill Dickey's mind, but it was nice to know what was on Pee Wee Reese's.

CHAPTER SIX

TOMMY

Tommy Henrich looks and sounds like a character right from the pages of a Charles Dickens novel. Character, indeed, has been Henrich's trademark since his minor league days, evidenced by his letter to the Baseball Commissioner Judge Kenesaw Landis. "Dear Judge Landis, I am playing baseball for a living in the Cleveland Indians organization and in my judgment the owner is not living up to our contractual agreement." The twenty-three-year-old Tommy went on for a brief paragraph, concluding with "I would be grateful if you would look into this matter, both for my benefit and for the general betterment of organized baseball. Sincerely, Thomas David Henrich. July 4, 1936, Massillon, Ohio."

Henrich risked his career and reputation. Landis looked into the matter and declared Henrich a free agent. Half the major league teams offered him a contract. The Yankees were one of the first and backed up the contract with $25,000. Henrich signed and after a month in their minor league system (Newark, New Jersey, Bears) was brought up to the Yanks to play along with Charley Keller and Joe DiMaggio, filling out one of the best outfields in the history of baseball.

Old Reliable played for the Yankees for eleven years, first in the outfield and then both in right field and at first base. (His life-time .282 batting average and 183 home runs say less about his contribution than his nickname of Old Reliable.) Game-winning hits by a left-handed hitter facing a right-handed pitcher were not chronicled as they are today, along with most base hits on Astro-Turf on a Sunday. Henrich was a game-winning hitter (or gamer) before the term was invented.

His air of professionalism was enough to satisfy Frank Crosetti, the keeper of the flame. Cro played with Ruth and Gehrig. He saw Joe D arrive and depart. He was the constant. Henrich loved to play and liked to practice. The right-field fence in the old stadium was just over four feet and the top was a railing just the right size, in Tommy's opinion, to jump on, balance for an instant, and catch a sure home run.

Cro used to marvel at the veteran right fielder's daily practice. Running to the fence, jumping and attempting to keep his balance long enough to snare a ball destined for the seventh row in the box seats.

"What's the chance you could make that play in a game, Tommy?" Cro asked one day. Henrich replied, "If I don't practice, none. If I do practice, fifty-fifty, and if I touch the ball and drop it I could be charged with an error."

Much later Cro, still in pinstripes, was telling a young outfielder of the value of practice even at the major league level. "What's to practice?" was the question to Cro.

Later on, the same player lost a ball in the sun during a Series game. Cro said nothing—the ball was lost and so was the chance to learn from Old Reliable. The young player was never called Young Reliable. Henrich and Crosetti, magnanimous in retrospect, agree that the ball lost in the sun could have happened to Terry Moore or Jimmy Piersall, two of the best outfielders of all time. They agree the failure was one of understanding. You become a Yankee because you have talent and use it. You stay here by getting better. Some guys never learned. More never got the chance.

"All that's been written before," the eighty-three-year-old Henrich admonishes his listener. "Let's talk about why none of us were included in the October Twelve group. After all, we had a lot to do with winning the first one." Henrich spoke the last sentence in a soft voice and then burst into laughter that had the timbre of church bells. A golfer in the mixed grill at the Prescott Valley (Arizona) Country Club, looked over at Henrich and smiled. A smile reserved for a treasured member.

"If you need any help getting back to your car let me know, Thomas," said the admirer.

"I'll manage," Henrich replied.

Henrich's exit from his obligatory white sedan reminded those watching not of Casey Stengel but rather of a youthful Connie Mack.

Roger Angell suggested in a *New Yorker* piece that Arizona was the best place to watch spring training, but he could not find his rental car in the lot, as all the cars were white. A modest defense against the Arizona sun. ⚾

—*Wes Westrum*

Henrich's sensitivity to the character issue is obvious. Thinking back on the guts it took to write to Judge Landis warmed his juices and stirred his soul.

"I don't feel, as some, that baseball is any different than any other business, and character or the lack of it plays a role. People will push you around if you let them. If you let them, many of them will do it more and start to like doing so. It's part of your job to make sure they don't. You don't need to be a student of Lenin. You just need to be a student of human nature. Alexander Pope said it: 'The proper study of mankind is man.' I have forgotten the year, but I will guess it was 1946. I have not forgotten the place, the visitors' clubhouse in Fenway Park in Boston. Happy Chandler was the Commissioner and I was the player representative for the Yankees. Allie Reynolds replaced me.

"The Mutual Broadcasting Company made a deal with baseball to pay for broadcast rights. Just how it all worked, I do not remember. I mean by this that anyone smart enough to be a player representative knew that we worked for the owners, it was their team, and we were employees. But I do know this much. When the deal was cut, it stipulated that all the money would go directly into the pension fund. It was the way the pension would be started. This may sound farfetched, and it may be that all the money was to go for only one payment to the pension fund. Sort of a pump priming. That may have been, all I know is what I am telling you.

"I didn't ask Happy how much money was involved, nor did I ask him when it would be paid. Instead, I simply asked him how it got from Mutual to the pension fund. I asked him five different times in front of the usual trunks that are scattered around a clubhouse and in front of several players and Frank Scott, our traveling secretary at the time, subsequently a players' agent. Happy, now morose, never answered my question. His failure to respond was duly noted by the others in the room while I was asking the questions, but none made a sound during my plea for information from the one man who represented the sport or business.

"Later on I learned the money was sent from Mutual to Happy's office and then to the pension fund. Tinker to Evers to Chance. I often wondered how long Happy held the ball on the relay and did anything end up in his glove, but that's for a book called *Baseball and the Federal Reserve.*

"Let's talk about those twelve guys. Boy, were they lucky." More laughter. "Stengel was not a clown when he became our manager in 1949. Spring training was the usual and nothing about it stands out. But the three-game exhibition with the Brooklyn Dodgers when we got back to New York holds vivid memories. We were lousy. Even a good team can look bad. We used to tell Crosetti, who liked to moan, that we will be all right when the bell rings, and the season starts.

"I don't really know how I felt. I don't know if I felt we were in the soup or that we were just in a slump. I know we played poorly against the Dodgers but I don't recall feeling we were lousy, just that we played that way and would probably come around. Charley Keller, who never brought attention to himself, stood up after the last game and, while never raising his voice, told us and himself, as well, a few things that would have made Knute Rockne go back to the drawing board before writing his next 'Win one for the Gipper' speech. I am not going to even attempt to repeat Keller's words. They would sound sappy and weak. The fact that this was Charley Keller and he was saying, we have talent but if we squander our abilities the American League is going to make fools of us, was stunning. Charley shivered everyone in the room. Stengel could have given the same speech and no one would have listened. Charley the Silent spoke, and we hung on every word.

"The Keller jump-start lasted a long time. By then, we had Joe back, the one guy who never needed a speech. We had a good team, and we got back into the habit of winning. It's a habit, you know."

"Only one of the twelve guys is in the Hall of Fame and I am sorry. Dozens of pitchers in Cooperstown would be delighted to change records and ability with Allie Reynolds. Baseball is about winning and Reynolds won. He not only won, he won the big games against the other team's best. Their best pitcher and their best players.

"Ted might sit one out against the Browns but not the Yanks. As for Rizzuto, to me it is a simple question. Where do you put your best player? You start with shortstop. He has to make the plays, the guy at third does too, of course, but he reacts. The guy at short is key, if you don't think so ask the high school coach in your town.

> I am not going to get into Rizzuto and the Hall of Fame except to say this much. The game is baseball, right? OK, then I will give you nine Ralph Kiners. You give me nine Phil Rizzutos and I will win. Ⓧ
>
> —*Tommy Henrich*

"I remember a big game playing the Indians, Bob Lemon pitching. Phil, not Stengel, gave Joe D the squeeze sign. DiMaggio was on third, and at that time batters, at least some of them, could give signs without getting an okay from the manager.

"Phil ran his hand down the bat and covered the end with the palm of his hand. That was our squeeze sign. It was not an easy sign for 'Tiny Hands' to give or relay. Small hands, short arms, long bats make giving the sign in a natural fashion difficult for someone like Phil. I remember he questioned the pitch and gave the sign again to make sure Joe saw it, which, of course, he had, the first time.

"Rizzuto, unlike Keller, liked to cut the pie a little. Most anyone can bunt the ball high and away. They can't always bunt it properly, but they can put the bat on the ball so when they go back to the dugout they can do so with their head held high. It takes a skilled bunter, and Phil was the best, to lay one down when the ball is low and inside, right at his head. Scooter dropped a fish, and Joe could have walked in with the winning run.

> My best pitch is anything the batter grounds, lines,
> or pops in the direction of Rizzuto. Ⓚ
>
> *—Vic Raschi*

"Let me say a few more words about those twelve men. At one old timers' game, Bauer got up with a man on first and you know everyone in the park wanted to see him hit one out. He sacrificed and moved the runner. That run won the game. Old habits die hard.

"At one of those games Vic Raschi and Allie and I were talking about the greatest third baseman the Yankees had and who was the best. Clete Boyer, Graig Nettles, Red Rolfe, and I said Bobby Brown. Lots of hooting, because as Eddie Lopat used to say, 'I hope you don't become a surgeon, Bobby. With those hands you could do some real harm.'

"The point I was trying to make is that of the third basemen we had, the one I would most like to see at the plate when the chips were down was Bobby 'Never Choke' Brown. I am not saying he should be in the Hall of Fame. I am only saying he could hit. Hit with the best of them. The American League is lucky to have him and we were lucky to have him also.

"Now do we have time to talk about my home run on a two-and-oh count against Don Newcombe to win the first game of the 1949 World Series to start those twelve guys on their way to fame and fortune?"

I think you just did, Tommy.

STANKY

Often, not every page, but every chapter for sure, I wonder about the value of what I am putting down on these pages. I know what it does to me and for me to take my thoughts back to Bassett, Virginia, or Minneapolis, Minnesota, when the Kansas City Blues played the Millers or St. Paul when we played the Saints. After all the years of drawing a paycheck from a baseball team, it is satisfying to know I still refer to "them" as "we."

Richard Sandomir, the *New York Times* TV sports columnist, wrote some nice words in a column titled "Scooter: The Second Final Goodbye" in September 1993. When I say nice words I mean it was an understanding article. I believe Mr. Sandomir always makes his readers understand what he is writing, but sometimes the subject of his words may wince a little. Not as much as when hit with a fastball in the ribs, but wince all the same.

The headline on the column written by a nameless headline writer was HOLY COWS AND GOODBYES: A READING BY PHIL RIZZUTO: "Friday's epochal event may have been Phil Rizzuto's last bovine melody behind the Yankee microphone after thirty-seven years."

The "event" was the game I did with Bobby Murcer and Tom

Seaver from the Skydome in Toronto. It was the last game of the 1993 season for WPIX and it may have been my last game as a broadcaster. Madison Square Garden Network, who owns the Yankee "rights," may, or may not, cut the same deal with PIX in 1994.

Most people in the New York area call WPIX, PIX. Mr. Sandomir then said, "If you missed Scooter's 1993 finale, here are excerpts from the Quintessential Phil, in all his glorious, surreal, and bizarre stream-of-consciousness."

In 1990 PIX and MSG had some of the same discussions they are having now. That is why he said "Second Final Goodbye." Why he said "quintessential and glorious and surreal" is that he writes for the *New York Times* and not the *Shopping Center News*. I know exactly what the reference to stream-of-consciousness was meant to convey and like the agile shortstop I used to be, I wish to jump right on that opportunity. None of what I have to say is defensive, rather it is informational, so read it in that vein. When people describe a speech or something written as stream-of-consciousness in nature, they are saying, in a nice way, they don't follow it.

I know the charge. I jump from topic to topic. It's true and Ted Williams does the same thing.

And for whatever it's worth, most people tell me they know where I'm going.

I played baseball a long time in New York, and the beat writers back then might ask one of us if we missed a sign, but we would not ask them if they ended a sentence with a preposition. In fact, we were not encouraged to talk to writers at all. We were treated like kids during that time. Speak when you are spoken to. Be seen but not heard.

Don Zimmer—who coached for the Yankees, managed the Padres, Rangers, the Red Sox and the Cubs—told me a great anecdote that illustrates the headline on a story and its content. It may also indicate that the Dodger players of that era had a little different relationship with their writers than we did with ours. We were the Yankees, proud, austere, snobbish, cold.

Let me explain Zimmer first in case you don't know him. He has been making a living in baseball almost as long as I have and he is one of its real treasures. If Zimmer did not exist someone should have invented him. When he joined the Yankees, Nick Priori, the Yankee clubhouse man, showed his usual good sense and put Zimmer next to Yogi. I guess he figured they could spit on each other. As it turned out, they became friends as good people often do.

Zimmer was an infielder on the Dodgers, and a good one, but when your team has Gil Hodges, Jackie Robinson, Pee Wee Reese, and Billy Cox on its roster, you better be a great one. Zimmer might have been one but never got the chance to find out. During the 1955 World Series he platooned. It was a left-hand–right-hand thing and during the middle of the Series he came in the clubhouse and saw he was not playing.

Milton Richman, a writer for one of the New York papers, came over to his locker and asked if Zimmer knew why. Zimmer of course didn't and added that he was a baseball player and he wanted to play. He said something like I know I can't take over for Pee Wee so I wish they would trade me next year. He did not say *"Play me or trade me,"* the plea heard so often in the clubhouse during that time. Not as often now, I would guess, when players are making two million a year.

"Don't play me. I don't want to get hurt," may be the cry today.

When you pay someone so much they are afraid to play because they might get hurt and can't make even more, something isn't working. Ⓚ

—*John Mize*

Walter Alston, the Dodger manager, was a tough guy from all I heard and the next day the news story carried this headline: ZIMMER RIPS ALSTON. Zimmer was dressing for that day's game when Buddy Bavasi, the Dodger General Manager, came storming into the clubhouse waving the story. He did not say, "William Donald Zimmer, I have spoken with your immediate supervisor, Mr. Alston. Would you please arrange to meet with me at your earliest possible convenience?"

What he said in front of the other twenty-five players was along these lines: "Zimmer, you no-good, ungrateful jerk, what the hell are you trying to do? We are trying to beat the Yankees. To win a World Series. And you pull this. I told you it was OK to play in Cuba this winter [an important source of income to Zimmer— $1,000]. Forget that, Zimmer, you no-good bastard." All the while Buddy was buzzing, he was waving the story and Zimmer was asking, "Did you read the story? Did you read the story?"

Buddy and Zimmer, from that point, were lost in words that contained no information, just anger and resentment. One of the Websters, and I guess they were all smart, said, "Anger is not an argument," but who was going to remind Buddy and Zimmer at such a time? Buddy flew off and Milton Richman, the writer, slid in—some ball players would like me to say he slithered in. When the hand flapping subsided, and the dust settled, Richman explained how the headline writer and the writer perform different chores for the paper. Then Milt added that if his story and the headline caused Zimmer to lose his chance to earn $1,000 playing winter ball in Cuba, that he [Richman] would write a check to cover Zimmer's loss. Zimmer was right. The story never mentioned manager Alston.

Try as I might, I cannot imagine something like that taking place in a modern clubhouse, unless it was on a TV show with Rod Serling called "The Twilight Zone." I can well imagine a general manager taking a player to task in front of others, always a dumb move, but the writer-player relationship, including the offer of blood money, went out with baggy uniforms. I liked baggy uniforms too, it made it easier to fool the ump into thinking the ball hit you.

However, baggy or, if you prefer, loose-fitting uniforms, made it all the easier for the big bad wolf to grab you while sliding into second, in the bad wolf's attempt to break up a double play.

The bad wolf I want to talk about here so I can give equal time to a New York Giant infielder, as I just did for Zimmer, a Dodger infielder, is actually a little bad wolf, Eddie "The Brat" Stanky. I am going to have a little trouble writing an even-handed version of this story, for two reasons. Over forty years later it still hurts. The second reason is I like stories where most of the characters are good guys, or at least well intentioned, and please don't tell me the road to hell is paved with good intentions.

If I failed to write about the time Stanky got the drop on me and not only made me look bad, but plagued me over the winter every time I had to explain my part, I would be a wimp. He made me look bad, it took less than a second. It helped his team win a World Series game. It was in the third game in 1951, the year Bobby Thomson hit the home run to put the Giants into the Series. The Giants won the first game behind Dave Koslo, Allie Reynolds lost, giving up two runs in the first. Eddie Lopat won the second game and we were even, going to the Polo Grounds, just over the Harlem River. I remember the second game because Stengel led off with Mantle and Bauer hit second, while I batted third. Both Mickey and I bunted for a base hit in the first inning. Wes Westrum, the Giants catcher, still does not believe it.

The Polo Grounds was three quarters of a mile from the stadium, a brisk ten-minute walk. The box score that day said Raschi LP, Hearn WP, Jones, Save. Anyone seeing the game knew the Yankee shortstop Rizzuto botched an important play.

Allie Reynolds lost the first game, Larry Jansen, the Giants righty, lost the second, and Rizzuto the Yankee shortstop played a role in losing the third game. ⓧ

—*Philip Francis Rizzuto*

I am not going to say Eddie Stanky was a dirty player. It's been said and written enough times by others, I don't need to add my two cents. I do need to say, considering the three times he broke my nose in the minor leagues and the number of times he had thrown dirt in my face in the minors and the number of times he slid into second base and grabbed that loose-fitting shirt I mentioned and pulled me down with him so my throw to the first baseman ended up in right field, I should have been ready for anything. I wasn't and I paid dearly. Still am, as you can see. In front of 52,035 paid and the press and TV, as Casey pronounced it, the Polar Grounds on October 6, 1951, with the Giants leading us, 1 to 0. Vic Raschi was strong and we knew he would get stronger, he always did.

Willie Mays, Hank Thompson, and Monte Irvin played in the outfield for the Giants. The first time in the history of baseball three black players performed for one team. ⓧ

Willie Mays had driven in Hank Thompson in the second. Vic had given up two hits and one run when the Giants came to bat in the fifth. Vic struck out their pitcher, Big Jim Hearn. Giant leadoff man, Eddie "The Brat" Stanky, had been called out in the second. Getting caught looking at a third strike makes you mad. It makes you mad on the playground at recess. Doing so during a World Series can give you a case of the vapors. Stanky worked Vic for a walk, giving them a runner at first with one out. Stanky stole eight times that year and was not a threat to run with a one-run lead. The next hitter, Alvin Dark, with his poker face and body to match, didn't fool Yogi and he signaled a pitchout. Gil McDougald, playing second that day, knew I would cover second, and Raschi delivered the high fastball to Berra, who came out of his crouch as the ball was thrown. Yogi was the only other player on either team that might have hit the pitchout, and he caught it—Yogi "Bad Ball-Hitter" Berra. His throw to me at second base had Stanky, who had to run, even though Dark could not reach the Raschi pitchout, dead in the water. The Brat was short by 20 feet. Stanky's description of what happened next is not much different than my own. Stanky says he was short by 12 to 15 feet but he was not short on brains. It was not, in his view, that he made a good play—I made a bad one. I made what he called an American League play. In other words, I did not take the ball out of my glove and tag him with the ball in my bare hand. I laid the glove, with the ball, I thought, firmly gripped in front of second base, all the better to make his foot touch it as he slid into second. My, what big feet you have. Big enough for the soccer-playing Philadelphia native to kick the ball out of my glove, and kick it so well that Joe DiMaggio, our center fielder, retrieved it.

By this time Pele Stanky was on third. Yogi was saying, "What's a catcher to do?" DiMaggio was thinking he should have been backing up his infielders even closer than he had been doing. I felt sick. Raschi never said a word. Not then, not ever. Sometimes I wish he had.

Dark singled, and Stanky scored. Giants 2, Yanks 0. Hank Thompson singled, moving Dark to third. When the inning was over, they had five runs. Whitey Lockman finished it off with a three-run home run. Whitey was in the dugout. Vic was on the way to the shower.

I didn't sleep that night. I recall the rain starting. I don't recall the line from Shakespeare but I knew where to look it up. "It droppeth as the gentle rain from heaven." The rain didn't keep me awake, my dumb play did, but it was a great rain. It gave us a day off and rest for our great pitching staff. Holy Cow, it was a good rain. We had better pitchers and most baseball people feel the day off gave us a chance to regroup and win the next three with the Big Three Reynolds, Lopat, and Raschi. Vic had time to rest up enough to pitch a whale of a game to finish them off in the last game. Hank Bauer got the winning hit and made a fine catch to end the game.

1949. 1950. 1951 World Champs. Holy Cow. We had won three times. Played before 774,702 baseball fans. Earned $17,811.00 and some World Series rings. If memory serves me, we all took rings at that time. Later on the team would offer other gifts to commemorate a World Series win. One year it was a silver box with all the team's autographs and another time it was a leather ice bucket like the one used by firemen even before the Yankees were a team. I have forgotten many of the awards and even some of the high moments.

I have not forgotten Pele Stanky and you can bet his memory is sweet.

So is my ring.

CHAPTER EIGHT

HANK BAUER

"I was pleased to learn that Jerry Coleman was not only my team-mate while we both played with the Yankees but that he was ob-servant. I watched him on some interview show talking about choking and what a World Series can do. He went on to say that he didn't like the word 'choke,' at least when it came to the Yan kees of our time. Each of us responded to pressure in a different way. He went on to comment about how much better I hit when playing in the World Series after starting poorly. I knew better than anyone what he was saying, I was just pleased and impressed that he knew it as well. Looking at my batting average for all nine (.167, .133, .167, .056, .261, .429, .281, .258, and .323) tells only part of the story. I go from bad to much better, but what really counts in baseball is not your average. Give me a team of two-out singles hitters and I will give you a second-place team. The numbers are better, but what was really better was when I got my hits. Jerry was right. Some of playing better has to do with playing more and I was lucky to have so many chances. Think of guys like Williams and Musial. Ted hit .200 in his one Series and Stan was lifetime .331 and .256 in three World Series.

"Going to the park every day was an adventure, because you didn't know if you were going to play or sit. Even looking at the other team's pitcher in the paper didn't give you a clue. Stengel used the book and threw it away.

"You couldn't figure him. But with the talent he had, it didn't make any difference. The best baseball player in our family was my brother Herm. Yogi told me that several of his brothers were better than he was. Makes you wonder, if the scouts—and I scouted after I played and managed—ever found more than one kid in a family that had a chance to make it. I know I didn't.

"If the Bauers and the Berras came up with four or five big league ball players, maybe there was something in the water in that part of the country. My home was just over the river from Yogi's in St. Louis. My brother Herm was killed in the war and never had a chance, and I guess Yogi's brothers stayed at home and worked so he would have a chance.

"Wes Westrum, the catcher for the Giants when we played them in 1951, told me my brother Herm was the best player he ever saw. Wes is not the sort of guy to give you a snow job so his comments meant a lot to me.

"The Yankee experience meant a lot to me, and to anyone who stayed around for a few years. Even players like Enos Slaughter. Enos spent nineteen years in the big leagues and played in over two thousand games, only about two hundred with the Yankees. Yet if you hear him talking at an old timer's game, you will hear the Yankees mentioned every other sentence.

"Right today, take Reggie Jackson. He went into the Hall of Fame as a Yankee. He played 2,820 games in the big leagues, 686 as a Yankee. The Yankee logo is like a college degree from Harvard. But like anything else, the Yankee name can also cause problems.

"So much has been written about the Copacabana flap, I don't want to add much to it but some of this may be interesting even today. It was Billy Martin's birthday party and several Yankee players and their wives ended up at the Copa to see Sammy Davis, Jr.

I don't need to go into all the names because the key words are 'Yankee player.' If we had been a bowling team from Far Rockaway, none of this would have taken place.

Sunday, May 12, 1991, the Red Sox honored Ted Williams and Joe DiMaggio. Ted spent half an hour in my office with Broadway Charlie Wagner and Dom DiMaggio. It just happened and it is one of my special memories of managing the Red Sox in Fenway Park. Ted talked for twenty-two minutes of the thirty, the three of us paying rapt attention. Here was the last .400 hitter in Fenway and I made a checkmark on my desk pad; he mentioned Yankee Stadium twenty-six times. ⑩

—*Joe Morgan*

"A guy at the next table was yelling racial slurs at Sammy. His comments not only were awful, but they were making it impossible for anyone to enjoy Sammy's act. Our table had words with his and because we were Yankee players, they had someone else to pick on and later on the Copa people got in on the act and someone popped one of the drunks. I know it was not me, and I know it was not Billy Martin. The whole baseball world knew it was somebody because the next day the headlines screamed—and when I say screamed I mean the *Daily News* used war-declared type—BAUER IN COPA BRAWL. The headline should have said, BAUER IN ROOM WHEN COPA BRAWL BROKE OUT. Let me say it was flat-out not a problem we caused, nor one we tried to keep alive, but we took the brunt of the heat. It gave George Weiss a chance to sell Billy. Casey couldn't save him. It gave me some first-hand knowledge that sometimes even if you are right, fighting something in court can be unwise, and it also gave me a chance to have a brief exchange with JFK before people would know those three initials.

"It happened while I was coming out of a dining car on the way to Washington, D.C. This good-looking guy said, 'Hi, Hank. How is everything at the Copa? Don't worry, it will turn out OK.' It took about as long to happen as it took to read these few words but I was not pleased to hear them, until I learned the good-looking young man was John F. Kennedy. I don't mean to say if John F. Kennedy said, 'Bauer, you are a butcher in right field,' I would be telling you about it now. I mean to say it was his way of giving me some support and getting my vote, come to think of it.

"We give each other a lot of support. Here is but one example. I hit a home run to tie a game and then Yogi won it with a home run in the ninth. When the press crowded around him asking, 'What was the pitch?' Yogi told them about the one I hit to tie the game. You don't forget about things like that. We played good and we got along good."

CHARLIE SILVERA

"Some of the baseball books say my nickname was 'Swede,' but if it was I never heard it. They used to call me Casey's illegitimate son, because some years I would only play in a handful of games because of Yogi's ability. I told Stengel this once and he came back, quick as a wink, and asked me if my mother had ever been in Kansas City.

"Stengel didn't spend much time with me and I am not saying he should have done so. I am saying he knew who buttered his bread and it was not Charlie Silvera. When I first came up and the Yankees were still trying to decide who should catch, Joe McCarthy was the manager.

"Even though he over time had to favor Yogi over me, I still think of him as a great manager, even better than Stengel in my book. Casey's focus was on himself, McCarthy focused on others. I know that my saying that will make some people say that I didn't play enough to have an opinion and I understand that. All I am saying is that if you don't pinch-hit for the first two months of the season you have a lot of time to see what is going on and I think I did.

"Billy Martin thought I picked up some information along the way and I coached for him in Minnesota, in Detroit, and in Oakland. Billy knew how to get the most from his players for one game or even a series of games. It's too bad the season was so long.

"Just making the Yankees was a thrill, even while in the bull pen I could look out and see DiMaggio and he was in the locker room. While I was in high school with Bobby Brown and Jerry Coleman—and what are the odds three kids in high school will play on one big league team—none of us ever thought we would meet Joe DiMaggio much less share the same shampoo Pete Sheehy put in the shower for us. I didn't see every game when Joe hit in 61 straight games in the Coast League when he played for the San Francisco Seals, but each of us—Jerry, Bobby, and myself—saw some of them. I can remember Joe as a Seal and a Yankee and he remembers me as Yogi's backup. Don't forget I was number two. Houk was my backup."

CHAPTER TEN

GENE WOODLING

"I am not interested in hearing about the prize you won for writing and let's make this quick. The world is not standing still waiting for another book about the New York Yankees. A book on the twelve guys? That's a twist, are you going to write a chapter on Silvera? You could because every one of us had someone pushing us, and Yogi knew Silvera was ready. Bill Dickey wore Yogi's number [8] before they gave it to Berra and sometimes in 1949 and early 1950 I thought Dickey was going to wear Yogi out. I played for seventeen years and I never saw anyone work, or be worked harder, than Yogi.

"We all knew that George Weiss brought Bill Dickey back to teach Yogi, but we didn't know that Dickey would push Berra so hard. Dickey worked him harder after the game than Yogi had to work during the game. Boy, did it pay off, as Spud Chandler said, he got good and he got good and fast. I wanted to play every day with the Yankees. When the Yankees eased Stengel and Weiss out and they ended up with the expansion New York Mets, they acquired me. It meant a lot to be wanted by two men from my Yankee days. Now Casey wanted me to play every day, but it was too late.

Just never got into step with Mr. Stengel, but I know he respected me and that was more important to me than having him like me.

"If you ever saw Casey walk, you knew it would be hard to get in step with him. Of all the nice things that happened to me in baseball the one that means the most is knowing that Casey told his writers that I was one of the players who did better after he left the Yankees. I really don't know why. I was sorry they sold me, and maybe I had something to prove. Whatever the reason was, I am glad Stengel didn't forget about me.

"They used to say the pinstripes make you better. The Phillies used them one year. One thing makes you good, you and your talent. We had a host of talent on that team and it's sad for me when I read about the death of one of us. Mize and Raschi were as different as any two men you could ever meet but they both knew what it took to win.

"Collins and Lopat didn't have that fire or at least it didn't show, but how they wanted to win. So when they die, it's a sad time for me. I don't stay sad long, I have too many blessings to count. One was playing on the '49 to '53 Yankee team. I played on enough teams to go back to more than one Old Timers' game. Most times going back to one of them is like seeing someone you met on a cruise ship a year after the cruise is over. You are all excited but it wears thin real quick. Not with that group of guys. The relationships are too thick, the personalities too strong to wear out.

"Having Stengel and Weiss, as much as you might rail against them, was part of it and don't forget we saw Joe play his last games and Mickey play his first.

"The farm I own near Akron was a working farm and I was the worker. Sometimes I would be out in the fields on a tractor and think about doing that as a young kid and of how that helped me learn that you can't just dream about making good, you have to wake up and make yourself do good or at least the best you can.

"I would stop at the end of a row and think back to Allie Reynolds's first no-hitter in Cleveland in 1951 when I hit a home run off Bobby Feller to win it for the Chief. I'd look over the field and wonder if anyone could be as lucky as I was right at this moment. Sure DiMaggio had me ten to one in memories, but he couldn't buy a newspaper at the corner without getting mobbed. I wouldn't change a thing. Well, maybe that last furrow is a little crooked. Like Casey's left leg.''

CHAPTER ELEVEN

BOBBY BROWN

Robert W. Brown, M.D. The two letters, M.D., are sufficient evidence for an army of parents to know their childrearing techniques passed muster. Passed with colors flying. Ink-stained wretches around baseball since January of 1984, when Dr. Bobby became the sixth President of the American League, sometimes joke the letters M.D. stand for "most difficult."

Dr. Brown is a tough interview. Some feel sharing a locker room with Joe D, Raschi, Reynolds, Lopat, Ford, Mantle, and Berra didn't give young Dr. Brown much practice in the art of being interviewed. Others give the Seattle native's interview style a different twist. "He didn't become President of the American League by talking to writers."

Not quite seventy, looking considerably younger, lean Bobby Brown pushes back in his chair and faces Camelback Mountain in Scottsdale, Arizona. Brown is in Arizona for his last spring training. He is serving his half of baseball, Bill White serves as President of the National League, without the benefit of a baseball Commissioner.

Fay Vincent recently walked or was ushered down the plank

and George Steinbrenner is now back at the helm of the good ship lollipop, also known as the New York Yankees. If the American League President has any reaction to Vincent's departure or Steinbrenner's return, it is not apparent. Brown replaced Lee McPhail, a one-time President of the Yankees, as President of the American League in January of 1984. His plan to retire in December of 1992, announced and printed in the Official American League Red Book, had been placed on hold, meaning Dr. Brown's tenure as American League President will be no longer than his days at third base for the Yankees.

Bobby played eight years with the Yanks, his playing career interrupted for twenty months while he served in the U.S. Army. Brown regularly missed spring training while playing for the New Yorkers, not because he was competing for another professional team, but because he was working toward his medical degree at Tulane University. Brown spent seven years in medical school during the time Vic Raschi was spending thirteen years at William and Mary, seeking his college degree, giving a whole new twist to the term student-athlete.

During the coming season, Brown would have to view video tapes of Nolan Ryan holding not a baseball but the head of Chicago White Stocking player Robin Ventura. Ventura, feeling the sting of a Ryan fastball in the ribs, charged the mound. Ryan put a hammer lock on Ventura and video tape would show Dr. Brown that Ryan delivered and landed six punches, to Robin's none. Bobby Brown would rule on the Ryan-Ventura main event, as he would prescribe medication, but not today.

Today he would savor the Arizona sun, his guest reluctant to offer a hat as protection. The sun seemed to be just what the doctor ordered and if the gracious Mrs. Brown, just leaving to run an errand, did not offer advice, none would be given. Slats Brown, to her friends in Fort Worth and baseball, hurried past, admonishing her husband, "Tell them, that is your story and you are sticking to it." Mrs. Brown, a stunning woman with voice to match, is gone.

This time was set aside to look back. The best part of making the Yankees was that it made so many memories. "Who said that?" questioned Dr. Brown. You did and so did most of the others in their own way, he was told. "Collective wisdom, I must say," commented Brown.

"Four of us were called up from Newark. Three stayed for the full ride, the five in a row. The Yankees were not going to win in 1946, the year we came up late in the season. The Yankees won 87 and lost 67. Not bad, but the Red Sox won 104 and lost 50, better.

"The 1946 New York Yankees had three managers. Joe McCarthy, Bill Dickey, and Johnny Neun. Not a normal year. They knew it was over and they wanted to see if we could play. Vic Raschi, Yogi Berra, Frank Coleman, and I all made the trip across the river. From Newark's Bears to New York's Yankees. From buses and boarding houses to Broadway and the Stork Club."

Now sitting out in the bright Arizona sun, Brown smiles to himself and says to no one in particular, "Never did get to the Stork Club and didn't live in a boarding house either, but it was all very different. Yogi played in seven games. He caught, but not well. But he hit very well. They knew he could do that in Newark, now they knew it in the Bigs. We both got eight hits but he was up fewer times than I was, so Yogi had a better average. If I forget, he reminds me. Yogi doesn't forget much. I will never forget how much knowing him, over the years, enriched my life. Yogi and Carmen Berra, you don't find better souls, anywhere.

"Raschi, who took all those years to complete his degree at William and Mary, didn't waste any time making an impression on the front office. He won two games. Frank Coleman dressed every day with the rest of us but never got into a game. Not in 1946. Not ever. Never played a game in the big leagues. Sometimes, I think about what he told his folks when he was called up. Then what he told them when he was sent back without so much as a time at bat. Walter Alston could at least point to his one time at bat. He struck out, but he got a chance. I don't think about Frank often, but when I do it is always with regret. His, not mine.

"Baseball hurts some while making others well. When I see someone like Bill Buckner make an error in a World Series [in the 1986 World Series Buckner's error on a slow bouncer by Mookie Wilson gave the New York Mets a victory over the Red Sox and the Mets went on to win the seventh game] it always brings a sadness. I know as well as the next person, perhaps better, that life and baseball works out to a winner and a loser, but when the loser is so clearly and publicly branded it takes something out of the winning."

Brown's views help to explain his decision to walk away from his medical practice in 1984. A different drummer played for Robert W. Brown. The eleven other players and their wives knew as much from the start. Sally Raschi: "We all knew Bobby was special, a lot of talent in one man, and when he became President of the league—the league our husbands performed in during those years—nothing changed. He didn't. Not in the least."

One thing did change. "A cardiologist sees and experiences a great deal of bleak times in a patient's life and I decided it was time for me to leave so I did. It was a good time to leave and playing in the American League and becoming its President was a once-in-a-lifetime opportunity. When it knocked I knew it was the only knock. I have taken a few since then," Brown smiles as he speaks, still enjoying the sun.

"So much has been written about the Yankees it is not a surprise to me that much of it is not accurate. It's been written that my father moved our family to California because the weather was better and I would have more time to play baseball. If Pudge Fisk is elected to the baseball Hall of Fame, I am going to send him a note and tell him he would have gotten in faster if his folks had moved from New Hampshire to Florida.

"Here is what happened if anyone is really interested. My father was considering a new job in California. We were living in Maplewood, New Jersey, and he asked or found out, at least, that the high school coach felt I had no chance of making the high school baseball team. That information and the job—my mother and some other things I am sure I will never know—entered into the decision.

"I was happy in Maplewood, it is a lovely small town. I was also happy in California. I was way beyond happy when I made the Yankees and played in a World Series."

Bobby Brown is given a handful of box scores from Yankee World Series games played from 1946 through 1953. The sun shines brightly, and Dr. Brown looks more like a cardiologist than either an American League President or a third baseman. The box scores were to be studied and palpated. Were a stethoscope handy, would the stack of papers be asked to take a deep breath? In bedside manner parlance, Dr. Brown is deep in evaluation.

Anyone fortunate to witness the examination must pay attention, listen, and take notes. "Willie Mays cost me a hit, in this game. [Fourth game 1951, Yankees 6 Giants 2, WP: Reynolds, LP: Maglie.] While he was running with his back to home plate trying to catch a ball I hit over his head. Much as he did when he caught the long drive against Vic Wertz in the same park, the Polo Grounds in 1954. That catch was captured on film and shown dozens of times, as one of the greatest catches in World Series history.

"My drive was not as long as Vic Wertz's but it was over his head and he was running the same way. He dropped the ball, it bounced up, and Willie recaught it. He fooled the six umpires [Barlick, Summers, Ballanfant, Paparella, Gore, and Stevens] and most of the fans. He fooled me. Willie knew it of course. So did some fans sitting in center field.

"One fan in center field had seen me hit a baseball several thousand times but this was the first time he had ever seen Willie Mays catch a ball, or recatch a ball, off my bat. You can imagine how my dad felt. He had seen me play game after game for years, usually from better seats, but this was the World Series and seats were hard to come by, even if you were a player. Someday I am going to ask Willie if he remembers the play.

"Every Series game is big. The Giants had won two of the first three, so if they win the fourth game they have us three games to one. Sal Maglie was pitching for the Giants. The Giants scored in the first when Monte Irwin drove in Alvin Dark, so when we came up, Allie Reynolds was down by a run. Some people felt he liked it that way. I was not one of them. Sal Maglie was not the sort of pitcher you looked forward to facing. He looked mean, and he was mean, and I had never faced him before. Ball players read the newspapers and when he struck out Joe DiMaggio to end the first, I was not thinking, We are going to get this guy, it is just a matter of time. I am sure none of us was feeling as if it was just a matter of time. Except maybe Woodling.

"Gene Woodling led off the second with a double, and I was elated. Then Hank Thompson misplayed Gil McDougald's fly ball and we had runners on first and second. Some of the Giants, even today, feel if Don Mueller, their regular right fielder, had not broken his ankle sliding into third in the Giant-Dodger Thomson H.R. game and had been playing right field, he would have handled the ball Gil hit. You can bet at the time no one on our team was thinking about it. We had the crafty Maglie thinking. Thinking about himself, the error, and maybe even Don 'Mandrake the Magician' Muller.

"I was thinking the four most important words a hitter can think, Get a good pitch. I did and if my hit had fallen, I would have gotten credit for an extra-base hit. Even when Willie made his phantom catch, Woodling took third. As it turns out, during my seventeen games in World Series play, I got eighteen hits. Almost half of them were for extra bases, had that one been a double, it would have been an even half. Frank Crosetti would say who cares? Not Willie for sure, and I have to say since we scored later in the inning and won the game, I can't either. But it gives me a good story to put in the pages of this book.

"I batted .357 for the Series and after the last game a writer ran out of people to interview and cornered my father. My dad said, 'My son is not the greatest ball player in the world but he is the best son.' Gave me a better feeling than getting a ring. It is a good feeling even today, like the sun, but it's time to look for a tree."

Brown is questioned about the examination of the forty-year-old box scores. "Life and death are perhaps as much a part of your medical specialty as base hits were a part of your life as a player. Does it strike you as unusual that these old box scores would evoke the reaction in you they seem to have generated?" Clear-eyed, Brown turns to look at the nearby mountain. "During the time I played these four Series—I missed '52 along with Jerry Coleman when we were called to serve in Korea—this country had perhaps thirty thousand medical doctors. The American League had four hundred players and only twenty-four or twenty-five of them were playing in the World Series. I was one of them.

"The 1953 Series was tough. I was in Korea as a battalion surgeon with the 106th Field Artillery, 45th Division. Jerry was sent home at the end of his tour [Coleman flew a total of 120 missions]. In fact, George Weiss called me in Korea, because I was in one place and he could reach me and asked me to locate Jerry. It was the only favor George ever asked. I was able to track Jerry down and was pleased to play a small part in his return to the U.S.

"I remember walking down the gang plank from the ship. It was anchored in Inchon Harbor—it was a shallow harbor and it was a long way to shore. The gang plank was more like a causeway and I remember thinking, I should be in New York wearing pinstripes not dressed in mufti carrying a canvas bag. It was the worst day of my life. We didn't react, like some did later about Vietnam, but I was not pleased to be there. It was not what you might call an important war, whatever that might be.

"Paul Johnson in his book *Modern Times* said the Korean War 'was launched for ideological reasons, without a scintilla of moral justification, or popular support.' He wrote one more sentence that stayed with me because I made a copy of the page, 'It killed 34,000 Americans, a million Koreans, a quarter of a million Chinese. It achieved no purpose. All its consequences were unintended.' When the major leagues meet about the value of the designated hitter in the American League, I try to keep Johnson's evaluation of the Korean War in mind. It's called perspective.

"Understand, I was sorry to be called up, but considering the 34,000 who gave their lives and the thousands wounded I was lucky and I bring it up because it was a sad day in my life. Even sadder if I had been Ernie Banks, because the one Series I missed would have been the only one he ever had. I played in seventeen World Series games, seventeen more than I ever dreamed I would play in when I didn't make the high school team in Maplewood, New Jersey.

"Even a bad experience has some good and I am sure I gained some medical insights while in Korea. I know one good memory. The first day I came ashore, I was driven to the base hospital and a medic, a staff sergeant, welcomed me, and showed me to an office. He said I was the MOD, medical officer of the day. In case you don't know it, sergeants run the Army.

"I looked around the bleak office and felt the same way. In a few moments, the sergeant wheeled my first patient into the office. A young GI wearing a softball uniform, at least that is what I thought. As it turned out, it was a baseball uniform. Softball is for the playground, I was told. Soft or hard the uniform was nothing like the one I might have been wearing that very same day in Yankee Stadium trying to get a good pitch to hit delivered by Carl Erskine.

"The X rays with the chart indicated no break but the patient had an acute sprain. His ankle was badly swollen. I took a good deal of time wrapping the ankle and telling the young man about the need to elevate his leg whenever possible. I told him to get some forms from the sergeant and that I would sign them to make it possible for him to miss some of his routine. Motor pool, I think it was.

"The reason I spent the time is I had plenty to spend. As he was about ready to leave, I asked him, 'Were you safe or out?' He laughed and said, 'Out, but the umpire was out of position.' He sounded like Yogi when Jackie Robinson stole home when the Yankees played the Dodgers in '57, or was it '56? I asked him a little about the game, and how much sliding instruction he had been given. He said a little in high school, but that sliding was just something you did. No one really teaches sliding, was the way I think he put it.

"I closed the door and moved the examination table and several chairs. I took off my white coat and folded it and put it on the floor. I may have opened the door and looked down the hall to see if the sergeant was coming but I prefer to think I did not. After I did all this, real and imagined, and I wish I had been watching the patient, I went over to the wall and sort of ran (I was in Korea—I was not crazy) in slow motion and in my best Frank Crosetti style, demonstrated the fade-away slide, making certain I raised my heel. While doing so, I told my rapt student, turning your toes up was the way to avoid what had just happened to him.

"I even replayed my slow-motion show and he left. I was moving the chairs back when the sergeant came in. 'Dr. Brown,' I was always pleased to be called Doctor and not by my rank, the corpsman said with emotion, 'Your first patient left here high as a kite. The guys on both baseball teams, ours and the other one, told him to stay away from the so and so army doctors. Go to them when you get shot and have no choice. Walk that sprain off and forget about it.'

"He went on to say that my patient not only said I was a good doctor, pleasing me and Tulane, he said that I knew more about sliding into third base than most anyone he had ever seen. It would be nice to end this in a Paul Harvey way and say the young man's name was Lou Brock. But it would besmirch my reputation as an honest man. I am sorry I have no idea of the name of that GI in Korea. I hope he likes to read about baseball as well as to play the game. I might find out someday."

CHAPTER TWELVE

JERRY COLEMAN

Picture a map of the Florida peninsula. It fits comfortably over the Republic of Korea, both the North and South. Jerry Coleman, Bobby Brown, and Ted Williams were hardly a comfortable fit in the service of their country during the Korean conflict, but they responded when called.

"Several writers suggested the Marines wanted to stock up their baseball team. Bobby was not a pilot, but rather a medical doctor in the Army Reserve, so I don't remember if he was included in the written speculation," Jerry Coleman ruefully commented while sipping coffee and petting his aged German shepherd, Casey.

Coleman's home is elegant, yet cheerful, surrounded by flowers and situated high in an exclusive section of La Jolla, California. Coleman's surroundings indicate no evidence of the handsome second baseman's Yankee past. He is the only member of the October Twelve not to display the plaque.

On display is the Pacific Ocean. "If you can't feel good when you pick up the paper and look out over the Pacific Ocean, coming back into the house and seeing pictures of yourself in baggy pinstripes is not going to help you feel any better." Coleman speaks as if he is summing up an important inning, not his outlook on life.

The room is silent, but heads nod assent. "People making cynical comments about the Marines needing a better baseball team were off base. The Marines needed more pilots. The inventory of men who could fly, if not today, but with a month or so of training was on empty. If they were going to fight in Korea, the Marines had to use their bench. Since Ted Williams and I had both flown in WWII, we were part of their roster.

Brown's role in Korea was in the Medical Corps of the U.S. Army. Williams and Coleman were Marine pilots. Coleman, credited with 120 missions, was awarded two Distinguished Flying Crosses. None of the trio picked up a bat while in Korea. Considering the size of the war zone, it is surprising the two teammates and their Red Sox adversary never met face-to-face.

Coleman recalled vividly one close encounter. "The ready room was like a dugout for Marine fliers and that damn red phone was like the phone to the bull pen. We were, it seemed, either in combat or on alert. We all watched that damn phone like it was alive. When the phone rang, we had to be ready to take off in moments. The waiting was worse for me than the mission.

"The mission was like a double play for higher stakes, you just did it. You simply performed and did the best you could. The waiting was the hardest part.

"Late one day we heard the radio crackle, 'MAYDAY, MAYDAY.' Everyone in the ready room and on the flight line fixed on the sounds filling the air. A Marine flier returning from a mission was in trouble. No one cared about his branch of service, all they cared about was that he was a flier. A frightened American, flying a wounded bird, desperate to limp back to K 6 or K 9. One of those K's, to tell the truth all those K's blend together. The only number that stayed with me was the number of my favorite aircraft: *Willy Sugar 8. WS8* on the rudder and painted on the cowl covering the engine. What shall stay, until God's last day for me, is the high drama of the event.

"The pilot all alone, leaking fuel, his plane on fire and wondering, as we all did, why are we here in the first place. He was alone, but perhaps five thousand men were intent on every scrap of information, and actively willing him safely back to earth. The stricken plane's radio was down, but others on his mission were flying close, in support of the burning aircraft. The tower at the K airfield, in that matter-of-fact voice: 'We have you, you are visible.'

"Hours pass, a matter of two minutes, the aircraft is down. After skidding two thousand feet, just missing a fire truck ready to rescue the pilot, the plane comes to a stop and the Marine flyer uses the emergency ejector as the plane is engulfed in flames. Eyewitnesses reported the tall Marine pilot came out of the cockpit as if shot out of a cannon, ripped off his helmet, and slammed it to the ground. A shaken and unsmiling Theodore Samuel Williams.

"The men in my unit knew I played baseball for a living and when word came over the radio the pilot was safe, we all cheered and then a while later, when we learned the flier was Teddy Ball Game, I said—I guess I would have to say I exclaimed—'Hey I know that guy.' It was a strange thing to say, but I don't recall anyone reacting."

Ted reacted to his recall to active duty in his book, *My Turn at Bat*. To say he was not at all pleased would be an understatement. Williams felt the same way about Vietnam as he did about Korea. No war is good and undeclared war is not only not good but also foolish.

Coleman is asked about his own brush with the Grim Reaper, and he gives the details. With three bombs under the wings looking larger than the single-engine Corsair, Coleman's plane experiences a sudden loss of power on takeoff. Training takes over and the three bombs are aborted, including one active bomb, sufficient to destroy the base. After dumping the bombs safely, the plane flips over and, still going 200 miles an hour, lands in the sand. Coleman is buried upside down in sand, unable to move or breathe.

"What a way to die, at least I could be right side up. That's really the only thing that came to my mind," explained Coleman.

"Thank God the rescue crew pulled me out. Casey Stengel asked me about the crash and the missions when I came back. He was really interested and was sorry I had been called up, not so much because he needed me but because it seemed a waste of time and he was right.

"They took two years, but what I remember most is that when George Weiss called Bobby Brown [he knew where to reach Dr. Brown] to tell me to write a letter asking to be released, I had flown all the missions the Marines would allow, and somehow Weiss knew that even though I didn't. George Weiss, the detail man. The detail uppermost in my mind was the group I was in really got on the ball and I was out and back home in a matter of days."

The seventy-year-old Coleman, looking fifty, clears his throat and his voice and face show heartfelt gratitude. "Baseball, let's get on with some baseball. Do you want to talk about the 1950 World Series? I carried those guys," laughed the 1950 World Series MVP.

"That last game, when Casey wanted Ford to get a shutout and Gene Woodling lost a ball in the sun and they scored, is an awful memory. Stengel showed Gene up in the dugout and it was cruel. I don't think Gene ever forgave the old man."

When told Woodling had not attended the victory party, Jerry comments, "I had forgotten that. We had so many."

When told that Woodling shows no rancor and even some affection and good feelings for Stengel, Coleman, with obvious joy, comments, "Guys like Woodling are able to rise above events. He did when we needed a hit and he did, if the report is true, when he needed to forget and forgive. I am proud I played with guys like that, but I didn't know it at the time. You tend to think about DiMag and Yogi." Coleman uses the name Crosetti employs for DiMaggio, DiMag. Most Yankee players use Joe D when speaking of the Jolter. At times DiMaggio and Rizzuto were known as the Big Dago and the Little Dago, but not by everybody and not for very long.

Coleman's admiration of Rizzuto does not extend to Scooter's appraisal of Stengel. "Stengel understood and knew his players. Their assets and their liabilities. He understood the front office and he knew how to use the press. Most of all Stengel knew that winning was more important than people. That is why he could beat Joe McCarthy.

"Joe was concerned how someone would feel if he didn't bat for himself—Stengel didn't care how anyone felt, even DiMag, and one time he hit Joe fifth in the order. No one, including Joe, could believe it but the old man knew that winning was all important and in a strange and remarkable way he made all of us feel that way as well. At least often enough for it to work. He made the chemistry, he had the horses, and he won.

"Rizzuto?" Coleman smiles. "He was fearless, the best inside double play man [the inside or pivot man on the double play is the one creamed by the sliding runner] I ever saw but he and Stengel never saw eye-to-eye. I joined the team with Stengel and that made it different. Not so different as to be all different but enough to matter.

"They say you are never old until you substitute regrets for desires and I guess I am old because I deeply regret my last conversation with Casey. It was in September of 1975. He attended a Padre game and came by to see me. You could tell he wanted to talk, I mean more than usual. I was gracious, but explained I had a pregame show to do and then the game and so I had to beg off. I am sure I said something about getting together after the game but the fact is we didn't and he was dead within the week. I still feel empty when I think about it. I attended his funeral but the time to talk was gone."

WORLD SERIES '49

I watched the 1993 playoffs and the World Series, making sure I listened to Jerry Coleman on CBS radio, and I was disappointed that no one I listened to said anything about the new Blue Jays from Toronto playing the old Blue Jays from Philadelphia. Sometime during my years with the Yankees the Phils were called the Blue Jays. You can look it up.

Right now I want to get started with the part of this book I have been looking forward to since the idea first surfaced, and a word to the new Blue Jays, if I may. If you are to win again and then twice more and tie us, in my opinion you will have done a lot more than tie. Considering the number of teams—just that alone—would make winning five straight even more of an accomplishment than ours was from '49 to '53. So, good luck and keep notes if you want to do a book like this. I wish I had.

The main reason I am sorry I didn't keep what the Navy used to call a day book, is that even the twelve guys who were on the team don't share the same mental pictures. One example. Vic Raschi's description of our four-game sweep of the Phils ("The Whiz

Kids") in 1950 would run along the lines of "They never laid a glove on us."

Yogi, who used to love to flap with Vic, says, "Take a look at the box scores. We didn't exactly kick the hell out of them." I did, and Yogi was right, but I am getting a year ahead.

Talking to Yogi Berra about baseball is like talking to Homer about the gods. (X)

—A. Bartlet Giamatti

One of the nicest things ever said about me that I didn't understand. (X)

—Yogi Berra

If this were a movie, the opening scene would have Steve Martin playing Casey Stengel giving us a pep talk in the Yankee dugout. Yankee Stadium, October 5, 1949. 66,224 well-dressed fans in attendance. Steve would say something like, "I planned to start all twelve of you guys but even though Burt Shotten is getting away with wearing street clothes and I have to wear the same funny suits you guys are wearing, they won't let me. So I am going with, well . . . I am going with just four of you. The rest of you stay ready."

The Yankees won, behind Allie Reynolds. He gave them just two hits. Don Newcombe gave us only five, Allie had two, Jerry Coleman had one, and Yogi and I went for the collar.

But we were off and running. Counting this game during the next five years we would play 28 World Series games. We would win 20 and lose 8.

Some totals that hardly would serve as evidence we were the Lords of Baseball. Total runs scored over the five-year, 28-game span: 94 for us and 78 for the National League. Total hits, over the five-year, 28-game span, 222 for us and 220 for them. The Bronx Bombers' home run numbers are interesting. We had 28 and the Dodgers, Giants, and Phils had 20.

As I said earlier, the idea to put the twelve players and manager and coaches on that plaque belonged to someone in the Yankee front office, but since so many changes have taken place in the Yankee organization, at this stage no one is certain who was responsible. At least one of the teams we faced, the Phils, had a reunion. The Yankees have honored me over the years in many ways, so please don't think I am the one suggesting something like that for us.

If a cloud hangs over the plaque, it is only over the plaque and how it came to exist. The role and contributions of the twelve were played out in the bright sunshine and are reflected in the box scores, on the radio, and in filmed accounts of the games played. Here is how they look.

Considering my early comments about my relationship with Casey Stengel, I was surprised to see that I was the only player to appear in all 28 games. Yogi was, you might guess, next and graced us with 27 appearances. Hank "The Man of the Hour" Bauer and Gene Woodling were tied at 26. Bobby Brown and Jerry Coleman also shared the same number, 14. The Big Cat, Johnny Mize, was called on by his "National League buddy" (as Stengel was called by some Yankee players) 15 times. Mize and the late Joe Collins shared first base and Joe appeared 19 times. I know it would please him to see those numbers. I hope it pleases Betty [Mrs. Collins].

Charlie Silvera got into one game, but he had a great seat for the other 27. Last the pitchers. I was shocked to look back and see Allie Reynolds's name 13 times. "Reynolds now pitching for Ford," would have been the way the PA announcer would boom out the names, one in the Hall of Fame [Ford] and one who should be in my judgment [Reynolds]. Vic Raschi's name is in 9 box scores and Ed Lopat's name is in 7. Considering what they did for that team over the years, perhaps the trio should be in the Hall of Fame.

Coleman, Bauer, Lopat, and Berra all managed in the major leagues.

All of us saw Joe DiMaggio's star shine. And we also saw, and in a few cases heard, his decision to step down while he still had more ability at the end than most guys had in their prime. His pride was an inspiration. Not only to the fans, who paid to see him, but to those of us lucky enough to be on the same team. You hear about great players that never got the chance to play in a World Series. A whole lot more never got to play on the same team with Joe DiMaggio. Day after day he would make your eyes pop, while breaking the other team's heart, back, or both.

DiMaggio was the best player I ever saw. Ⓚ

—*Yogi Berra*

We twelve also saw Mickey come on the scene. Introverted and talented, and then Billy Martin, extroverted and limited, except in desire. A good time was had by all. Silvera, Brown, and Coleman were all twenty-four years old even though as I write this I don't believe it. I was thirty-one and the three pitchers were just over thirty. Bauer and Woodling were twenty-six, and as I put these words down those of us still living are old enough to carry on a conversation with Stengel and understand it. Well, maybe.

Over 68,000 paid to see our last game in 1949 when we beat the Red Sox while the Dodgers were beating the Phils in Shibe Park 90 miles away. The Dodgers won 9 to 7 in ten innings behind Jack Banta. Raschi pitched our last game, and Jerry Coleman drove in three runs to clinch the game. Both flags were decided on the last day of the season, and twenty million fans watched major league baseball that year.

Only 66,224 fans attended the first game of the Series. They used to call these games Subway Series and it was the third time we would face the Dodgers. It was the sixteenth time the Yankees played in a World Series. It was my fourth. My first under Stengel. Branch Rickey was the President and General Manager and George Weiss filled that role for us. A whole lot of warmth in the front office for both sides. A.B. "Happy" Chandler, onetime governor of Kentucky, was the Commissioner of Baseball and he threw out the first ball for the afternoon game.

Halberstam's *Summer of '49* represents me as not wanting to look foolish in that game. I never remember wanting to look foolish. I do remember the feeling of getting the bat on the ball and running into the out at third base. Something Cro told me never to do. I explained to Crosetti, whom I respect deeply, that I wanted to draw the throw to third to make sure the run scored. An out for three runs is a good trade anytime. ⑩

—*Jerry Coleman*

The games were played at two o'clock, if memory serves, and the way the sun was in the late afternoon I used to wonder why they didn't play them at high noon. I wondered, but of course never said anything.

Jim Turner, our pitching coach, and Stengel started Reynolds, who was 17 and 6; the Dodgers started Don Newcombe, who was 17 and 8. The press made a lot of Newcombe's five shutouts. We lit a candle to Joe Page in our bull pen. The next day I read in the paper that Ty Cobb had been a guest at the game, and I am sorry I didn't get a chance to meet him. I did years later, and he was what you would call focused. So was Newcombe. He struck out DiMaggio and Billy Johnson and Cliff Mapes in the second. Johnny Lindell had a single in that inning but when the other pitcher sends three guys back to your bench holding on to their bats, Lindell's single to right did not bring to mind the first robin of spring.

Jerry made an error in their fifth on Furillo's ground ball and Hodges sacrificed him to second. Allie walked Campanella, giving the second-guessers' fodder. Shotten let Newcombe hit and Allie struck him out, Yogi held on to the foul tip, and then Pee Wee Reese forced Furillo at third. Still no score.

In the bottom of the fifth, Newcombe struck out the side again, getting Johnson, Mapes, and Jerry Coleman. In the top of the sixth, Allie walked Spider Jorgensen. Giving up a walk to start an inning is not the worst thing that can happen to a pitcher, but it's high on the list. I am sure someone said or wrote that Allie started to bear down on the next hitter, Duke Snider, and struck him out.

Jackie Robinson drove Allie's fastball deep to center and Joe D made a fine catch, and Reynolds struck out Gene Hermanski to end the inning. I would like to say that Joe's catch saved the game. I would like to, but I can't. It was just one of hundreds of great catches he made. I can say this. Never once did I ever turn to follow a ball hit to the outfield that I did not see Joe moving toward the ball. Most of the time he was in full stride, but he was always moving.

Allie singled to left to open the next inning. Having your pitcher open an inning with a hit is way up on the list of good things and having the next hitter be a good man with the bat is fine and dandy as well. Hindsight tells me I should have been ordered to bunt. I was not and hit what I would like to remember as a shot to third, to force Allie at second. Tommy Henrich flied to center and Yogi struck out.

Allie set them down in the seventh, getting Campy for his sixth to end the inning. Allie was getting a lot of Dodgers on called third strikes. That's the worst kind.

The eighth inning was a blur of strikeouts. Newcombe, Jorgen-sen, and Snider for them. And Mapes and Reynolds for us. Snider struck out three times in that game, as did Mapes. You can bet they both still remember, and I will bet it didn't ever happen to Duke again in a big game. Jerry got a double and I hit a fly to center, leaving him at second. Everytime we get together we talk about it. Usually he brings it up.

The game lasted two hours and twenty-two minutes, and here is the way things stood at two hours and twenty minutes. New-combe had given up four hits and struck out eleven. Allie had given up two hits and struck out nine. Newcombe needed to get three more outs to force the game into extra innings: Tommy Henrich, Yogi Berra, and Joe DiMaggio.

The first pitch to Henrich was a ball, and Newcombe followed with another. A youthful Henrich had not been afraid to write to Judge Landis, and the thirty-six-year-old first baseman was not go-ing to bail out on Newcombe's hard curve. He caught the pitch almost perfectly and dove it well over Furillo's head in right for a game-winning home run.

A heady way to start our odyssey from Yankee Stadium to Eb-bets Field to the Polo Grounds to Shibe Park, and our five straight series victories.

The second game, also in our park, was played the next day, the sixth of October 1949. Stengel used six of the twelve for this game. Raschi, a 21-game winner, was rested after clinching our last game and Stengel started Charlie Silvera in place of Yogi. Yogi had struck out and grounded to short in the first game. Stengel might have been concerned about Yogi's sore thumb, broken ear-lier in the season, or he may have thought the righthand–hitting Silvera had a better chance with the Dodgers' pitcher, Preacher Roe, a lefthander.

Almost four thousand more fans paid to attend the second game and Silvera still believes it was to see him behind the plate. Raschi was sharp and put them quickly away in the first. I singled for the first hit in the second, and with Henrich, Hank Bauer, and Joe D to drive me in. It was just a matter of time. I am still waiting.

Jackie Robinson doubled to left to start the second. I didn't get to know Jackie well, but you had to respect the way he played and the way he handled himself. When he died, Yogi's comment about Robinson as a player was, "He was a hard out." As usual, Yogi didn't waste words. Nor did Jackie.

The next batter, Hermanski, lifted a long foul way down the line back of first base. Jerry Coleman ran a long way to make the catch for the out, but with Jackie's speed he ended up on third. Marvin Rackley grounded to third. Hodges singled Jackie home and took second on Lindell's error.

Vic gave Campy an intentional walk and struck out Roe. Not bad. Jackie leading off with a double and an error could have been a whole lot worse than one run. It was early. The hit by Gil Hodges had been just beyond my reach and I remember thinking Vic was just a bit too fine. We put Newcombe away and we can get this lefty. We beat Mel Parnell, who won 25 for the Red Sox, so we can take the Preacher Man. He was 15 and 6.

In our third, Silvera popped to third and Vic grounded to Reese. I got on when Pee Wee made a rare error and stole second. Henrich grounded to Reese to end the inning. Vic struck Jackie out to start the Dodger fourth. Then Hermanski tripled to deep center when the ball took a bad hop over DiMaggio. Hank Bauer, backing Joe up, retrieved the ball from the base of the wall and held Hermanski to the triple.

Rackley hit a slow roller just over the mound and Jerry Coleman made a sparkling play, charging the ball and throwing under-handed, cutting down Hermanski at the plate, saving a run and making Silvera look good. I knew right then why Jerry had been the toast of Wellsville when he played in that small upstate town in New York.

Jerry now does the San Diego Padres games and I am told when a Padre makes a good play, someone in the booth hangs a star on a fishing pole and waves it at the crowd. If someone in the Yankee booth hung out a star for Jerry on that play, he would have been scalped and George Weiss would have hung the scalp from his belt. It was a great play and kept the game close.

Campy opened the fifth inning with a single and when Lindell bobbled the ball in left, he tried to get to second. Johnny threw to Jerry in time to nail him at second. Jerry doubled in the fifth but was left stranded by Silvera and Raschi. After seven innings, it was still one-zip. Johnny Mize pinch-hit for Silvera, getting a single, the first of many key hits. Snuffy Stirnweiss ran for Mize. Casey, the chess man, pinch-hit for Raschi, and Bobby Brown took a called third strike. Something he seldom, if ever, did. His lifetime batting average in World Series play is .439. He didn't earn it—and I am told it is the record—by keeping the bat on his shoulder. Casey had me bunting and when Roe dropped the ball I was safe at first. It was the second error of the game for the Dodgers. Henrich and Bauer made the last two outs. Joe Page held them in the ninth and Gus Niahros made his only appearance in a World Series. Yogi kept a lot of catchers on the bench and he did it for years. In this second game he let two of them out of the bull pen, in one game.

DiMaggio, at age thirty-four, with bad wheels, legged out a hit to open the ninth and Lindell, Billy Johnson, and Jerry Coleman left him on first. Game over. Winner Roe. Loser Raschi. Two hours and thirty minutes of what might have been. It was one for the books, however. It was the first time that two 1–0 shutouts came in one Series. Considering the number of records they are keeping today, that record may have to be amended, and they will have to add in a qualifier—in the Eastern time zone.

The next day we took the bus to Brooklyn. Ebbets Field was full, 32,788. It always seemed full, but the crowds did vary, by sometimes as much as a thousand fans. It seemed to me, and I had seen many games in that park as a kid, that the fans could reach out and touch you, and sometimes you were afraid they would. No team ever had more loyal fans than those Dodgers. Going back to Brooklyn was like going back home for me, but no one made me feel welcome.

Ralph Branca and Tommy Byrne were the pitchers. Tommy, a lefty, had won 15 for us and Branca had won 13 for the Dodgers. Byrne hit Reese in the leg to open the second. Eddie Miksis popped a ball up right near our dugout and Yogi made a good catch and threw out Reese trying to take second. It was a good play by Yogi and not a great move by Pee Wee and I bet he was sorry he ran.

Over the years a lot of people thought because Yogi didn't look like Bill Dickey, he couldn't play like Bill Dickey. I never saw anyone quicker than Yogi. His feet and hands were as quick as anyone I ever saw. In sheer quickness, no one, not Joe D nor Mickey, was a match for Yogi. I used to wonder why he could never find his wallet.

Our third opened with a walk by Cliff Mapes. It was the first walk given up by Dodger pitching. Jerry was caught looking and came back to the bench tight-lipped. Tommy, a very good hitter, singled. Mapes took third and I drove him in with a fly ball to right. Henrich walked and Yogi popped up, but we were one up.

In the fourth, Gene Woodling doubled off the scoreboard, but stayed at second when Mapes hit a soft ground ball to Jackie Robinson.

In the Dodger fourth, Reese took a strike from Byrne and then hit a long home run to left. Byrne got Miksis, but gave up a hit to Furillo and walked Robinson and Hodges to load the bases. Casey came out. I always felt that it didn't matter what the pitcher said to Stengel. When he moved from the bench, he had already made his mind up to leave the guy in or take him out.

He sent Tommy to the shower and brought in Joe Page. It was the sixty-first time Page had come into a game that season. Ebbets field was a sea of noise. They loved the Dodgers and while the Yankees were respected, they were hated like a rich uncle, only you couldn't boo your rich uncle. Least not so he could hear.

Page popped Luis Olmo up and first baseman Henrich reached into the stands to make a fine play. The sort of play you would see four or five times on TV if it happened today. Duke Snider grounded to Coleman. It could have been a whole lot worse and Page took the crowd out of the game.

After Reese's home run, the fifth, sixth, seventh, and eighth innings were a series of strikeouts, popups, and ground balls. If you were selling baseball, those innings would not have been a good film clip. If you were a Dodger or a Yankee fan, however—Branca was sitting us down, fourteen in a row, and Page wobbled at times, but didn't give a run—the events were high drama.

When Pie Traynor played third base for the old Pittsburgh Pirates, they used to say "so-and-so doubled down the third base line and was thrown out at first by Pie Traynor." In other words he was that good. In the Yankee ninth, with the score one to one, Henrich singled and was thrown out by Robinson. He was that good.

Henrich is pleased that the play is remembered by some as a smash of that velocity, but in typically Henrich fashion, he downplays the batted ball. "I hit the ball well and he made a good play," said Henrich from his home in Prescott, Arizona. Berra walked. DiMaggio popped up and Bobby Brown singled to right. Berra on second, Brown on first, Woodling walked, loading the bases. Mize, pinch-hitting for Mapes, singled off the fence, Berra and Brown scored and Woodling was on third. Bauer ran for Mize and Coleman drove in the final run of the game for the Yankees. In one half-inning, six of the October twelve contributed to a victory but as Berra said years later, "It ain't over until it's over."

With Page still pitching, Hodges grounded to Coleman. Olmo hit a home run into the lower left field stands. Dodgers 2, Yankees 4. Snider struck out. Campanella hit a long ball to left, it hit the top of the railing and jumped into the stands and the Dodgers were at home and behind by one run and Page had pitched over five innings.

Bruce Edwards pinch-hit for Branca. Edwards was the sort of player you liked to see do well. He stayed in the minors a long time and paid his dues, and then played in the shadow of Campy. It was not to be. Page struck him out looking. The game drained me back then and going over it again was a tonic. I knew how it was going to turn out, but it was a blast even so. Gave me a good excuse to call Tommy Henrich. Next time, collect.

Having just said that the last game was a blast, I will have to come clean and tell you I laid a bomb the next day. The fourth game was in Ebbets Field, October 8, 1949. Eddie Lopat started for us and Burt Shotten came back with Don Newcombe. At the time it seemed like an unwise move to me. Pitchers need rest. Guys that throw as hard as Newcombe need it even more. I know this is easy to write now, but I can only tell you that Jim Turner was not alone in thinking Newcombe needed more time.

When I led off on the second pitch with a solid single and Tommy Henrich followed with another to right, it looked like we would chase Newcombe in the first inning. Runners on first and third, nobody out, and Yogi batting third at the plate. Joe Hatten started warming up in the Dodger pen and don't let anyone tell you that does not bother the guy pitching. Just a few moments earlier the manager has given you the ball and made you believe you are his favorite in the world. Two hits and he is getting the hook.

Yogi hit a ground ball to third and Eddie Miksis caught me on third in a rundown and the umpire called me out for leaving the basepath. Then Campy threw out Henrich, who should have been staying close to first while the rundown was taking place.

I can promise you that Henrich and I were red-faced and if he brings it up I change the subject. To close the loop on that first inning, DiMaggio walked, Brown walked, loading the bases, and Woodling lined out.

The game was still scoreless starting the fourth. Lopat was a master. Some American League hitters felt the more you saw Lopat, the better chance you had to catch on to him. To the Dodgers it was a whole new experience.

Joe led off the fourth. He hit a line drive at Snider. Duke caught the ball with no trouble but it was well hit, and if it had sunk a little it could have gone to the wall. By this time the bull pen was quiet. Brown doubled off the wall. Woodling walked. Mapes doubled down the left field line and Brown and Woodling scored. Pitcher Lopat doubled, scoring Mapes. Joe Hatten replaced Don Newcombe. I singled and to continue our base running, Lopat was out trying to score. But we had three runs and had knocked a great pitcher off the mound.

Heinrich walked to open the sixth. Yogi singled to right. Miksis made an error and Berra and Henrich were on second and third. No one out. They put Joe on, why I will never know, to pitch to Brown. Bobby tripled and we were now six runs ahead. Game was half over and we were up by six. Piece of cake. In their sixth, Reese led off with a single. Billy Cox, batting for Miksis, got an infield hit. Duke Snider hit a shot close enough so I could step on second and throw to Henrich at first, pure textbook. WOW! Robinson singled. Reese scored. Then Hodges singled. Then a whole lot of them singled. They singled Lopat like it was batting practice. They pecked us for four runs and Stengel brought in Allie Reynolds. Spider Jorgensen, pinch-hitting for Erskine who had started the sixth, was the first hitter the Super Chief faced. It seemed to me the Dodgers had been hitting for an hour, but it took Allie only three pitches to put an end to the firestorm.

Brown, Coleman, and Reynolds made out in the eighth inning and I led off the ninth. I walked on four pitches. Henrich singled me to third. Yogi was the batter and Jack Banta was pitching for the Dodgers. On the second pitch to Yogi, catcher Campanella makes a snap throw to third. Crosetti looked at me and I looked at him. Stengel looked at both of us. I can still make my neck hot by thinking about it. Yogi flied to right and I would have scored had I been on the base instead of trying to find a spot to hide in the dugout. Allie Reynolds was masterful in the last of the ninth: one, two, three, including a pinch-hitter named Dick Whitman. It was his only time at bat in a World Series for Brooklyn and he was struck out, but by a great, great pitcher, Allie Reynolds. We would meet Dick again. He was sold that November to the Phils and we played them next year. But first, the last game of 1949.

Since we were up three games to one, it would be foolish to

suggest we were worried. Stengel and some of his coaches may have been and told the press something to make them happy but the players didn't think it would go seven games.

Game 5, October 9, 1949, Ebbets Field. Stengel gave Vic Raschi his second start and Shotten selected right-hander Rex Barney. As I mentioned, the team went by bus. If your wife wanted to attend, and all of them did, it was up to them to make arrangements. Sally Raschi, like many of the Yankees family, found a lot of their "real" family showing up in October. Extra guests in small apartments, taking longer in the shower than expected, should not affect the way your husband pitched, and in Vic's case I am sure it didn't, but Sally's memory of this game may give some insight into what it meant to be a World Series wife. Before or after one of the games in Brooklyn, Vic had scouted around for a parking place for Sally and her party. Parking in Brooklyn was murder. Vic located a spot, told the guy what he would like and for all I know gave him a baseball. He did pay in advance, that much I know. So all is well in the Raschi house. Vic's on the bus, off the bus, dressed, and warming up. Sally and her brood are making the drive to Ebbets Field. You can almost hear it. "Turn here, Mother," "Wait, your dad said to take a right. Oh, there it is." They found the lot, started to pull into what seemed to be a full lot, and found out it was. The cars were jammed in to increase profits, as expected—what was not expected was the short-term memory loss of the attendant. Vic Raschi paid for a place? News to me, but you can see we are full.

Resourceful Sally started looking for a place on the street and her good looks and charm influenced a police officer to come to her rescue. Perhaps he could hear the National Anthem, and convert the anguished look on her face into happiness. Sally, with his help, was able to park and in the rush to leave, she slammed the car door without turning off the motor. You can blame it on the noise, frustration, or anger. Whatever the reason, the policeman unlocked the car and turned it off. Not in time for Sally Raschi to see her husband's first pitch, but she saw enough to know he won the game, and the Brooklyn police won a fan.

First inning. Rizzuto and Henrich walked. Rex Barney was, with good reason, upset, but when he tried to pick me off second base, he threw over Pee Wee's head into center field. That often happens to pitchers and the rest of us. We try to make things better not by stopping what got us in the soup but by trying to erase the event that put us in the fix.

George Will told me about what he calls the hole theory. It goes like this: "When you are in one, stop digging." ⓧ

—*Philip Francis Rizzuto*

Now I was on third, while Yogi was striking out. Joe D hit a ball so deep I was able to walk home and Tommy took third. We had scored first, and then Bobby Brown hit a shot through the box, and we had two runs. Woodling walked, and Mapes struck out. A very good way to open and I am sorry Sally missed it.

Vic set the Dodgers down in order and even worked Barney for a walk in the second after Coleman made the first out. I moved Vic to second with a sacrifice. I don't know what could have been in our mind at the time and sure don't know now. When I say "our mind," I mean Stengel, as he called the play. I do not recall bunting for a base hit, with our pitcher on first, and I fail to see the wisdom of giving up a run to move Vic to second. Let me beg the question by saying it was years ago, and while it may have been important at the time, it isn't anymore. At any rate, Tommy made out, and Vic got ready to face them in the second. He quickly disposed of Robinson, Hermanski, and Hodges.

Yogi opened the Yankee third with a topped ball back to Barney and Duke Snider made a great catch on a long drive by Joe D. The whole park was alive, Snider was a great ball hawk and the

Dodger fans understood the drama of one great player robbing another. Brown walked and Woodling singled to center, the fleet-footed Brown going to third. (I told Dr. Brown I would find a way to say he ran well, so I have.) Jerry Coleman drove in Brown. Shotten brought in Jack Banta and here is an example of how the Yankees of that era could make the other team begin to doubt their ability. If not ability, at least their last decision. The first man Banta faced, our pitcher, Raschi, singled in a run. It was a solid hit. We had them down by five. Rizzuto's routine fly ball ended the inning.

Give the Dodgers credit, and we always did. They came back in the next inning and scored. Campy doubled their first hit, Banta moved him to third, and Reese drove in the run.

In the fourth inning DiMaggio hit his sixth World Series home run. It was his only home run in that series and he would hit two more, for a total of eight, putting him in seventh place for most home runs in World Series history. Mantle (18), Babe Ruth (15), Berra (12), Duke Snider (11), and Lou Gehrig (10), are the first five on that list.

After four innings, the Yankees were up 4 to 1. Thanks to Woodling and Coleman, we added one more in the fifth. Raschi had little trouble in the last of the fifth, and Shotten brought in Carl Erskine to open the sixth. "Oisk," as the Dodgers fans used to call him. He walked me, Henrich singled on a hit-and-run, and I made it to third in time to hear Frank Crosetti's lecture "Picking Off Runners at Third, for Fun and Profit." Yogi hit a fly to center to drive me in. DiMaggio popped to second and Brown tripled off the right field wall, scoring on Jackie Robinson's throwing error. Erskine was gone, perhaps thinking Stan Musial was playing third for the Yankees because that is the way Brown hit that triple, and Joe Hatten came in to pitch. Woodling greeted him with a double. Mapes lifted a fly ball for the last out, but we had three more.

The top of the sixth was crucial. Duke Snider wasn't the Dodger Captain, Reese was (I never felt a baseball team should have one), but he sounded the alarm bell with a double. Robinson walked and Yogi went out to the mound. Something Raschi didn't like, but Yogi knew what he was doing. Hermanski singled and Snider scored and Jackie went to third on an error by Mapes. Vic struck out Hodges, got Rackley, but walked Campy to load the bases. Shotten pinch-hit for Joe Hatten with Billy Cox, an excellent hitter, and Vic struck him out.

The Dodgers brought in Erv Palica to open the seventh and they must have wondered why they hadn't used him earlier as he put away Coleman, Raschi, and Rizzuto on what seemed like nine pitches.

In the seventh Vic started giving up some hits. Reese and Snider hit the ball hard and he walked Jorgensen and Hermanski. Jim Turner came out, and Vic was always glad to chat with Turner. He had managed Vic in Portland, Oregon, and Vic admired and respected Turner. In Vic's view Turner helped him make it to the big leagues. He had been ready to quit when Turner took him under his wing. Turner could say the same thing to Vic that Yogi may have just said, but Vic would listen to Jim. After a while everybody listened to Yogi, but this was before that. Hodges came up, hit a threerun homer, and Stengel, for the third time in the series and the sixty-third time in the season, called for Joe Page. Joe struck out Olmo pinch-hitting for Rackley, but the score was now 10 to 6. The four runs pumped up the Dodgers, none more than Duke Snider, who made a circus catch off a drive by Henrich. Yogi made an out, DiMaggio walked, and Brown singled him to second. Woodling hit a fly ball to left to end the inning.

Page was as pumped as the Dodgers and the only hit of the inning by Bruce Edwards was erased by Pee Wee hitting into a double play, Page to Rizzuto to Henrich. Paul Minner came in to pitch the ninth and the lights were turned on, the first time that had ever been done. The umpire in chief made that decision. Some writer suggested the home team makes that decision, but it is the crew chief. Jerry doubled and I singled but we were not able to score off Minner, making his lifetime World Series ERA 0.00.

In the bottom of the ninth, Miksis batting for Jorgensen opened with a double. Page struck out Snider, Robinson, walked Hermanski and struck out Gil Hodges to end the season.

Yanks win their first of five, but who knew? Who could?

CHAPTER FOURTEEN

WORLD SERIES '50

George Will spends several thousand words writing about how a baseball game changes. How the pitcher in a particular inning needs to do certain things to carry on to victory. As a baseball person, and after over fifty years in baseball I can use that descriptive term, I was pleased that Will's book, *Men at Work*, spent so many weeks on the best-seller list. My reasons are twofold. George Will is someone I sometimes see in press boxes around the American League and it is nice to nod to a best-selling author and see him nod back. The other reason is that anything that increases interest in baseball is good for business. George Will's book has accomplished that end.

Sadly, I didn't (and I wish to choose my words here) like what he did. To my way of thinking, George took a simple game and complicated it, and by doing so the game did not become any more interesting. I am not alone in this opinion, as a great many baseball people feel as I do, but you can bet they are not going to say so out loud. The reason I am not fearful of doing so will be obvious in the next few sentences. I know more about baseball than George

Will. George Will knows more about writing books or letters to a friend, for that matter.

Here is my view of this book thus far. I hope the reader understands that the twelve of us liked and respected each other, and that we all had some skills to bring to the clubhouse—that we were lucky to be included in the group, even if some people question the number twelve. You will note Joe Collins did not make the 1949 box score. Not only were we fortunate to be on the Yankee teams of that five-year period, but being there made us better.

Can you guess how valuable it was to have DiMaggio, Henrich, and Berra hitting before or after someone like myself? I saw pitches as a Yankee I would have seen once a month had I played on some other major league teams.

Whenever we played the Indians, we always saw the same three guys: Bob Lemon, Early Wynn, and Mike Garcia. Whenever we played Detroit, we never saw a second-line pitcher. If a Yankee of those days hit .290, he was really a .330 hitter. ⚾

—Bob Kuzava, New York Yankees, 1951–54

We walked through the '49 series. I loved doing so (except the pickoffs) but what I like is not the issue. Having you turn the page is, and at this stage I am like George Will's pitcher in that middle inning. What do I do next to keep you along on the journey? One thing I am not going to do is what I believe so many others have done and that is to write things that are not true, just to make something interesting. Nor am I going to dwell on hate. I said my piece on Stengel and may let some other punches fly, even as I understand my obligation to the departed.

Seems to me it's time to get on with the Whiz Kids.

We didn't of course waltz from one October to the next. Detroit, under Red Wolfe, the old Yankee third baseman, won 95 to
our 98, and Boston and Cleveland didn't send us a telegram as we
left St. Pete after spring training saying "We concede." Let me tell
you it was tough.

We really were tough in the mental sense—as Yogi puts it, we
were self-confident. When you have Raschi, Reynolds, and Lopat
and then the front office (no matter how much you may dislike
some of them, Mr. Weiss) comes up with a jewel like Whitey Ford,
it does something for the whole team. World Series money was an
important part of our pay. Receiving $5,627 after we beat the
Dodgers meant I could stay at home with my family that winter
and not have to find a job. During that time most players did something during the winter. Can you even imagine that now?

When you think you know baseball, you don't. 〇〇

—*Yogi Berra*

Almost every few pages I learn something about the team or
something that happened to it or one of its members that I didn't
know. Sally Raschi's phantom parking space is but one example.

Another is the story of Vic Raschi's selection as the Yankee
starting pitcher in 1950. Eddie Sawyer, the Phils manager, was slow
to announce his starting pitcher. The time the manager tells the
pitcher and the press is his business and Eddie was taking his time.
Turner and Stengel told Allie that he would start when Robin Roberts started. So when Sawyer shook up the baseball world by starting his ace relief pitcher, Jim Kostanty, he made the decision for
our team. Jim ran a sporting goods store in Oneonta, New York, a
small college town. I got to know him quite well, and for some
strange reason that eludes me now (like why I didn't keep going to

the eye doctor and using Johnny Mize's bat after 1950), we seldom talked about the 1950 Series. We talked about his business, his family, my family, but very little about what I want to tell you about now.

We opened in Philadelphia, three days after the season, after the Phils beat the Dodgers on the last day. Dick Sisler's home run won it for them and it was a great moment in that old ball park.

The six-foot-two Konstanty walked Woodling to start the game and for four innings, Mize, Brown, Bauer, Yogi, and I were hitting the ball but no one was running by Cro at third to score. Joe D was hitless. Both pitchers were masterful. Woodling, looking for all the world like Pete Reiser, crashed into the wall trying to catch a popup off Eddie Waitkus's bat. This happened early in the game (first inning) and I remember thinking how important Woodling was to our chances of getting some runs.

In the fourth, Brown led off with a double and took third on Hank Bauer's deep fly to center. Woodling was a key hitter. He was also a guy you had to like, because he was so open. If Stengel couldn't feel Woodling's occasional rancor in the clubhouse at those moments, his skin had to be three inches thick. Woodling got up to a nice hand, and as I said, everyone watched the pitchers. Jerry Coleman was MVP of the 1950 Series, and he started earning the award by driving in his boyhood pal, Brown, with a long fly to left. We were up by one. And that's the way the game ended. Vic went the full nine, giving up but two hits, and they left three on. We got five hits, the only extra-base hit was by Brown, and left nine on. Casey was groaning about the number of men left on base and who could blame him? When George Will talks about the critical times of a game sometimes he loses me, but when the game is over and your team left eight or nine or more men on base, you've squandered some chances.

Announcers are fond of saying, and I am guilty as well, that the runner is in scoring position when he is at second base. If the batter hits one out, the batter was in scoring position, so what they really mean is the more times you get men on base the more chances that the next event, a hit, a walk, or in some cases a wild pitch or a passed ball, will help you end up with more runs than the other guys.

We stayed in Philly for the second game. The first one took two hours and seventeen minutes before 30,746 paid. This one will run three hours and six minutes before 32,660. Both games were in Shibe Park on October 4 and 5, 1950. This was only the second time in thirty-six years the Phils had been in a World Series.

Shibe Park looked more like a factory than a baseball park but it was storied in baseball so every time I played a game, despite the crummy clubhouse, I felt like I was playing in a museum. Shibe Park was the home of the A's, so we knew it well. Lou Gehrig's four straight home runs were hit in this ball park. Ted Williams got six hits in seven times at bat here in 1941 to keep his average over .400, and the year after we played the Phillies, Jackie Robinson made a circus catch in extra innings and then hit a home run to beat the Whiz Kids (I guess they still were even though we won in 1950). That win set up the '51 Giant-Dodger playoff that put the Giants in next year's World Series with the Yankees. Hallowed ground for a baseball person. Just a vacant lot now, occupied partly by the Deliverance Evangelistic Church. Not only is this book about twelve men, some of them now dead, it's about four ball parks. Three of them gone, one torn down and rebuilt on the same ground.

Shibe Park was alive this day as Allie Reynolds faced Robin Roberts. Roberts had a wicked fastball and Reynolds was even faster. I would have paid to see these two guys. Woodling beat out a bouncing ball to Granny Hamner at short to start the game. It was a close play. I popped up and Yogi singled to left, Woodling taking third, DiMaggio at the plate. Joe and Mize both popped up. Roberts was 20 and 11 for the season and he showed us why in the first.

Allie was sharp and the only well-hit ball in the second was a drive by Richie Ashburn. Bauer just missed a shoestring catch. Reynolds got two ground outs, a strikeout, and ended the inning.

In our second, Brown led off with a line drive well played by Ashburn. It is the sort of play that Ashburn, now a Phillies announcer, would call a line shot. I know because I have heard him when driving back from Cape May, New Jersey. Bauer fouled to Jones at third. Jones was called "Puddin' Head." I will take "Scooter" any day. Roberts walked Coleman, and someone broadcasting the game or writing about it said that Roberts let up after getting two quick outs. Don't believe it. Roberts owns a golf course outside Philly, and when I played a round several years back, we talked about it.

His version: Jerry was tough to pitch to, because he hit the ball both ways. Meaning he did not have a pattern of hitting.

Reynolds singled Jerry to third. Woodling hit another roller to short and Jerry scored our first run. Mr. MVP was on a tear. Reynolds was on second, and I missed a chance for an RBI when I flew out to Ashburn. Sort of a routine fly out.

In their second Allie struck out Puddin' Head and then Hamner tripled. One out, man on third. Crosetti's rule is you have simply got to score. Allie worked his magic on Seminick and Goliat and they didn't.

In the third Mize got a hit but DiMaggio, Brown, and Berra made out. The Phils' third was sort of a replay of the second except this time it was Waitkus wasting a double after Roberts struck out.

In the Yankee fourth, Bauer popped to short, Coleman doubled, Allie walked, and Woodling and I failed to drive in the base runners.

Roberts set us down one, two, three in the fifth and Mike Goliat hit a shot between first and second and Jerry Coleman made a stunning play, but hurried his throw and Goliat beat the toss. Base hit. Roberts's attempted bunt was snatched by Allie Reynolds and I was sure we could hold them again. Waitkus hit a ground ball to Coleman. His last play, moments earlier, was one of those, "Oh Doctor Hang a Star on That One," but Jerry never touched this one. The ball was what we call an easy chance but it took a good hop for the Phils and ended up in right field. Goliat was on third. Ashburn flew out, Goliat scored. Tie ball game. Sisler fouled out to Mize.

Brown led off the sixth with a single. He didn't score, in fact he was still on first when Reynolds struck out swinging to end the inning. This one dinky hit, at least to me, is an example of how memory can play tricks. I played in all 28 games but it was not until I spent time going over all of them, the way Dr. Brown might examine the history of one of his patients, that I realized how valuable he was to our five wins. I don't see him often. When an ex-teammate becomes president of the league it kind of puts up a wall. He doesn't, the job itself does, and when I do see him we don't talk much about individual games or innings.

Mostly we talk about Frank Crosetti. You can be sure Frank knows the value of Bobby Brown's bat, and now that I have taken the time to revisit, I do as well. Do you suppose I have said enough nice things about Dr. Brown to be in line for a free physical?

In the eighth inning several things happened that to me indicate how hard it is to manage a team, any team. Dusty Baker was just voted the National League Manager of the year, in 1993. I saw part of what he had to say on CNN. He talked about second-guessing and that as the manager he had the first and only guess and that if he were to do anything different next year it would be to make sure he remembers that and not let the second-guessing keep him awake at night. I was pleased Dusty got the job and won the award, but I thought to myself, Lots of luck, Dusty. You are going to need to change human nature, yours and others', to accomplish that goal.

Eddie Sawyer removed one catcher, Andy Seminick, for another, Ken Silvestri. I don't know all the reasons, maybe no one does, but Seminick had a bad leg. Sawyer put a pinch-runner (Putsy Caballero—those Whiz Kids had some great names) in the seventh when Andy walked. Here was Sawyer's thinking. Seminick is the better hitter even with a bad leg, but now that he may not come up again in the game, I can run Putsy and bring in Silvestri. Sounds good, but what about the bad leg in the first place? Just how much does the bad wheel hamper Seminick? Is the supposed superior hitting ability of Seminick . . . well, you could go on and I will not but I did want to make you think. I also wanted to talk a bit about two moves Stengel made, because I knew more about them and I wanted to give more of one example of managerial chess play.

After our eighth, when DiMaggio, Mize, and Brown were retired like ducks in a shooting gallery, Casey replaced Mize at first with Johnny Hopp, and Brown, at third, with Billy Johnson. As was the case with Sawyer, Stengel was acting on what the MBAs call "information." Mize and Brown were just up and in order for them to come up again we would need to bat around. Since Mize and Brown are more "hitters" of the ball than they are "catchers," it stands to reason Stengel was making the best use of the tools George Weiss placed in his tool box. He was also giving Hopp and Johnson a chance to play in the World Series, but scratch that from the list of reasons right quick. Casey, and he was not alone as a major league manager in this respect, was not the least concerned about playing time. This was a move made on what might happen during the rest of the game, namely, on the chances of the left and right side of the infield needing a "catcher and thrower" of the ball since the hitting time clock had just been punched.

I hope I have done an adequate job of showcasing Stengel's thinking. More importantly, I hope the other players on the team think so. Here is my thinking and it may be one reason I never managed. Putting in someone to play short, or any of the infield positions late in the game, barring injury to a player, is dangerous. Here is why: Johnson and Hopp, to keep this to Casey's move, are bound to be tight. A sort of "I-hope-I-don't-have-a-tough-chance-right-away" thing. Believe me, that is not the way to field. You want a "hit-the-ball-to-me" attitude, and you want it from the first pitch. While Hopp and Johnson are tight, Brown and Mize are maybe—and considering the two players that is a big maybe—thinking, "They tell me I can't field and maybe they are right." Lastly, the chemistry and balance of the team are changed, the comfort zone, if you will. I can't say for sure but I will bet that Joe McCarthy would not have made those changes.

In the Yankee ninth, Woodling and Rizzuto (the platooning guru) grounded to second and Berra (just a plain guru) popped up.

In the bottom of the ninth, Vic faced Jones, Hamner, and Dick Whitman, a pinch-hitter (two World Series in two years). They had two men on, and Mike Goliat hit into a double play, Rizzuto to Coleman to Hopp. The throw from Jerry was a ball Mize could have handled with ease. Extra innings.

Sawyer brought in his third catcher, Stan Lopata, and I don't have a clue why he did.

Our first hitter in the tenth was Joe DiMaggio. Joe hit Roberts's fast ball into the upper left field stands. The Yankees were up by one. Johnson struck out and Johnny Hopp flew out to left. Hank Bauer grounded to Hamner.

Reynolds needed to get three more and we are up two games to zip and I knew he could do it. We all did, Allie most of all. Jackie Mayo, pinch-hitting for Roberts, walked. It was the only time he came to bat in a World Series. Waitkus sacrificed Mayo to second, and Allie got Ashburn to pop the ball up to Johnny Hopp. Dick Sisler was called out on strikes and we headed back to Yankee Stadium.

Crosetti, after watching him for years, said DiMaggio only had one weakness. He didn't attend Mass often enough. ⓧ

—*Philip Francis Rizzuto*

Let me make one more comment on Casey's or on any manager's concern for the way one of his players felt. I just spoke about Brown and Mize. In Johnny's last year, 1953, Mize was in striking distance of a pinch-hitting record. I don't recall the number, say it was eighteen, what was important was the record. John didn't think about it at the time, but when you are seventy years old and someone doing a game of the week or some nationally televised game says something like, "The record was held by Boom Boom Brag-don," that old Boom Boom feels good and the next time Boom Boom buys gas, the kid at the pump may ask, "Are you the guy they were talking about on TV last week, Mr. Bragdon?" It all comes under the heading of recognition and never downplay its importance. In 1953, Johnny Mize knew the number of pinch-hits, and he also knew that our winning was more important than that record. That, as they now say, was a given. As he told me, he needed one more to tie or break the record and we were playing the Washington Senators in Griffith Stadium the last game of the season. They were way down, late in the game—let's say, 9 to 3— and I will bet I am not far off, even though when Mize told me, he was not highlighting the score, he was pointing out Stengel's be-havior. I don't want to go into a long thing on pinch-hitting, so let me just say most baseball people would not think the Yanks and the Senators playing the last game of the season would need to make extensive use of pinch-hitters. It seemed to John Mize that if manager Stengel was going to need one he would be the one called on. Wrong, Casey called on Billy Martin. I didn't hear this, so if you have read another account, you may have a different version, this one is from Mize to me. But later in the clubhouse Mize al-lowed, to use the Georgia term, that he was disappointed not to have been given a chance to pinch-hit.

Casey said, "I was going to use you next."

Game 3 of the 1950 World Series was played in Yankee Sta-dium before 64,505 on October 6. Ken Heintzelman, a five-eleven left-hander with a won and lost record of 3 and 9, was pitching for the Phils and Eddie "The Junk Man" was going for us. Lopat was 18 and 8 and was pitching in his second World Series. It was Heint-zelman's first and only time and I do not write this to put him down. A whole lot of people would be proud of one game in the big leagues.

I never recall anyone calling Lopat Junk Man or even Junk in the clubhouse, or Old Reliable for Tommy Henrich, or the Big Cat for Johnny Mize. The one exception was Scooter, his name was the same for the other players and the fans. ⊗

—*Reliable Source*

Eddie Waitkus opened with a hit off Lopat but then he got three quick outs and I walked to open our half of the first. Jerry Coleman hit a soft liner to Granny Hamner at short and the alert Phillies shortstop doubled me off first. Crosetti was going to get the ruler out. It was not a heads-up play on my part and Lopat knew I knew as much and didn't say a word. Yogi walked, meaning I should have been on second with one out and DiMaggio at the plate. Joe flied to right.

The second inning ended with no score, Hamner singled off Billy Johnson's glove and Seminick singled, but Goliat and Heintzelman were not able to get the ball out of the infield. Bauer, Mize, and Johnson made outs for us.

Lopat held them in the top of the third and the bottom didn't start with a bang for the Yankees. Cliff Mapes popped to first, Lopat was caught looking, but I walked and stole second, and when Andy Seminick's throw was high and ended up in center field, I ended up on third. Put that ruler away, Frank. I stole second on the second pitch. Some people don't like to run on the second pitch. I think you run more on the pitcher and the way he is making that particular delivery than on the count. The pitcher's delivery and the batter are the important considerations. You don't run if Babe Ruth is hitting, for example. But he wasn't. MVP Coleman was and he singled to center, scoring me easily. Jerry ran into the third out at second and was credited with a hit, a single. We were one up.

In the fifth and sixth innings only two hits were flashed on the Yankee Stadium scoreboard. Neither one for the Phils. DiMaggio and Lopat came through but were left stranded.

In the sixth Lopat had two quick strikeouts, Ashburn and Jones, then Del Ennis doubled into the left-field corner. Sisler hit a shot over my head and when Hamner missed a bunt attempt, Yogi picked Sisler off first base. Considering Hamner started off the seventh inning with a solid single, Yogi's play was crucial.

After the single in the top of the seventh, Seminick sacrificed Hamner to second. Mike Goliat singled, Hamner crossed the plate. Heintzelman laid down a great bunt so Yogi could not get to it and Waitkus made the last out but they had broken the tie, and it was 2 to 1, the first time they had a lead.

Mize, Johnson, and Mapes went down in the bottom of the seventh, and they went almost as quickly in the top of the eighth, sending four men to the plate but not scoring. Ashburn, Jones, Ennis, and Sisler failed to solve Lopat's junk.

In the last of the eighth Woodling hit for Lopat, popped to Hamner, then Rizzuto bounced to third and Coleman and Berra walked. Sawyer came out to talk to his pitcher and Heintzelman then walked DiMaggio. Getting two men out and walking the bases full must stay with you. At the time, of course, it didn't stay with me but looking at the inning now, well, it's different. Sawyer came out and brought in Konstanty again. The mostly Yankee crowd gave Heintzelman a nice sendoff. Not a standing ovation, but some people stood and gave him a nice hand.

Casey sent Brown in to hit for Hank Bauer, and Bobby fouled three pitches before hitting an easy grounder to Hamner. He booted the ball and Coleman scored. Jackie Jensen ran for Brown and Mize popped up to third, leaving three men on.

Woodling took Bauer's spot in left, showing the depth of the Yankee bench, to open the top of the ninth. Big Tom Ferrick was now on the mound. Hamner greeted Ferrick with a double and felt better, I would guess, about his error in the previous inning. I know I would've. All of us felt good that DiMaggio was playing center

Had James Joyce written this book, he might have called this photo *Portrait of the Scooter as a Young Boy.*

Yogi Berra—the greatest catcher of the modern era. As Casey would have said: "The numbers don't lie. You can look it up." Or as the late Bart Giamatti, former Commissioner of Baseball, once put it: "Talking to Yogi Berra about baseball is like talking to Homer about the gods."

Gene Woodling said of Mickey Mantle: "No one including Babe Ruth hit them consistently as far as Mantle. Mantle was unbelievable. I don't think he ever realized the talent he had."

Gene "The Rock" Woodling was the only Yankee Stengel ever
regretted trading, and when Casey went to the Mets, one of the
first things he did was bring Gene back.

Pitching coach Jim Turner said you only had to tell Whitey Ford once.

Yogi Berra called Joe DiMaggio the best player he ever saw.

Dr. Bobby Brown went on to become a distinguished
cardiologist and is currently President of the American League.

Furman Bisher of the *Atlanta Constitution* said that Johnny
Mize's induction into the Hall of Fame came twenty years too
late.

Here's Scooter trying to learn how to bunt.

Jackie Robinson said that Allie Reynolds was one of the finest competitors he had ever played against. There were some who thought he threw as hard as Bobby Feller.

People forget that Charlie Silvera played six weeks in 1949 and hit over .300. Without him, we could not have won the pennant.

Whitey Ford—Chairman of the Board.

Superstar Ed Lopat specialized in slow curves, slower curves, and change-ups. The batters, who thought they could take him downtown, went home cursing. Yogi said he could catch him with a Kleenex. Here he is later on as a Yankee coach.

Jerry Coleman, the decorated Marine Corps pilot, is kneeling on second base like he owns it. He has been the television announcer for the San Diego Padres for over twenty years.

Allie Reynolds said Vic Raschi was the strongest pitcher on the
Yankee team.

Toward the end of Joe Collins's career, he had other opportunities to play major league baseball, but he chose to retire a Yankee.

field for us because the moment Hamner hit the ball, I whirled to see Joe on the run and I said to myself, triple or inside-the-park home run. Almost any other man playing center would have made Hamner's day. Seminick sacrificed Hamner to third, Billy Johnson to Joe Collins. Collins had replaced Mize at the start of the inning.

They put Goliat on, perhaps to encourage Sawyer to pinch-hit for the next batter, Konstanty. Here came Dick Whitman again. Yankee Stadium was still buzzing several hitters after Hamner's hit, an indication of just how great Joe played that ball. Whitman bounced the ball to Collins, who nailed Hamner at the plate. Waitkus made the last out and we had dodged a bullet thanks to the skill and speed of DiMaggio. I always love a great defensive play because it does so much to discourage the other team. If I was thinking that Hamner had a chance for an inside-the-park home run, imagine what *he* was thinking. When he got to home plate he found Yogi waiting with the ball.

Top of the ninth, with Russ "The Mad Monk" Meyer, a six-one right-hander with a 9 and 11 record, pitching for the Phillies. Jimmy Bloodworth, a name I always liked, was now playing second. Billy Johnson lined to left. One out. Monk struck out Mapes, two outs. Holy Cow, Joe saved our bacon and this guy is murder. Woodling hit a shot to Bloodworth. He couldn't handle it and they gave Gene a hit. I hit a similar ball to Bloodworth and it went off his glove a few feet from second base and Woodling was safe. Again no error and Woodling and my hits were wonderful examples of the "inches" in baseball. A few inches and Bloodworth picks my ball up and touches second or feeds to Hamner and I am out at first.

Coleman, first-ball hitting, strokes a single between Mayo and Ashburn and we are three up. We are at home, Ford is getting his first World Series start after winning nine straight games after coming up from the minors.

Final game. October 7, 1950. 68,098. Time of game two hours five minutes. Ford vs. Bob Miller, who was 11 and 6 that season. Whitey, and I am sure we called him Ed at the time, walked Waitkus to open the first. Ashburn made out and Jones hit a ground-rule double, two men on. Del Ennis hit a hard, high bouncer to third and Brown made a good throw to nip Waitkus at home. Jones holding at second. Ford, as Jim Turner said, "had the guts of a burglar" and he showed it by striking out Dick Sisler. Here was a kid from Long Island, who spent part of the year in the minors, starting the last game of the World Series. It is one thing to do what I did and start playing in one of them like I did, in 1942, with Keller and Dickey and Spud Chandler. But pitching, now that is another kettle of fish. Not that I want to come back as a pitcher, thank you.

Mike Goliat booted Woodling's ball, who led off for us in the first inning as he had the other games against the Phils. I led off, hit second as well as some other spots in the lineup. With Casey you had to wait until you opened the clubhouse door and looked there to know if you were playing and where. I grounded to third, moving Woodling, and then Yogi singled him home. One up in the first inning. Miller now faced DiMaggio. His wild pitch was so wild, Yogi made it to third. Joe doubled, Yogi trotted in with the second run. Sawyer was out quickly and you just know that Miller was gone, but could he bring in Konstanty again? Yes, and it was Jim's seventy-seventh appearance of the year. You have to wonder what pitching seventy-seven times does to an arm. The answer has to be, bad things, but again I am not saying Sawyer was wrong. He had to go with his best and, knowing Jim as I did, I am sure he wanted the ball. He got Mize to ground to second, moving Joe, but then Bobby Brown grounded to second also and Sawyer looked like a genius.

The second and third innings were what the announcers like to call sparring rounds. After this book if I announce any more baseball games I am going to become self-conscious, and if Bobby "Golden Boy" Brown reads this, he will say "It's about time."

Dr. Brown got that name because he got a bonus to sign with the Yankees. I don't think he likes it now and liked it even less back then. The bonus was not much of anything considering what they get today and was not that great even in those days. Some writers,

however, gave him the name, and it stuck. You will not see it here
again.

Del Ennis opened the third by beating out a slow roller down
the third base line. Sisler flied to right. Hamner singled to right,
sending Ennis to third. Next, a strange play that would be replayed
until you were sick of seeing it. Seminick hit a slow roller to Mize,
who stepped on first for the force and threw to Yogi, nailing Ennis
at home. Andy Seminick's bad leg kept right on running. When
that sort of decoy play happens most infielders think they missed
something and run around trying to tag someone. "When in danger, fear, or doubt, run in circles, scream, and shout." That last of
the fourth was another good inning for Konstanty. He struck out
Joe, gave up a single to Mize, but allowed no runs.

In the fifth Ford struck out Goliat and gave up a single to Konstanty. It didn't matter, as he got Waitkus and Ashburn. They had
to be disheartened, but if they were, you would never have known
it. A lot of that had to do, as far as I was concerned, with the guts
of Jim Konstanty. Wish I had told him that.

In the sixth, Jones was called out to open the inning. Ennis hit
a ball to Brown, who made an error. Ford never shrugged, and he
kept the ball in on Sisler. Double play, Coleman to Rizzuto to Mize.
Side retired.

Last of the sixth. Yogi had what they now call a "good at-bat."
He worked the count full. Fouled off several, he likes to say twelve
or fifteen, and hit a home run to right field. Berra's second. His first
was a pinch-hit home run in 1947. The first one in World Series
history. Konstanty was not unnerved, but he hit Joe. Mize then hit
a hot shot past first base that Waitkus could not handle and Mike
Goliat, backing up, made a fine play and threw the slow-running
Mize out at first. Joe took second. Brown tripled a frozen rope to
center and DiMaggio scored, making Goliat's play mean even
more. Bauer lined to left and Brown scored. Jerry Coleman made
the last out, but we had three more runs. Three games up, five runs
up, we have a magic man on the mound. Holy Cow, does it get
any better than this?

In the seventh Casey did his hippity-hop and Mize and Brown were on the bench and Billy Johnson was on third and Hopp was at first. Ford set down the side and opened our seventh by striking out. Woodling singled and was caught stealing. He spent seventeen years in the big leagues (as opposed to my thirteen) and only stole 29 bases vs. 149 for me so I wonder why was he running?

The top of the ninth had Jones hitting a solid single to left center off Ford. Ford then hit Del Ennis on the leg. Two on. Sisler bounced to Coleman, who forced Ennis at second, with Jones going to third. Sawyer sent Ken Johnson, a pitcher, in to run for Sisler although Johnson is not listed in *The Baseball Encyclopedia* as having any World Series experience.

Ford struck out Hamner to chalk up his seventh and we needed one more out. Andy Seminick drove a high fly to left center and Woodling got under it but lost it in the sun and dropped the ball. Jones scored and Johnson made it home all the way from first. Andy Seminick, with his bad leg, stopped at first. Jack Mayo ran for Seminick and Stengel was running up and down in our dugout, showing up Woodling. Something a manager should never do, even though he may be upset and with good reason. Ford lost his shutout. Woodling, however, catches that ball most of the time. This time he didn't and showing him up was bush, anyway it wasn't over. There I said it.

Now it's 5 to 2. Stengel went out to talk to Ford. Mike Goliat hit a shot just under my outstretched glove for a single. Mayo went to second, Stengel to the mound. Allie Reynolds came in from the bull pen, and to tell the truth I didn't even know he was out there. Sawyer sent Stan Lopata up to pinch-hit for Roberts, who had come in to open the eighth. Allie struck him out on four pitches. You can find this half-inning described in half a dozen books as three pitches. Trust me. It was four. It was four pitches in a row and two World Series parties. Back-to-back. Gene Woodling didn't attend. I don't blame him.

CHAPTER FIFTEEN

WORLD SERIES '51

The '51 Series opened in Yankee Stadium, before 65,673 people on October 4. Allie Reynolds, 17 and 8, with two no-hitters, and 126 strikeouts, was the Yankee pitcher. The Durocher-led fairytale Giants started Dave Koslo, 10 and 9 with 54 strikeouts. The Giants had won 39 out of 47 games to force the three-game playoff with the Dodgers. Bobby Thompson was still trying to come back to earth and Durocher was trying to figure out how to replace Don Mueller. Mandrake the Magician was an uncanny hitter and a fine outfielder. His nickname referred to his ability with the bat, but his glove was what they had trouble replacing. His broken ankle mended but over the years baseball people feel when Mueller went down so did the Giants. Mueller had been injured in the ninth inning of the Bobby Thomson home run game the previous day, and the Giants simply didn't have time to figure out what to do, with the World Series starting the next day. So 16 or 17 hours after Russ Hodges screamed "THE GIANTS WIN THE PENNANT, THE GIANTS WIN THE PENNANT, THE GIANTS WIN THE PENNANT EEEEEOOOOOEEEE! THE GIANTS WIN THE PENNANT!" The

Yankees were ready for them, just over the Harlem River at 161st Street and River Avenue. Yankee Stadium.

The morning of the first game someone stole Wes Westrum's catcher's mitt. By the time he discovered the theft, it was too late to go back to the Polo Grounds for a spare. He borrowed one from Charlie Fox. (Years later both of them, Fox and Westrum, managed the Giants after the team moved to San Francisco.) I bet they always made sure their catchers traveled with a spare mitt. As for the Yankees, we would have been better off if someone had stolen Monte Irvin and held him hostage.

In the first inning, Allie got Stanky and Dark and then he walked Hank Thompson. Irvin singled, moving Thompson to third. Whitey Lockman hit a ground-rule double into the left-field stands. One run in and Irvin on third. Bobby Thomson, the next hitter, was at the plate when Irvin stole home. They said it was a high pitch. They said Allie didn't look Irvin back to third. They also said you don't expect a runner like Irvin to steal home in the first inning. Maybe you do if the manager is Leo Durocher.

After the play, Monte dusted himself off and Bobby walked. Considering what had just happened 60 feet and 6 inches in front of him, you could understand why Allie was a bit wild. Then Willie Mays flied to right. Rough inning for Allie, catcher Berra, and the whole team. The start of a rough series for Willie. He would score only one run, and manage only four hits. Even the great ones stumble. We didn't use computers in those days but I will bet a ginger snap you would look long and hard to find a Reynolds-pitched game where he gave up two runs in the first inning.

> Irvin stole home. It was the first time it ever happened to me in a World Series and the last time in baseball. Ⓧ
>
> —*Allie Reynolds*

In the bottom of the first I singled. My most vivid memory of that inning is Monte Irvin robbing Hank Bauer of a two-run homer. Steal home in the top of the first, then rob Bauer in the bottom. Ouch. I hit the ball hard, Hank creamed his, and instead of coming right back and matching them two and calling one, it was still 2–0. DiMaggio ended the inning, hitting a fly to right.

We did get one back in the second, when McDougald doubled, Coleman singled, and Hank Thompson made an error, allowing Gil to score.

> The first time Hank Thompson played right field for the Giants during 1951 was in the World Series. ⓧ
>
> —*Wes Westrum*

Collins forced Jerry at second. Allie Reynolds singled and Mickey Mantle walked. I came up with two out, my team one run behind, and the bases loaded. I grounded out to first base and the ball was hit well enough to get by Lockman but he threw me out to Koslo covering first. It was close but the three men left didn't care.

In the Giants' fifth Irvin tripled over DiMaggio's head. Something not too many hitters did to Joe. It was Irvin's third hit in a row. In case you were wondering, in his first World Series, Mickey played right field and Hank Bauer was in left. DiMaggio was in center.

> I played the first game of the 1951 World Series like I didn't belong. ⓧ
>
> —*Mickey Mantle*

In the Giants' sixth, Allie got Mays but Westrum singled and after Koslo sacrificed, Stanky walked. Alvin Dark, another future Giant manager, hit a three-run homer off Reynolds. Irvin followed with his fourth hit in a row, but was left on when Lockman grounded out. Lockman grounded out and they were grinding down Allie.

In the last of the sixth, Berra, McDougald, and Coleman made three quick outs. Casey seemed like he was always moving. Moving and talking for sure. As a kid in Brooklyn I used to read and hear people talking about cigar-smoking pols meeting in smoke-filled rooms. Back rooms, always back rooms. Stengel and his brain trust held their meetings in the Yankee dugout. In full view of their bench, our bench and several thousand people. During those first few innings, Turner, Bill Dickey, and Cro were scratching their heads. Casey couldn't bring in Allie, because he was already in, so he took Allie out and Bobby Hogue, a little-used right hander, took the mound. Hogue disposed of three hitters, including Mays and Westrum. Casey pinch-hit for Hogue in the next inning, Bobby Brown struck out swinging. Collins and Mantle both failed. The inning ended, and Tom "Plowboy" Morgan came in to pitch the eighth. We had some good nicknames, just like the Phillies. We were also in a deep hole, 5 to 1, and Dave Koslo was making the folks in Menasha, Wisconsin, proud. Putting those haughty Yankees down, one by one. The people back in Menasha knew Koslo as Koslowski. The same way people in Scranton, Pennsylvania, knew Joe Collins as Kollonige. Looking back on this game, as I did to come up with these name changes, I was pleased to note the October Twelve group got all but one of the seven hits off of Koslo. Kollonige, Coleman, Berra, and Reynolds each had one. I got two. (I would have settled for one in the second inning.)

As far as I know, no one in our family ever thought about changing our name. Back then, I was thinking, how are we going to score some runs? I was trying not to think about the shortstop leaving three men stranded. Yogi and I were able to come through with base hits in the eighth inning but we didn't score. Morgan had pitched well. He even managed to get Irwin so it was still 5 to 1, going into the ninth. Morgan struck out Mays and Koslo to end the inning and it was the last of the ninth and the Yanks were down to three outs.

Coleman walked. Mize pinch-hit for Collins and popped to Dark. Woodling, pinch-hitting for Morgan, took a third strike. Not that it mattered in this game but he didn't take many third strikes. Mickey made the last out of his first World Series when he flew out to Mays in center. In Mickey's last World Series, in 1964, he hit a three-run homer in his second-to-last at-bat in the seventh game. It wasn't enough. St. Louis beat the Yankees three games to four. Yogi was the manager. He took two teams to seven games, each time losing the final game. Once in each league. They also said he couldn't manage. They said he didn't look like a Yankee. They said he couldn't catch, but nobody ever said he couldn't hit.

> The world needs more people like Yogi Berra. They don't need to look like him, just be like him. Kind, thoughtful, interesting, and humble. Ⓧ
>
> —*Bobby Brown*

Game 2. Yankee Stadium. October 5, 1951. Casey and Turner chose Ed Lopat and Leo Durocher sent Larry Jansen to the mound. Lopat was 21 and 9 for the year. Jansen, the pride of Verboort, Oregon, had been 23 and 11. Jansen needed to pitch well. He had eight or nine kids to feed. Another great matchup. 66,018 people thought so, showed up, and all of them stayed.

> After getting two walks off Koslo, I was afraid to look
> at the lineup card for today's game, but of course I
> had to. Hitting first, playing RF Mantle. Ⓜ
>
> —*Mickey Mantle*

Lopat got Stanky, Dark, and Bobby Thomson quickly in the first inning.

Yesterday, when Irvin stole home, some of the Giants were saying, Allie didn't "look" Irvin back to third. As Cro would put it, "Who's to say? Who's to say?"

Today in our first inning, it was time for *us* to pull a shocker.

Wes Westrum, the Giant catcher and one of the brains in baseball, told me he can still "see the first inning" in his mind's eye. I should have asked him if he ever got his catcher's mitt back, but you always think of those things after a conversation. The Giants didn't know much about Mantle. We didn't know that much about him. Don't forget this was his first year and he played in only 96 games. We knew about his speed and power, but it takes looking back to really appreciate his ability. Baseball people I respect have called Mantle "the best two-strike bunter that ever played the game." He dragged one, a Hang-the-Stars!-Oh-Doctor bunt right past righthander Jansen that even had Cro fighting off a smile.

I was the next hitter and since I had a reputation as a good bunter, Westrum and Jansen, Durocher for sure, were looking for me to bunt. Knowing that, I was more interested in getting a good ball to hit as I could feel Thomson at third and Lockman at first straining to charge. Even a world-class bunt from my bat would not be unexpected.

The unexpected bunt is the best bunt of all, and I was trying to act like I didn't know what I wanted to do. For some strange reason I remember seeing Stan Musial just before the game. He was close to the Giants' dugout, and some of our guys were kidding Gene Woodling that his batting instructor was attending the game. Woodling and Musial had the strangest batting posture I every saw. Early in the count—I know it wasn't two strikes—I bunted past the mound. Lockman hurried his throw to Stanky trying to cover first and I was on with an error. I can tell you even now it pumps me up to think how good it felt to take it right to them, and to do so in the first inning. The park was alive. I'll bet even Stan the Man, a National League fan, of course, was impressed with the way we started—more importantly, the Giants were.

McDougald singled Mickey home and I had to stop at second. Joe grounded into a double play, Dark to Stanky to Lockman, and Yogi struck out. Now it was our turn to be shocked, but the truth is we were not. Sure we lost a chance to run up some runs, but we had one and we had them thinking.

Irvin got another hit in the second—he had eleven in the Series—but Mays, Lockman, and Westrum made outs and we started the bottom of the second with Woodling and Brown coming up empty. Then Joe Collins hit a long home run for his second hit of the Series and we were up by two. Lopat made the last out and went right to the mound. Today he would be told to wait for a commercial. Mind you, I am not fussing about commercials. Just saying what happened.

Lopat and Jansen worked quickly. The game lasted just over two hours, and both sides went down without much action until the sixth, and then something took place people still talk about and write about and like the old telephone game we played when we were kids—the more times the stories are told, the more they change. Here is mine. Willie Mays lifted a fly to center, right center. It looked to me like the center fielder's chance. I watched Joe make the catch. I always did. If someone called me today and said I am going to fly out to San Francisco and hit fungoes to Joe DiMaggio, I would go along to watch.

Mickey said he was going for the ball and Joe said the three words they say at every level of baseball, *"I got it."* It's like Yogi wrote it for the game. No wasted words. Not "It's mine, get away." Just three little words.

At shortstop I didn't hear them but Mickey did as he gave way. As he gave way so did his right knee when his spikes caught in a drain. He went down faster than if he was trying to fall down quickly. It was like a huge invisible hand pushed him down. Willie and Mickey were both strong and at the time didn't have an ounce of fat. They used to kid and say you could strike a match on one of them.

On the grass in center field, Mickey looked like a broken bird in pinstripes. He was carried off the field on a stretcher and Mickey was never the same again. It's been written that Mickey blames Joe and all sorts of other fault yarns. I don't believe them and I don't think you would be wise to either.

Bauer replaced Mickey, it may have been the only time he did so. Considering Mickey's impact on baseball it may come as a surprise that Mantle's injury was not a front-page story when it happened. He was a rookie but his speed and power alone made him special.

The sixth inning was routine if you want to call a great catch by DiMaggio off the bat of Hank Thompson routine.

In the Giants' seventh, Irwin led off with his sixth hit in seven at-bats. Lockman followed with another single to center, hit so well Irwin held at second. Willie tried to bunt but Bobby Brown whipped the ball to second in time to force Lockman. Irwin took third and the fleet Willie beat my throw to Collins at first. Lopat walked Westrum, loading the bases. Hank Schenz ran for Westrum and Bill Rigney hit for Hank Thompson.

Durocher and Stengel loved to make moves. If they had been basketball coaches, players would have been moving all the time, up and down the court and off and on the bench. Bill Rigney, another later-to-manage-the-Giants player, hit a fly deep enough to right to score Irwin, and Mays moved to third after the catch.

Ray Noble, a catcher, batted for Larry Jansen and fouled to

catcher Berra. The Giants scored but left two on. Noble stayed in the game and Clint Hartung took over in right. Clint Hartung is the answer to the question, Who was the most ballyhooed player ever as he came into the major leagues? Mantle had his share but I think for sheer hype Clint was the winner. It was a shame. Too much pressure on a kid can be just as bad as not getting a chance at all.

George Spencer came in to pitch for Leo and the Giants. Spencer's slants were effective and Joe D, Yogi, and Woodling all grounded out.

Inning number eight. Lopat got Stanky, Dark, and Bobby Thomson in much the same fashion: one, two, three.

Bobby Brown opened the last of the eighth with a sharp single over second and Billy Martin made his debut. I wonder how he would feel about my describing it that way? Somehow I think he would be pleased. He was special and wanted to be treated that way. It was no secret that Billy was Stengel's pet and it was also clear that Joe and Casey were not pals. Not even close.

But Billy was able to pal around with Joe and somehow it didn't seem to matter. Billy had something and now he was excited to be in a game, if only as a runner.

Billy Martin was one of the most complex baseball men I ever saw. He got me several jobs after I managed the Red Sox and I would have to say I admired him and I was loyal, but you just knew he wasn't going to die in bed. ⚾

—*Billy Jurges*

Joe Collins grounded out and Billy moved to second on the play. Right in the middle of things. Just the way he liked it.

The Junk Man, Eddie Lopat, was going to help himself. Bobby Brown's hit gave him the first base runner since the second, so he drove in Martin with a single. Boy, was he proud. And so were some others, Vic and Sally Raschi, Earlene and Allie Reynolds, and Libby Lopat. Those six were like a family. A happy family. They were great pitchers and it helped that they were as close as they were.

Bauer and Rizzuto flew out but thanks to Lopat's stinging hit,we and he had a cushion. McDougald moved to third and Coleman came in to play second.

Lopat faced Monte Irwin to open the ninth. His seventh hit in two games. Coleman made a good play on Lockman's smash and forced Irvin at second. Willie grounded to McDougald at third, who got Lockman at second. Coleman, in the game for moments, handled the ball twice. Hartung hit a smash at Joe Collins at first behind the bag, Lopat moved quickly to the bag for the relay and the victory. A five-hit jewel by the Junk Man. Eddie's second victory in a World Series.

Game 3, in the Polo Grounds before 52,035, at the time the largest crowd to see a World Series in a National League Park. The National League had smaller parks. I guess that's just the way it worked out.

Durocher picked Jim Hearn, who had been 17 and 9. He struck out 66 over the year but walked 82. The Yanks ran out one of the big three, Vic Raschi. The Springfield Rifle finished the season with his usual numbers, 21 and 10. Strike outs, 164. Walks, 103.

Gene Woodling led off for the Yanks while Mickey watched from Lenox Hill Hospital. Mickey's father had gone with him in the cab to Lenox Hill. Mickey leaned on his dad while getting out of the cab. They both fell and ended up in the same room. Cab? That's right, a cab.

Woodling led off the first with a popup to Bobby Thomson, and I singled to left. Westrum threw me out trying to steal second and when Gil McDougald singled off the short 279-foot wall, I was sorry I had run. Joe D flew to left. Inning over.

Maybe I should change the word "sorry" to "disappointed." Considering what Gil did, and that if I had waited I would have been on second or maybe even third, I was disappointed.

Raschi hit Stanky to open the Giants' first, but Dark flew out and Bobby Thomson struck out. Monte Irvin walked and you can bet that Lopat and Reynolds got on Raschi about his fear of pitching to the red-hot Irvin, but they did so later. Much later, like next spring in St. Pete. Lockman grounded to McDougald playing second.

In our second, Yogi legged out a roller, but was left on. More kidding here, about Yogi's speed, but not today. Brown grounded into a double play, the pitcher's friend.

Thomson doubled to open their half of the second and then Mays drove in his only run in the Series and his first in World Series play. He would drive in five more. Mays played in 20 World Series games and his batting average was .239. As I have said, even the great ones run into slumps, in some ways that is why baseball is so wonderful. Even Mays and Ted Williams, two accomplished hitters, could fail to come through in a short series.

That RBI was it for Willie and the Giants as Westrum, Hearn, and Stanky made outs. Stanky took a third strike. Still makes me smile to think about watching him go back to the dugout. The Giants were the ones feeling good. They had taken an early lead.

In our third we blew a chance to get back and then some. Alvin Dark made a throwing error on Bauer's ground ball and they had just given us four outs to start the inning. Stengel put the bunt on and Raschi bunted the ball back to pitcher Hearn and he got the lead run at second, but the relay throw from Dark to first was wild and Raschi was safe. He was safe at first but he tried for second on the overthrow and was out. The pitcher's friend in an unusual package. Woodling walked, another break, and I grounded to first.

The fourth inning was nothing to write home about, or to do much writing about here either. Since I already covered the meeting at second base between Edward Raymond Stanky and Philip Francis Rizzuto, I will skip it here. I do have to say this: Bobby Hogue replaced Raschi. The score at the end of the fifth inning was Giants 6, Yankees 0.

I led off the eighth inning for the Yankees. Casey used to kid— and I was never sure he was kidding—"If you get hit by a pitch that brings in the winning run, collect fifty in cold cash." With uniforms as loose-fitting as they were, maybe some guys even tried to do it but if they did I never saw money change hands.

Jim Hearn nailed me on the arm and the pain was not worth even a hundred dollars. Not only that, but my getting to first was not a big lift when you are down six-nothing. I know all about that "the longest trip starts with the first step" stuff. I am just telling you how I think I felt after making a two-base error and getting ready to spend a sleepless night.

McDougald singled to center and I had adequate time to speak with Edward Raymond Stanky, while Joe D popped to third, but I didn't. Didn't even glare at him. I took my lead and watched the hitter and Cro in the third base coaching box like he was the most important man in the world. He was to some of the Yankees, like Coleman and Brown, and I was not far behind.

Yogi hit back to the mound and moved the runners. Bobby Brown walked. Bases loaded. Joe Collins, the next hitter, walked me in and we were finally on the scoreboard.

Sheldon "Available" Jones came in to pitch. Later on the Giants had a pitcher with the name Sherman "Roadblock" Jones. I was always confused about the two of them. I mean, I was confused looking back. Bauer bounced back to the mound, and all we had to work with was three more outs.

Johnny Mize, batting for Joe Ostrowski (Joe had replaced Hogue as our pitcher in the seventh), hit a fly to right. One down. Woodling hit a deep home run into the right-field stands for the Yanks' second run. Then I hit a fly to deep center (yes, it was deep) and McDougald popped to Lockman. Game over. Two hours, forty-two minutes.

The mighty Yankees were down two games to one. Could the press be correct? The Giants were on a roll. Could our cake walk to a third flag have rendered us fat and happy? They had won 52 of their last 63 games, and were hot, and we had just been held to five hits. They'd knocked Vic out of the game and the Series. Woe is me.

Like most my age and even younger, I am not a fan of indoor baseball. I know all the reasons for having an all-weather dome, and I suppose if I owned a team I would want one, just like I would want a George Weiss to be my General Manager. Getting back to 1951, it rained enough to cancel the next game. "It droppeth as the gentle rain from heaven." It did for Shakespeare in *The Merchant of Venice*, and it did for the New York Yankees.

The rainout gave us a day off. Good for us and not good or at least not as good for the Giants. Why? We were down. It seems to me a day off is always good when you are down. If you are playing golf well you can't wait to get to the next hole. At least it is that way with me. The main reason the rain helped us is that it gave our pitchers an extra day to rest. If you gave Reynolds, Raschi (note, I just said they knocked him out of the game and the Series), and Lopat time, the Big Three would find a way to win. As you will see they did. Hitting and some good defense helped.

Giving Allie Reynolds time to rest and time to seethe is bad for the other team. He came back in game four, on Monday, October 8. Hank Bauer in right field, leading off. Mantle still in Lenox Hill Hospital, watching on TV.

First inning. Sal "The Barber" Maglie pitching for the Giants. 49,010 in the stands. The crowd was down. Sunday's rain washed out a big crowd. Bauer walked. The Barber struck out the Scooter. Sounds sort of quaint. It wasn't.

Berra lined to center. The Barber struck out Joe D, the Yankee Clipper. I will leave the rest to you. Half-inning over and Reynolds took the hill to begin the last of the first.

Stanky lined to short. Dark doubled off the wall. Allie faced fellow Sooner Hank Thompson. Hank grounded to Coleman at second and Dark went to third. Irvin singled (his eighth hit) Dark home and they were up again. Irwin tried to steal second and Yogi's throw was high, but I was able to leap for it, make the grab, and come down hard to tag Irvin, with Lockman at the plate. We had given up a run, but getting Irvin, the guy who killed us in the first game and hurt us in the others, was a good trade-off. Not a great one. But it gave us a good feeling running back to our dugout.

Woodling opened the Yankee second with a double down the left-field line. Woodling's ball was just fair but he was on second. McDougald hit a roller to Bobby Thomson at third, who booted the ball, and we had runners at first and second, no one out.

Bobby Brown hit the long fly to Mays in center field that was caught, dropped, and recaught by Willie. The umpires missed it, but it was witnessed by Bobby's father from his grandstand seat and by some other fans sitting in center field. You can see why the ball hit by Brown and caught by Mays stayed with Dr. Brown all these years. Had the umpire ruled a trapped ball, the bases would have been loaded. Instead, Collins drove Woodling in for the tying run, and then Allie flew out to right. Hank Bauer's batted ball hit McDougald, giving Hank a single, but McDougald made the third out.

No score in the third but Joe DiMaggio picked up another hit.

With one down in the Yankee fourth, Brown drove the ball deep in the hole at short and beat Dark's throw. Maglie went to 3 and 2 with Joe Collins and lost him. With two strikes, Allie Reynolds singled, driving in Brown, moving Collins to third. Allie's elation was shortlived as he was caught rounding first. Mays to Dark to Lockman.

"I was surprised Willie got to the ball so quickly and then threw in one motion," Reynolds explained "Fact is, he made a good throw on a base runner who wasn't thinking—me."

Bauer made the third out, grounding to third.

Bottom of the fourth. Dark doubled again, but was left on base, when Allie got Thomson and Irwin on strikes, and Lockman.

In the Yankee fifth, after I popped to second, Yogi punched a hit to right and Joe D hit the first pitch into the left-field stands. Home run number eight. It would be his last. DiMaggio number seven in all-time World Series home runs. Yogi (by now wearing number 8 on his back) scored ahead of Joe and the Yanks were up 4 to 1. This was the first time in the Series we scored two runs in one inning. Woodling and McDougald made the last two outs, and Allie walked Hank Thompson to open the Giants' fifth.

Willie hit into another double play, Reynolds to Rizzuto to Collins, and Westrum walked. Lucky Lohrke, hitting for Maglie, popped to second. Lucky got his name when he missed a team bus in the minor leagues and most of the team was killed in a bus crash. I know we were lucky to see the last of Maglie and I will bet if Leo had to do it again, he would not have taken Maglie out. Leo only had one guess. I had two.

Available Jones came in to pitch the sixth and Brown doubled to left center. Collins moved Bobby to third with a fly to left, but Allie's ground out to third held Brown at third and Bauer popped to second. Inning over but Sal the Barber was gone and we were up by three, and still had the Super Chief.

Allie struck out Stanky to open the Giants' sixth and then Dark stroked his third double just over third base. Dark's seventh hit of the Series. He was stranded again.

In the seventh, I hit Jones's first pitch, and Yogi and Joe D made out, but Woodling walked and we had two on with two out. I had a big lead at second, and Westrum threw behind me and I took off for third. Edward Raymond's throw hit me in the back as I was going to third and the ball got away from Bobby Thomson, allowing me to score on his two-base error. Woodling took second. The ball in the back didn't hurt. Not then. Not the next day. McDougald singled Woodling home and Brown flied to center to end the inning, but we had another two-run frame.

Jerry came in to play second and Gil McDougald took over for Brown at third. Allie got Dark on a double play, Reynolds to Rizzuto to Collins, to end the eighth.

The Giants brought in Monte Kennedy to start the ninth and he made quick work of Berra, DiMaggio, and Woodling, the last two on strikes. What a way to pitch in your first World Series. Pop up a Yogi and hang a K on Joe and Woodling.

Hank Thompson walked to open the bottom of the ninth. Then Allie gave up another single to Irvin, number nine. Lockman flew to left, and hero Bobby Thomson drove in Hank with Irvin going to third. You can bet he would have a tough time stealing home today. Then Mays ended the game, hitting into his third double play of the day. Rizzuto to Coleman to Collins. It took three of us to end this important game and while it didn't mean much at the time, it does today.

We were now even with the Giants and had one more game in the Polo Grounds, and then we would go back over the river. The game lasted almost three hours. Left on base, Yankees 8, Giants 5.

Game 5. World Series. October 9, 1951. Polo Grounds. 47,530. Two hours and thirty-one minutes.

Lopat was to pitch again after winning game two and he would face Jansen, as before. Woodling in left and leading off. Stanky leading off for the Giants. Leo, still concerned about the loss of Mueller, decided to start Clint Hartung in place of Hank Thompson.

The Giants scored first when Dark and Irvin both singled, and when Woodling misplayed a ball, Dark scored. Irvin now had ten hits.

The second inning was scoreless and Lopat opened the third inning by hitting an easy roller to Jansen, then Woodling and I walked. Yogi hit a smash to Lockman and I was out at second but Woodling moved to third. Joe D singled, scoring Woodling. Irvin booted the ball and Yogi was on third and Joe on second. Leo decided to walk Johnny Mize and pitch to rookie McDougald as first base was open. After Gil hit a grand slam, the flood gates opened too. It was only the third slam in World Series history. Brown singled and Collins hit a fly to Mays. Inning over but the Yanks were up by four.

In the Giants' third, Lohrke pinch-hit for Jansen and struck out. Dark and Thomson came up empty.

Monte Kennedy started the fourth inning. He got Lopat on strikes. Woodling walked and nine years after I hit my first World Series home run, I hit my second. Off Monte Kennedy of Amelia, Virginia. If I ever meet Monte, I am going to drive him over to Bassett and buy him lunch. On the map it looks to be about an hour.

Joe got one more hit to extend the inning, but the scoring was over for the fourth.

The fifth was scoreless.

In the sixth inning George Spence came in to pitch for the Giants and after an out, I singled to left and Yogi followed with a hit to right but when Hartung made an error, I was able to score. Mueller was missed—here was another time his broken ankle hurt them. Mize doubled in Yogi and we had another two-run inning. It was now 9 to 1.

In the Giants' sixth Bauer replaced Collins in right as Joe went to first to take over for Mize. Lopat gave up a single to Irwin, his eleventh hit, but he did not score. The official scorer was seeing the white spaces in his scorecard disappear, as Stengel juggled his chessmen.

In the Yankee seventh, Brown walked and Joe Collins beat out a bunt. I am sure it was his first. Stengel put in Jerry Coleman to run for Brown. Lopat bounced to the mound, moving both runners.

Woodling walked, his third of the game. Bases loaded. Rizzuto walked, Coleman scored. Leo bought Al Corwin in to pitch. Al delivered a wild pitch and we had another run. Yogi hit a fly ball but not one long enough to score a run, then Joe D doubled in Woodling and Rizzuto to end the scoring in the inning, and the game. Final score: 13 to 1.

As long as this is about the October Twelve, I guess I should say that in the ninth Woodling tripled but tried to turn it into an inside-the-park home run and was thrown out at the plate, Hartung to Stanky to Westrum. Shows the Yankees were still eager for more and the Giants were still in the game. But we had them down and it was downhill to the stadium and downhill for the Giants.

The sixth game drew 61,711 and was played October 10, 1951, in Yankee Stadium. It would be the last time Joe DiMaggio would ever wear a Yankee uniform. If Yankee fans had known this would be his last game, not a park in the country would have held the crowd.

David Halberstam wrote in his *Summer of '49* that DiMaggio had become "somewhat of an icon." Many of the fans attending the game who held Joe in the highest esteem would not understand the use of "somewhat" when it came to Joe D. If baseball of that era had an icon, Joe was it.

Raschi and Koslo were the pitchers. Vic, under the mother hen pitching coach, Jim Turner, since he was taken out of game three on October 6. Four days' rest was just right for Vic and Sally knew where to park near Yankee Stadium.

In the first inning the Giants didn't score but Lockman doubled and was stranded. In the last of the first, Coleman singled and Yogi doubled off the wall. The ball was hit so hard it came back to the infield and Coleman could not score. Joe D came to the plate (his fifty-first World Series game—at the time a record). Leo decided to put Joe on to load the bases. McDougald was the next hitter, this time he flew out to Mays, Coleman scoring. This game the Yankees broke on top. Mize made the third out.

The second and third innings were scoreless and in the fourth Rizzuto, Coleman, and Mize turned a nifty double play, so I wanted to make sure it made this page.

In the Giants' fifth, Willie Mays singled to DiMaggio in center and took second on a passed ball to Yogi with Koslo at the plate, then Koslo flied to right with Mays taking third after the catch. Vic walked Dark. Lockman beat out a hit down the third base line. Then Irwin made the last out of the inning. Irwin was held hitless in the sixth game.

In the Yankee sixth Coleman was called out on strikes and Yogi followed with a single and took second on a Thompson error. Leo Durocher ordered Joe D walked again to pitch to Gil McDougald. Koslo delivered a wild pitch and Berra and DiMaggio moved. Berra was on third and Joe on second when McDougald hit a humpback liner to Bobby Thomson at third. Johnny Mize worked out a walk and the bases were loaded.

Hank Bauer worked the count to 3 and 2 and the runners were on the move as Bauer just missed a home run. By the time Irwin got the ball back in, Hank was on third, and Berra, Di-Maggio, and Mize had crossed the plate. It would be the last time Joe DiMaggio scored a run for the New York Yankees. Yanks on top, 4 to 1.

Joe Collins took over for Mize at first to open the seventh. Mays singled. Bill Rigney, now a guru for the Oakland A's, pinch-hit for Koslo and singled to right. That was enough for Stengel, who brought in Johnny Sain to face Stanky. Raschi showed no sign, but was disappointed to be replaced. Stanky hit a soft fly to right. Sain struck out Dark. Lockman hit a fly to DiMaggio for the last out Joe would record as a New York Yankee.

Leo Durocher brought in Hearn to pitch the last of the seventh. Sain grounded to short. Hearn gave me a good pitch and I hit a ball deep in the hole and beat the throw. Coleman fouled to Lockman. Berra grounded to second.

Top of the eighth. Sain handled Irvin, with help from Bauer, who made a fine catch. One out. Bobby Thomson pops to McDougald at third. Two out and Sain was strong. Hank Thompson walked. Westrum singled over second. Thompson stopped at second. Davey Williams ran for Westrum, Mays walked, loading the bases. Ray Noble pinch-hitting for Hearn was called out on strikes by home plate umpire Ballanfant.

Last of the eighth inning. Noble catching, Larry Jansen pitching. Joe DiMaggio's last Yankee hit was a solid double to right. McDougald bunted and Jansen's perfect throw nailed DiMaggio at third. Collins flied to left and McDougald was caught stealing for the third out. Three more outs and the Yankees would be champs for the third time in a row. One more and Stengel would tie Joe McCarthy's record of four in a row.

Top of the ninth. Sain gave up a single to Stanky. Dark beat out a bunt down the third base line for his tenth hit of the series. Lockman singled, loading the bases. Stengel, moving around the dugout like a wave machine, brought in Bob Kuzava during the rally. It was Kuzava's first World Series.

Irvin greeted Kuzava by flying to left and Stanky scored. Both runners moved up. Bobby Thomson flied to left. Dark scored. Score: Giants 3, Yankees 4. Two out. Leo sent up a pinch-hitter for Hank Thompson, Sal Yvars, a little-used catcher who lined to right to end the game.

Moments after we moved up the short runway to our clubhouse, and before the room was opened to the press, Joe DiMaggio said these few words: "I just played my last game. I can't play like I could and it's time to give it up. Thanks for everything." I know what I heard and I also know all that went on after he said that. The attempts Del Webb and Topping made to get him to change his mind. Part-time player for more money and who knows what more went on. They were businessmen and this man to them was an asset. To us, he was a leader and a gentleman.

> After spending five-plus games in the bull pen, I was sure I would not get into a game. I wasn't thrilled to find the bases loaded, but I knew Jim Turner had confidence in me, which gave confidence to me. ⓧ
>
> —Bob Kuzava

The reason I said that I knew what I heard is that Joe was so low-key that Allie Reynolds, who was right next to Joe, didn't hear what Joe said. Allie was not alone. Big Pete Sheehy, who ran the clubhouse for years and who loved Joe and was loved in return (the clubhouse is now named in his honor), heard what Joe said. And I am sure he heard even more.

We were teammates of one of the great players of all time. Pete had a special place and there was only one. One place and one Pete.

They only gave one World Series MVP award. I was lucky to win it in 1951.

CHAPTER SIXTEEN

WORLD SERIES '52

Crosetti would hit infield every day and toward the end of the drill, some of us would begin hot-dogging and he would get on us right away. When you beat Cleveland to win the American League Pennant by a slim margin—we won 95 and lost 59 to their 93 and 51 in 1952—it's good to have someone working you over every day.

Stengel couldn't do it and I am not saying it was his job, or that he wasn't good at it when he was a coach. He may have been. I am just trying to let people know how important Crosetti was to a good portion of the team. Turner and Cro were crucial.

The Dodgers, meanwhile, won under Chuck Dressen, beating the Giants without a playoff. Once was enough for Bobby Thomson.

The first game was in Ebbets field. October 1, 1952. Some were saying the Yankees were getting a little long in the tooth. True, they had a thirty-six-year-old shortstop, but at my age, a thirty-six-year-old shortstop is hardly long in the tooth, so let me get out of this by saying the Yankees, as far as age was concerned, were a balanced team.

Allie Reynolds started the game for the Yankees, and he faced

Rookie of the Year Joe Black. Dressen had taken a page from Eddie Sawyer's book and started Black, a relief pitcher. Unlike Konstanty, Black had started two games during the season, while coming in from the pen fifty-four times. Dressen, the Dodger manager, spent some time with the Yankees prior to his Brooklyn assignment and his imperious manner had rankled several of the Yanks.

Starter Reynolds was one example. "Dressen would try to make himself look good by making you look bad," was Allie's comment and Reynolds wanted to show Dressen he knew when to throw a curve and he wanted the win, too.

With the usual near-full house of 34,861 in Ebbets Field, Black set down Bauer, Rizzuto, and Mantle in order. Reynolds did the same to Cox, Reese, and Snider.

In the second, Black did it again. Berra, Collins, and Irv Noren. Noren was playing right field for the first time in a World Series.

Reynolds, a 20-game winner for the Yankees during the '52 season, who had the best ERA in the league, 2.06, worked carefully to Jackie Robinson to lead off the last half of the second. He lost Robinson on a 3 and 2 count to a home run to left.

> Mr. Halberstam said in *The Summer of '49* that I threw at hitters and at black players, in particular. During 13 years of regular-season play, I hit six batters. My recollection is that they were all white. By comparison, the late Don Drysdale hit 154 batters. ⓧ
>
> —*Allie Reynolds*

Campanella singled off the wall, but was thrown out by Berra when be tried to steal second. Andy Pafko was at the plate when

Campy ran, and I am surprised he attempted the steal. Even more so looking back. He stole only twenty-five times in ten years. Yogi stole thirty times but it took him nineteen years. He never stole a base during a World Series. Pafko grounded out. Hodges topped a ball back to Reynolds, but they were up by one at home and they had done so early.

Gil McDougald led off the Yankee third with a home run also to left and getting right back is always good. The Dodger fans were going bananas and Gil put a lid on some of the noise. Billy Martin in his first World Series as a starter struck out. Then Black struck out Reynolds and Bauer was caught looking. Holy Cow!

At six-five, Don Drysdale delivered his 90-plus m.p.h. fastball with a big sidearm motion—"all spikes, elbows, and fingernails"—that made right-handed batters think they were under a rocket attack from third base. They say that halfway through some of his games the groundskeeper had to come out and sprinkle sand in the batter's box. Batters' fears were justified. Big Don hit 154 batters, about 1 every 22 innings. It's the all-time record. Off the field, Drysdale was always a considerate gentleman, but [on the field] he broke one batter's hand and was suspended for throwing beanballs. He threatened to sue and was reinstated. Adding to the terror, Don had a temper and everyone knew it. After giving up one home run, he threw the ball into the stands. He claimed it "slipped." Ⓧ

—Total Baseball, *edited by John Thorn and Pete Palmer*

Allie induced Furillo to pop to Berra, Black took a third strike, and when Cox walked, he was thrown out stealing, Berra to Rizzuto. The next day the *New York Times* said it was a spectacular play. They meant my catch and tag, not Yogi's throw. This was a Yankee inning. I mean, our side had been struck out, but we came right back and put them away and even though it was the bottom of the order, when Carl Furillo is hitting eighth, you have a mighty fine team.

I started the fourth with a single and then Mickey beat out a bunt down the line at third and we had two runners. Yogi forced Mickey at second, but we had men on the corners with one out. Joe Collins hit a line drive well back in right field and Furillo took away our breath and a chance to score with a great throw to the plate. The term today is "awesome" and it was. I love defensive baseball and a throw like Furillo's was worth the price of admission. I was just sorry it happened when we were the other team. Noren grounded to second. Two left on.

Going to a memorial service for Don Drysdale was very hard for me. He was a hard pitcher to face and I am lucky I didn't have to do it very often. We shared a room once during a golf tournament in Florida and he let me use his car. It was a brand-new Ford station wagon, 1957 I think, and I lost the keys. I never lost my respect for him. He hit a lot of batters. One more reason to like playing in the American League. Ⓚ

—*Yogi Berra*

In the last of the fifth, they left two on and Snider's double off the wall was wasted, as well as Robinson's walk. Campy ended the inning by grounding into a double play, Martin to Collins.

McDougald walked to open the fifth. Billy Martin got his first hit, a single down the left-field line. McDougald was out trying for third, and Billy took second on the Pafko throw. Reynolds grounded out. Andy Pafko made an "Oh Doctor," a diving, sliding play on Bauer's drive to right.

Reynolds put them down: one, two, three to close the fifth.

Rizzuto struck out to start the sixth and Mickey singled to left. Yogi forced Mantle at second, Hodges to Reese, and Collins rolled to first.

Allie Reynolds caught Black looking for the first out in the Dodger sixth. Cox popped up and Allie had two quick outs and the score was still tied. Reese singled and took second on a Reynolds's wild pitch with Duke Snider at the plate. Reynolds, pitching out of a stretch, delivered and Snider hit a long home run over the rightfield scoreboard.

McDougald errored on a Robinson smash and Jackie took second when Reynolds tried to pick him off first, but threw wildly. Campy grounded to short, but the damage was done. The Yankees were down, 3 to 1.

Noren walked. A leadoff walk in the seventh, when you are down two runs, is just what the doctor ordered. Gil McDougald hit into a double play, Cox to Jackie to Hodges. I will bet you one of those ginger snaps that after the DP, Stengel got up and moved around the dugout, but I didn't see it.

Martin grounded to Cox, who threw him out. Allie got the Dodgers in apple pie order in the last of the sixth and Casey took him out in the eighth inning.

He would have been the first batter except he was lifted for a pinch-hitter, Gene Woodling. You can bet Allie was sorry to be taken out but when his old teammate from Wilkes-Barre tripled off the wall in right, he was pleased. Black was thinking, Is this what they meant when they said the Yankees keep coming at you?

Bauer hit a run-scoring fly to center. Yanks down by 1. Rizzuto flied to right. Black struck out Mickey to end the inning.

Stengel brought in Ray Scarborough for his only World Series appearance. He struck Black out and got Cox on a ground-out to third. Two out and Pee Wee Reese at the plate, home run to the lower left-field stands. Snider grounded back to the mound but they had one more.

In the top of the ninth Yogi flied to center, Collins hit a soft ground ball to Jackie, and Irv Noren was caught looking to end the game. We lost eight games on the way to winning five straight Series in a row. This was one of the most disappointing. I know it hurt Allie, the Dodgers only had six hits but three of them were home runs. We left four on, they left two. Game time: Two hours and twenty-one minutes.

Game 2. Ebbets field. October 2, 1952. 33,792, almost 2,000 over capacity. Brooklyn loved the Dodgers and they disliked the Giants and Yankees, in that order. Raschi, 16 and 6 for the year, started for the Yanks and Carl Erskine was on his familiar mound for Dressen. "Oisk" from Anderson, Indiana, was 14 and 6.

Bauer led off with a single to right center. Casey put on a hit-and-run but I missed the pitch and Campy threw out Bauer. Then Erskine walked me. Mickey struck out, and with Woodling at the plate I was out stealing. Not a good way to start.

Raschi said, "Never you mind," and put them down in the bottom of the first.

In the second Yogi singled but was left on. In the bottom half, the Dodgers loaded the bases but could not score when Erskine flied to center to end the threat.

Raschi walked to open the third, but was out when Hank Bauer hit into a double play. I grounded out. Inning over.

The Dodger third saw Cox called out on strikes. Reese singled. Snider, the Dodger center fielder, could not run like Mickey, few could, but he could run well enough to beat out a bunt, and Reese was on second. Jackie forced Snider at second on a good play, Collins to Rizzuto, Reese going to third. Campanella singled him home, and Pafko struck out to end the inning. But they were one up and had scored first.

Mickey doubled off the right center field scoreboard to open the fourth. Woodling grounded Mantle to third, and Yogi drove in the tying run with a fly to right. Collins tapped back to the mound.

In the fourth Hodges struck out but Yogi dropped the ball and had to throw out Hodges at first. Then Raschi got Furillo and Erskine.

McDougald walked to open the fifth, stole second, then Billy Martin singled, Gil scored, and Billy took second on the throw to the plate. Vic Raschi was called out on strikes, and Bauer walked. A passed ball by Campanella let Bauer go to second but Campy recovered in time to throw out Martin at third. I grounded to Reese.

In the last of the fifth, Raschi again put them away quickly but Yogi dropped a third strike and this time had to throw out Snider.

Inning number six opened with Mickey bunting. Woodling singled to center, Mantle holding at second. Erskine wild-pitched the runners one base. Runners at second and third. No outs. Yogi walked to load the bases. Dressen called Billy Loes in to pitch. (A Long Island righty to go along with our Long Island lefty, Whitey Ford, who was in the U.S. Army at the time.) Joe Collins drove the ball to Robinson, who was able to tag Berra but his throw to Hodges was dropped for an error, allowing Mantle to tally the run and Woodling to take third.

McDougald beat out a bunt and Woodling scored. Runner on first and one out. On the first pitch from Loes, Billy Martin hit his first of five World Series home runs. Raschi and Bauer struck out to end the inning. But we had five big runs.

The Dodgers did not threaten in the last of the sixth and the seventh was also scoreless. Loes left for pinch-hitter Rocky Nelson, who walked. Also on the bench and ready for Dressen, but not used, was another Rocky. Rocky Bridges, as well as Rube Walker, later a coach with Yogi when Gil Hodges managed the Mets, and Dick Williams, who would later manage the Oakland A's to a seven-game victory over the Berra-managed Mets.

The eighth inning with Ken Lehman pitching (Dressen did not use Ralph Branca, Clem Labine, Ben Wade, Moore, or Joe Landrum in his pitching rotation during the Series) opened with a Berra single. A Collins walk, and three outs, by McDougald, Martin, and Raschi. Raschi was very strong in the last of the eighth, getting Snider, Robinson, and Campanella.

The ninth inning was over with only one base runner; Martin singled, and Raschi had thrown a gem. A complete game giving up only three hits and striking out nine. Game time: Two hours and forty-seven minutes.

Game 3. Yankee Stadium. October 3, 1952. 66,698. Eddie Lopat pitching for the Yanks and Preacher Rowe, another left-hander, going for the Dodgers.

Lopat not only started the game but drove in the first run. In the third, after Rowe had given up two walks, one of them an intentional pass to Martin, Eddie drove in Bauer. I made the last out of the inning, but we were up early at home and when your pitcher drives in a run, it gives everyone a lift. Even Cro almost smiled. I am sure Jim Turner did when he clapped Ed on the back. Raschi, Reynolds, and Lopat were like his children.

In the third Carl Furillo hit a ground-rule double when the ball was touched by a fan. A Brooklyn fan. Reese beat out a bunt down the third base line, Furillo going to third. Jackie Robinson drove in Carl with a fly to center. Campanella hit into a double play and we held them to one run.

Collins, Mantle, and Woodling went quickly in the last of the third.

Both teams missed chances to score in the fourth and Cox singled to open the Dodger fifth. Roe sacrificed Cox to second, Berra to Martin. Reese drove in Cox and they went up by a run in the last of the inning. Yogi and Woodling singled but did not score.

As Yogi would remember it years later, "Three hits, a single, a double and a home run didn't mean a thing on that team if you didn't win. No one said anything to me after the game. I would have been surprised if they did."

In recent years there has been a tendency to rate Berra as the second-best hitting catcher of the modern era—behind Johnny Bench. I have always found this comparison puzzling. Berra leads Bench in batting average by nearly 20 points as well as in RBIs and total runs scored, despite the fact that Yogi had fewer at-bats. Bench leads only in total home runs and ties Berra for Total Average. As for Yogi's overall contribution to his team, Yogi's teams outperformed Bench's. Ⓧ

—*Philip Francis Rizzuto*

Jackie Robinson singled to center to open the eighth inning, the Dodgers still ahead. Campanella singled and Jackie moved to third. Pafko flew out to Woodling and Jackie beat the throw and they were up 3 to 1. Yogi was charged with an error on a pop-up from Snider and then Duke popped up again to short. Casey had Hodges and Cox walked to pitch to Roe and he grounded out.

Woodling struck out in the last of the eighth inning and we were down to five outs. Berra hit one of his many home runs into the left-field stands. Bauer and McDougald made outs and the game moved to the ninth.

Carl Furillo grounded to short. Reese singled to right and Jackie singled to left. Stengel brought in Tom Gorman to face Campanella, Reese on first, Robinson on second. The Dodgers keystone combination pulled off a double steal. Campy popped up and with Pafko at the plate, Berra was charged with a passed ball and two runs scored. Pafko singled and Snider fouled out to Berra to end the inning but the Dodgers were up 5 to 2.

In the last of the ninth, Johnny Mize, pinch-hitting for Gorman, drove a home run into the right-field stands but one run was all we could manage. Martin popped up. I flew to center and John Sain, the pitcher, pinch-hit for Joe Collins and to tell the truth, I had forgotten that move. Sain also flew out to center and Lopat lost, giving up eleven hits while we managed six, and Lopat had one of them. The Dodgers left ten men on base so it could have been worse. For us, I mean. Jerry Coleman and Dr. Brown were both serving in Korea and most times the games were tape-delayed broadcast. For their sake I hope so. Bobby and Jerry both told me that they knew soon enough.

Game 4. Yankee Stadium. October 4, 1952. 71,787. Webb and Topping and Weiss could not be happy with the Series thus far but we were drawing well. Joe Black and Allie Reynolds hooked up again, in a rematch of game one. Reynolds had nothing to prove to Chuck Dressen, but he wanted to anyway.

Allie struck out Cox to open the game. Then Reese singled and Snider was safe on Billy Martin's throwing error when Duke hit the ball through the middle and Reese was on third. Reynolds was in the soup. He struck out Robinson on a called strike and got Campanella swinging.

I won 7 games in the series and struck out 62 batters. These were two of the most satisfying. ⓧ

—*Allie Reynolds*

Mickey walked in the last half of the first, but McDougald, Rizzuto, and Mize made outs.

No score in the second.

In the third, Pee Wee Reese singled off my glove. The sort of shot you think is a hit but can be called an error depending on who makes the call. Reese was credited with a hit and I was credited with the put-out, Berra to Rizzuto when Pee Wee tried to steal second.

In the last half of the fourth, Mize led off with a home run to left and Snider stole a home run from Yogi with a leaping, one-handed catch, as the ball was going into the stands, that Yogi still can't believe. Woodling and Bauer made outs while Yogi was shaking his head and the game moved to the top of the fifth.

Andy Pafko singled, Hodges walked. Furillo bunted the runner up, Mize to Martin. Dressen put on a squeeze play and when Black missed the pitch, Yogi put the tag on Pafko. I would like to say that Reynolds put his hand on Yogi's shoulder and said, "Nice job, kid," but I can't because he didn't. Then Black walked and Cox popped up to Berra.

The Yankees left two on in the last of the fifth, and the sixth inning for the Dodgers was too much Reynolds. Mize led off with a double in our half of the inning; Berra, Bauer, and Martin left him on second.

In the seventh Hodges hit into a double play, Rizzuto to Martin to Mize. Martin was the sort of baseball player you had to admire. He used every bit of his God-given talent, and I can think of so many over the years who did not. I don't mean guys, like Wakefield or Hartung, I have mentioned before who were hyped out of the game. I mean guys like Joe Pepitone, who had a host of talent but didn't use it. As hard as Billy worked, he could never make a double play like Jerry. No matter which side of it he was on, the tag side or the throwing side. If he threw the ball to you he would sort of hide it, so you had to look for it and that could mess up your timing. If he was taking the throw, he could not come close to Jerry's smooth leap and throw to first, but Billy was a great one and a fearsome manager. He was a fearsome, fearless sort of guy.

In the Yanks' seventh Allie struck out. Then McDougald and I made quick outs and Allie needed six outs.

Furillo singled over my head to start the top of the eighth. George "Shotgun" Shuba, a name I always liked, pinch-hit for Black and lined out to center. Rocky Nelson came up again, this time for Cox, and struck out. Then Reese flied to right. Danger passed.

> Can you imagine how bad Billy would be if he didn't have baseball. Ⓚ
>
> —*Casey Stengel*

Johnny Rutherford came in to pitch the eighth for the Dodgers. I would like to say after a pit stop, but the publisher may edit it out. Mantle tripled over Snider's head and scored when Reese threw the relay into the stands trying to nail Mickey at third. Mickey scored on the error. Mize walked, Collins ran for John. Yogi lined out to right and Woodling grounded to third, moving the runner, but Bauer was called out on strikes.

Reynolds got Snider on a fly to Mickey, put a called third strike past the great Jackie Robinson, and Campy grounded to third. Game over. Reynolds shut them out on four hits. Series tied at two.

Game 5 was played on a Sunday. October 5, 1952, before 70,536 in Yankee Stadium. Carl Erskine back on the mound for the Dodgers after his loss in the second game. Stengel, with no rain to rest his pitching staff, selected Ewell "The Whip" Blackwell to pitch. Blackwell had been a big winner for the Cincinnati Reds, winning 22 games in 1947, but the right-hander who came at the hitter by way of the third base coaching box, or beyond, had developed arm problems. It was a gamble, but Blackwell knew how to pitch and, as the writers said, his heart was not hurting. He had come to us from the Reds on August 28 of that year. A trade arranged by Weiss for Stengel for just this need. The need? Nine well-pitched innings.

Billy Cox singled off McDougald's glove and was on with the

first hit. Reese flew out and Snider hit into Blackwell's friend in both leagues, the double play.

The Yankee leadoff trio, McDougald, Rizzuto, and Mantle, came up empty.

Second inning. Robinson walked. Shuba, playing left field, singled, Robinson going to second. Then with Campanella at the plate, Jackie stole third. Stealing third in the second inning was daring, and if Jackie was not that he was nothing. Blackwell, reaching back, struck out Campy. Then Pafko singled to right and Jackie scored. Hodges walked the bases full and Erskine bunted on a squeeze play to Blackwell and The Whip got Shuba on a force to Berra at the plate. Billy Cox then forced Erskine at second. Only one run. Blackwell wasn't feeling good but it could have been a whole lot worse.

Mize grounded out to open the second for the Yanks. Yogi walked and Woodling was the victim of daylight robbery. Pafko went back to the left-field stand (the railing was about five feet then) and leaped just as the ball was going into the stands. What a catch. Turned a two-run home run into a long fly out. Bauer flew out to end the inning.

No score in the third and fourth innings.

Hodges walked to open the fifth. Erskine bunted and Blackwell threw late to second. No one out and two on. Cox sacrificed both runners. Then Reese hit a long fly to deep left and Hodges, by now on third, scored. As Frankie Frisch used to moan, "Oh, them bases on balls. Oh, them bases on balls." Snider then hit a two-run homer and Robinson ended the inning by striking out. But they had a three-run inning and a four-zip lead.

Dressen, in fine Durocher fashion, brought in Furillo to play right for his great arm and moved Pafko to left. Shotgun Shuba going to the bench.

Erskine walked Bauer. Martin singled, Bauer stopping at second. Irv Noren, hitting for Blackwell, came up with a run-producing single and Martin went to third. McDougald forced Noren at second, Martin scoring. Rizzuto singled. Mantle fouled to

Cox, Johnny Mize hit a ball into the left-field stands for a three-run homer and Yogi ended the inning with a fly ball. It was Johnny's third home run in three games and he was on his way to being named MVP, and the Yanks were up 5 to 4.

Sain came in to pitch the sixth. He was met with a double by Furillo but Carl was left on base. Woodling, Bauer, and Martin finished the last of the sixth in order.

In the Brooklyn seventh Erskine was out on a fly to center, and Cox beat out a roller to third. Reese bunted Cox over and Snider drove him in with a single to center. Score tied and Snider took second on Mantle's throw to the plate. Stengel put Robinson on. Furillo flied out to deep left center to end the inning. Score tied at 5.

No scoring in innings eight and nine.

Tommy Holmes came in to play left to start the last of the ninth. Holmes, a Brooklyn native, spent most of his playing career with the Boston Braves and this was his second World Series. Playing for Boston in 1948, when they lost to Cleveland 4 games to 2. The score remained tied, and after nine innings the umpires ordered the lights turned on.

Top of the tenth. Sain struck out Campanella, and then got Holmes and Hodges and it was our turn to turn off the lights and go home.

Sain grounded out, McDougald hit a soft fly to left. Rizzuto grounded to third. Lights still on.

Dodgers' turn. Top of the eleventh. Sain struck out Erskine, Cox singled off McDougald's glove. With the hit-and-run on, Reese singled Cox to third. With two strikes, Snider doubled. Cox scored, Reese holding at third. Casey ordered Jackie passed. Furillo hit into a double play, McDougald to Berra to Mize.

Last of the eleventh. Mantle rolled to Carl Erskine; Mize was robbed of a home run when Carl Furillo made a great catch in right. Yogi took a third strike to end the game. Turn out the lights. Yanks lose 6 to 5 and the Dodgers are up three games to two.

Erskine gave up hits in only two innings, pitching nine no-hit innings but not in a row, this was an Erskine gem. Great pitching and great outfield play for the Dodgers. Game time: Three hours.

Game 6 back in Ebbets Field. October 6, 1952. 30,037. Raschi for Yanks and Dressen selected young Billy Loes for the Dodgers. Loes had pitched well in the Dodgers' pennant drive. The Dodgers had won 96 games to our 95 during the regular season. Winning by four and one-half games to our two.

Both pitchers controlled the game during the first, then the second, and then the third innings.

In the Yankee fourth Mantle popped up but then Mize walked, and Berra came up. Yogi hit into a double play but when Reese threw wide to first and Yogi moved to second, the Yankees had a break but couldn't capitalize when Woodling lifted a fly to center to end the inning.

Raschi struck out the side in the last of the fourth, but Campanella came up with a hit during the inning. Still no score.

The fifth inning was also scoreless.

We failed to score in the top of the sixth and Snider hit a leadoff home run in the bottom of the sixth. Then Vic got Robinson, Shuba, and Campanella in order, but the damage was done. We were in Brooklyn—if they win it's over and the outfield play of yesterday would be on everyone's mind. Making great plays in the outfield is something you can almost will and it helps to have over thirty thousand believers rooting you on.

In the Yankee seventh Yogi led off with a home run, his second of the Series, and we were back even. Woodling followed with a single and went to second on a Loes balk. Noren was called out on strikes. Martin popped to third. Two down. Raschi hit a shot off Loes's leg and Woodling scored. McDougald walked and Rizzuto grounded out. I was disappointed but we were up by one.

In the last of the seventh, Raschi struck out Hodges, Furillo grounded out, and then Loes singled, stole second. A pitcher, mind you. But it went for naught when Cox struck out.

Mantle, the first hitter in the eighth inning, hit a long home run to left field. 3 to 1. Woodling singled but was left on base. It sure was nice to have that extra run.

Last of the eighth, Collins at first. Mize popped to first in the top of the eighth inning and I know this is second-guessing, but with apologies to Betty Collins, Casey should have had his head examined for taking Mize out. Reese grounded out to open the inning. Snider hit his second home run of the day and his fourth of the Series. Raschi got Robinson on a fly ball, but then Shuba doubled to left center and Stengel walked to the mound with his mind made up. Reynolds came in to take over for Raschi. Raschi's words to Reynolds were, "Think you are up to it, Chief?"

"Let's find out," answered Reynolds. Sandy Amoros ran for Shuba and Allie struck out Campanella.

Holmes took over in left again and Reynolds was the first batter up in the top of the ninth. Allie tapped back to Loes. Gil McDougald beat out a slow roller to third. Rizzuto singled down the left-field line sending Gil to third and Dressen brought Roe in to pitch. Preacher walked Mickey, probably worried about another home run, to load the bases. Then Roe fanned Collins and Berra lined to right.

Last of the ninth, Bauer in right. Allie struck out Rocky Nelson, Pinch-hitting for Hodges, to open the inning. He walked Furillo. Pafko pinch-hit for Roe. Andy Pafko popped a short. Cox grounded to third to end the two-hour-and-fifty-six-minute game. We came from behind, won, and the Series was going to seven games. Raschi got the win and Reynolds got the save. My feeling now, this far removed from the event, is that we were just pleased to be going to seven. That was enough. Get a good night's rest and be ready for the last game.

Game 7. October 7, 1952. Ebbets Field. 33,195. Joe Black returned to pitch for the Dodgers, with his one victory and one loss record. Ed Lopat pitched for the Yanks. Lopat pitched eight and one-half innings on October the 3rd and was ready. As the announcers would say over and over again, this was it. Lopat could rest all winter. Both teams had their backs to the wall. Had one of us thought, we might have said we were going to take this thing one game at a time, but that cliché wasn't in use back then.

Black got McDougald to start the game. I tried to bunt, but got the ball down the line and Hodges tagged me out at first. Then Mickey struck out.

Lopat struck out Cox, who led off every game but one for the Dodgers, but Yogi dropped the ball and had to tag him out. Reese hit sharply to Gil McDougald at third, and was safe on the throw. Gil's first of two errors. Lopat struck out Snider and Robinson flied to right.

No score in the second inning. Shuba drilled a ball through the box, almost hitting Lopat, another reason I would not want to come back as a pitcher. When a ball is hit that hard, you have no way of getting out of its way. You can get hit at the plate, but it's not like being hit by a batted ball.

The third inning was one, two, three for both teams.

Leading off the fourth, I knew they were ready for a bunt. That is what happens when you are a little guy and bunting is the way you keep bread on the table. I faked around a little, but had no intention of bunting. Then I got a great pitch out over the plate and turned on it and doubled down the line. Holy Cow, I thought I was back on Long Island, playing for the Boston Blackhawks, a semi-pro team I had played for when I was sixteen years old. Bill Jurges, the Cub shortstop, had a brother on that team, but I was not thinking about him or the Blackhawks. I was just thinking how good it felt and how quiet the fans were. Mickey hit a shot to first and I went to third. Mize hit a home run just foul and then singled and I scored. Yogi hit into a double play but they had to score two runs to win.

Lopat started the top of the fourth by giving up a base hit to Snider. Robinson beat out a bunt down the third base line, and then Campanella did the same thing. Teams used to send scouts to watch each other before they played, and the scouts would come back with a "book" on the other team. Bill Skiff was one of the scouts who worked for the Yankees. If the book had an index, bunting did not have a Campanella reference. Bases loaded. Stengel took Lopat out and brought in Allie Reynolds. This was the third time the Chief would pitch in seven days. You had to worry, but you also knew mother hen Turner was in the loop, as they would say today.

Allie faced Hodges who lined to Woodling, and Snider scored. Allie, covering home, dropped Woodling's throw, allowing Robinson to take third. Reynolds struck out Shuba, and Furillo grounded out.

Four full innings. 1 to 1. A tired Reynolds on the mound for the Yankees. Joe Black had given up two hits, for three bases.

Gene Woodling hit big home runs in both of Allie Reynolds's no-hitters (1951) and Woodling hit another to open the Yankee fifth. Then Noren popped to third, but Billy Martin singled. Reynolds and McDougald both made infield outs.

Allie struck out Black to start the bottom of the fifth, and then Cox doubled and Pee Wee Reese singled and the score was tied. Reese took second on Woodling's wide throw to Yogi. Robinson and Snider both failed and the game was getting as tight as a drum. When it happens you can do nothing about it, I mean the tight feeling. You can take deep breaths but don't let them see you. The best thing you can do is to tell yourself, you have been here before and you got over the hump, so you can do it again. If you have been in a war, you can tell yourself, this isn't all that important. No matter what you do, when the game is tied in the sixth inning of the seventh game, you are going to be tight.

Leading off the sixth, I lined to short. Mickey hit a home run out of the park, really out of the park, into Bedford Avenue. It was his second home run in two days. Then Mize singled and Dressen brought in Roe. Yogi struck out. Woodling singled. Bauer, pinch-hitting for Noren, was at first on Cox's error. Bases loaded. Billy Martin hit a fly to center. But we were up by one. Black was gone and I wished we were playing in Yankee Stadium so we could feel the crowd.

The most accurate measurement of a player's offense may well be Tom Boswell's Total Average. Boswell divides a player's total bases by the player's
total times at bat. Using this measurement, walks
count as much as singles, a home run equals four
singles, and the really great batters hit around
1.000.

According to Boswell's statistics, Hank Aaron's
Total Average is .983, Willie Mays's TA is 1.026, and
Mantle's is 1.118. In other words, the greatest hitter
of the last thirty years is Mickey Mantle. You can
look it up. ⓧ

—*Philip Francis Rizzuto*

Ralph Houk pinch-hit for Reynolds to open the seventh, and
grounded to third. Gil McDougald singled and I sacrificed him
over. Mantle singled him home to take a two-run lead and Mize
fouled out to Furillo.

Roy Campanella singled to start the last of the seventh, but was
erased when Hodges hit into a double play. The '52 series was a
nightmare for Hodges, one of the nicest men in baseball and a great
player. He came to the plate twenty-one times without getting a
hit. Shuba grounded out to end the sixth.

Raschi came in to pitch for the departed Reynolds and Vic
walked Furillo. Mize was now playing first, and then the pinch-
hitter Rocky Nelson, batting for Roe, popped up. Cox singled, Furillo held at second. One out and two on, Reese walked to load the
bases. Snider and Robinson, the next two hitters. Raschi had
pitched seven and two-thirds innings just twenty-four hours earlier

and bringing him in seemed like an error. It did at the time and it still does, but knowing my feelings about Casey, you can discount my comments. I don't recall Vic or Allie ever saying anything about it. They were that way, it is called professional. But at this late date and at my age, a reader merits candor so you just got it.

Vic might have been able to face one batter, but even so he was not like Allie, who could start and come in from the pen. I guess that is about enough of that, as my mother used to say. I will say this: When Stengel called for left-hander Kuzava—Bob Kuzava, the same guy who had been a hero last year but in a far different ball park, Ebbets Field was not for left-handers. Baseball people always said that, but then if you said that about Preacher Roe they would clam up. Kuzava was not a Roe, but he came in when called and it took guts to walk in to face those two hitters. Snider worked the count to 3 and 2 and popped up weakly to third. Then with the bases still loaded—FOB as they used to say, Full of Brooklyns—Jackie hit a high, wind-blown fly and Joe Collins lost it in the sun. It was the first baseman's ball. Kuzava was blocking my chance, if I had one, to catch the ball. All of a sudden Martin dashed in, running like Groucho Marx but as fast as Mel Patton, reaching out like a guy trying to keep something from falling off a truck, and caught the ball. It was not a run you would like to see over and over in your mind like DiMaggio's, but he made the catch and saved our bacon. You don't give the other team four outs in the last of the seventh, in the seventh game.

Erskine came in for the Dodgers in the eighth and after Yogi lined to right, Woodling did the same. Bauer walked and Martin hit a fly ball to Snider.

The last half of the eighth inning is a little cloudy—not the game, the memory. Not only mine but some of the reports gone over for this book. It's been written that Ralph Branca was ejected by umpire Larry Goetz. If so, I can't recall the argument. I do know this much: With Kuzava on the mound, Campanella struck out. Hodges was safe on McDougald's second error, and Pafko pinch-hit for Shuba and struck out. Furillo flew out to left. Three more outs.

Holmes playing left for Brooklyn. Kuzava grounded to second. McDougald singled. Rizzuto popped up to Cox, Mickey grounded to first. Kuzava needed to get Bobby Morgan pinch-hitting for Carl Erskine and he did. Billy Cox hit an easy groundball to second and Reese flied to left. We won, and even now, over forty years ago, it seems like a tough win. But we won. We tied the Joe McCarthy Yankees of 1936, '37, '38, '39. That team had won over the Giants twice, the Cubs once, and the Reds once to win four World Series in a row and now we had tied them. We'd tied the Yankees. We were the Yankees. Not the Yankees of '36 to '39, with names like Lou Gehrig, Tony Lazzeri, Frank Crosetti, Red Rolfe, Charley Keller, Twinkeltoes Selkirk, Joe DiMaggio, Bill Dickey, Tommy Henrich, and Lefty Gomez. But we were Yankees all the same and if we won one more, we would have five in a row. It seemed after beating this team in this way, it would go on. Coleman and Brown would be back and so would we. Game seven lasted two hours and 54 minutes. Seemed like a long weekend.

WORLD SERIES '53

The Dodgers and the Yankees would meet once again in the 1953 World Series. The record was clear: The two New York teams were the best in baseball. The Yankee record of four straight needed no press agent hype, and the Dodgers had won flags in the tough National League three out of the last five years and lost on the last day of the season the other two. The two best teams in baseball. That much was for sure. The next seven games would tell the tale, who the best in baseball was.

Yankee Stadium. September 30, 1953. Baseball Golden World Series. It had been fifty years since the Boston Red Sox won the first World Series, beating the Pittsburgh Pirates 5 games to 3. Correct: 5 games to 3. Since they didn't play a series the next year and, for the most part, the World Series operated in a seven-game format, maybe they took a year off to fine-tune the event. Whatever the case, the '53 fall classic was billed as "golden."

> The infamous Black Sox series of 1919 was won by the Cincinnati Reds five games to three. The 1920 and 1921 World Series were also a best of nine affair. Cleveland of the American League won five games to Brooklyn's two. The next year, 1921, the Giants won five games to three to beat the Yankees. It was the first time Miller Huggins and John McGraw would meet as managers in a World Series. ⑱
>
> —*Tony LoCastro*

Allie Reynolds and Carl Erskine warmed up before 69,374. Dressen and Stengel in the dugouts masterminding the games, Weiss, working for Webb and Topping, watching from his box next to the press box. I would spend many more years in that press box and one much like it when they redid the old park, but all that was ahead of me. Today I was a veteran (meaning older) shortstop trying to help my team and hang on to my job. During the '53 season, I played in 134 games. In 1954 the total dropped to 127 and then in '55 to 81, and then in 1956 I was released after playing in 31 games.

I can hear Walter Huston saying the words, "The days dwindle down." But this was September and I was eager to trot out to short and let Joe Collins at first throw me a few nice one-hop ground balls, and I would toss it over to Gil McDougald at third. Gil would look at the ball, like he could see something on it, and flip it to Reynolds on the mound. Batter up. The cast of characters included Reynolds going for his seventh victory in a World Series, and catcher Campanella, who had driven in 142 runs during the year while Snider was hitting 42 home runs and Erskine was winning 20 games.

Junior Gilliam singled right through Allie's legs to open the first inning, but failed to score when Reynolds held Reese, Snider, and Robinson in check.

The Yankee half of the first started with McDougald popping to second, a Collins walk, and Hank Bauer's triple, scoring Joe. Yogi struck out and Mickey walked along with Woodling, loading the bases. We had drawn first blood, we were at home and with two out and the sacks full, as Billy Martin stepped up. Billy hit a shot over Robinson's head into left center for the second triple off Erskine and we were up by four. I grounded to third to end the inning.

To open the second, Allie hit Campy. You can bet he was not throwing at Roy. Dressen pinch-hit for Erskine, after two outs by Hodges and Furillo, with Wayne Belardi. Belardi struck out. He would come to bat two times in a World Series and strike out and ground out. I hope he is glad he got the chance.

Dressen brought in Jim Hughes to pitch. Hughes had been 4 and 3 for the season. The last of the second and the third were scoreless.

In the Yankee fourth, after Woodling flew out to center, Martin bunted, beat it out, and in true Jackie Robinson style went all the way to third on throwing errors by Hughes and Furillo. Carl Furillo made very few errors—few of these were throwing errors. I grounded to short, Billy holding, and when Allie walked, McDougald forced him at second. But we were still up by four and the Super Chief was living up to his name.

Allie struck out Hughes to open the fifth and then gave up a home run to Junior Gilliam to right. Reese flied to right, Snider doubled, and Campy flied to deep left.

Duke Snider made a fine catch of a hard drive by Joe Collins to open the Yankee fifth. One out for Hughes, Bauer flied to right. Berra hit another long home run and we had the four-run lead back. Mickey grounded to second.

Allie gave up a leadoff home run to Hodges—Hodges's first

World Series hit—to open the sixth inning and he still regrets the pitch.

"It just got away. Away from me and he hit it away. Way away. I can't hit a golf ball that far anymore," says Allie.

Reynolds could hit a golf ball, he was one of the best golfers in baseball. Reynolds then got Furillo but gave up a single to Cox. Shotgun Shuba, pinch-hitting for Hughes, on 2 and 1, hit a two-run homer into the rightfield stands.

> I can still see that ball, I could see it well that day, I just couldn't quite get to it in time to reach it. ⚾
>
> —Hank Bauer

With the score 5 to 4, Stengel brought in Johnny Sain to pitch for Reynolds. Sain got Gilliam but walked Reese. Snider singled to right, Reese taking third. But we got out of the inning when Robinson grounded to third.

Dressen brought Clem Labine in to pitch the last of the sixth. Woodling, Martin, and Rizzuto, numbers 6, 7, and 8 in the lineup, failed to produce a run. Batting in the eighth spot was new for me, but as Yogi said, "It doesn't make any difference where you bat, it's how you bat." His meaning as usual is clear. If you hit well, the manager finds a way to use you in the best spot for the team. I was glad to be hitting anywhere in the lineup.

Seventh inning. Sain still on the mound. Campanella singled to left, Hodges hit a shot to me at short and was on with his second hit. Furillo singled, scoring Campanella to tie the score. Cox bunted and Yogi snatched it and threw out Hodges at third. Labine did the same thing with the same results, this time Yogi got Cox at third. Then Gilliam fouled out to Berra to end the inning. One of Berra's finest innings, of many.

Years later, when a young Al Downing was pitching to an older Berra, they had a meeting before the game and Yogi suggested he would handle anything in front of the plate. Al, not wanting to question Guru Berra, went to Ellie Howard and told him of the conversation.

"Kid, if Yogi wants the ball in front of the plate, you just try to beat him to it, see if you can," explained Howard, another in a long line of catchers playing in the shadow of the Hall of Famer.

Sain opened the last of the seventh looking at a third strike, and then McDougald flied to Snider. Collins hit a home run into the right-field stands. Bauer and Berra singled and Ben Wade came in to pitch. Wade had been 7 and 5 for the season. He struck out Mantle to end the inning.

Sain made quick work of Reese, Snider, and Robinson in the Dodger eighth.

In the Yankee eighth, Woodling led off with a ground ball to Robinson. Billy Martin singled to center and stole second while I was at the plate. Wade walked me and Johnny Sain doubled to right center, scoring two runs. McDougald lined out. Collins scored Sain with a single. Wade struck out Hank Bauer. 9 to 5, Yanks.

The Dodgers did not threaten in the top of the ninth and Sain had a World Series victory. It was his second, giving him two more than his pitching coach, Jim "Milkman" Turner. He would remind him, but not today. The game had taken three hours and ten minutes.

Game 2. Yankee Stadium. October 1, 1953. Two left-handers, Lopat and Roe, were selected to pitch the second game before 66,786.

Gilliam, playing second base, led off, grounding out to short, and then Reese tripled to right when Hank Bauer fell, Mantle alertly backing up the play to save a run. Spider popped to Berra and Robinson, hitting fourth and playing right, flied to Mantle. Lopat was pleased to have the inning behind him.

In the Yankee first, Roe walked Woodling and Collins, Bauer

hit a long fly to right, and Woodling took third. Berra flied to right and Woodling scored, Collins taking second on the throw to the plate. Mantle walked, and Roe hit McDougald to load the bases with two out. Martin flied to short center.

The second inning was full of action but short on runs. Hodges walked and stole a base. Cox received an intentional walk, but Roe made the last out when he hit a ball off Lopat's glove that allowed Collins to make the put-out at first.

In the Yankee half, I led off with a double and took third when Furillo booted the ball for a one-base error. Roe struck Lopat out. Junior Gilliam made a good play on Woodling's hard smash and nailed me at home. Collins grounded to first.

The third inning was also scoreless.

With two out in the Brooklyn fourth—Robinson and Campanella—Hodges and Furillo both singled. Cox doubled into the right-field corner and both men scored. Roe struck out but they had us by one.

We managed to get Martin to second base in our half of the fourth but that was it.

The game remained 2 to 1 in favor of the Dodgers in the fifth and sixth innings.

In the Dodger sixth with one out, Furillo doubled off the wall. Cox grounded to third, Furillo holding. Roe struck out. Before the game was over the Dodgers would strand ten runners.

In the Yankee sixth, Yogi walked and Mantle flied to left. Stengel put on the hit-and-run and McDougald missed the pitch and Berra was caught between first and second. Then Gil struck out.

In the Dodger seventh, Gilliam, Reese, Snider, and Robinson failed to tally.

With the count 2 and 2, Martin opened the Yankee seventh with a home run to the left-field stands. Rizzuto, Lopat, and Woodling followed with three quick outs, but the game was even.

In the eighth, Furillo ended the inning with a double play, Martin to Rizzuto to Collins. In the Yankee half, after two out, but with Bauer on with a single, Mickey Mantle hit a home run well back

in the seats in left and we were up by two runs. McDougald flied
to left. Lopat shut them off in the top of the ninth, by getting Cox
to ground to short, then giving up a hit to Roe's pinch-hitter, Dick
Williams. Getting Gilliam on a fly to Mantle. Walking Reese on
four pitches.

Two men on, Snider, with 42 home runs during the regular
season, at the plate. Snider grounded to second. Snider was to
speak with Don Zimmer of the memory just after an Old
Timer's game in Dodger Stadium. Snider in 1992, fit-looking following triple bypass surgery, said, "You hate to make the last
out in any game, recess to sandlot to spring training. But in the
Series, when you feel you should be able to hit Lopat's slow
stuff, it really stays with you. Lopat won seven Series games.
That helps a little. Hitting four home runs when we beat the Yankees in 1955 helped a lot."

Game 3. Ebbets Field. October 3, 1953. Vic Raschi for the
Yankees and Carl Erskine for the Dodgers. Raschi had been 16 and
6, Erskine 20 and 6. This would be the last eight innings Raschi
would ever pitch for the Yankees. He was St. Louis–bound next
spring in a contract flap with George Weiss.

Vic, don't ever have a bad year. Ⓧ

—*George Weiss*

As 35,270 looked on, Erskine struck out McDougald and Collins to open the first inning. It would get worse, much worse. Bauer
grounded to Reese.

In the Yankee second, Yogi walked and took second on a wild
pitch. Then Mickey looked at a third strike; Woodling grounded
out, moving Berra to third. Billy Martin walked and I looked at a
called third strike.

In the third, Erskine got two more strikeouts and the Dodgers went out in order. Connie Mack, always called the grand old man of baseball, at least it seemed that way, was watching and must have been thinking, This is a crackerjack of a game, boys. Not for us, Connie, and since you are an American Leaguer, not for you.

No score in the fourth, but one more strikeout for Erskine: Mantle.

In the fifth inning Billy Martin singled. I followed with a single. Raschi bunted both runners over, and when McDougald singled in the first run, Martin, I took third. Joe Collins looked at strike three and Bauer grounded to second. We scratched out a run. Erskine was making his mark in the record book with strikeouts.

Bottom of the sixth. After one out, Robinson doubled to center. Jackie could drive the pitcher nuts and Rasch balked him to third. Cox squeezed Jackie home with a bunt. 1 to 1 tie. Erskine singled, but Vic got Gilliam and Reese to end the inning.

In the Yankee sixth, Erskine got two more strikeouts and the Dodgers got a run in the last of the inning when Snider led off with a base hit followed by a Hodges's walk. Then after Campy and Furillo made outs, Furillo striking out, Robinson singled home the go-ahead run. Cox struck out to end the inning.

The seventh inning was scoreless.

Collins struck out, his third time in this game, to open the eighth. Bauer lined a base hit to center, Erskine hit Berra with a pitch. One out and two on. Mantle struck out swinging for number 12 for Erskine. Woodling singled to center scoring Hank Bauer and Berra took third. Billy Martin grounded out to end the inning. Score tied.

In the Dodger eighth, Hodges grounded to short. Campanella hit a long home run to make the score 3 to 2, and Furillo grounded to third. After Robinson's single, Cox popped up to Martin.

The Yanks were down to their last three outs. Don Thompson took over in left for Jackie Robinson. Don Bollweg took over for me at the plate as a pinch-hitter and struck out. Raschi was also lifted for a pinch-hitter. It's been reported that Mize sat next to Stengel all during the game telling Casey how he could "hit this guy." Since I seldom sat near Casey during a game I cannot say for sure, but I would be surprised. John was surprised when he became Erskine's fourteenth strikeout victim. Johnny felt bad when he came back to the dugout and I don't think anyone spoke to him. I know Casey told Irv Noren to bat for McDougald and he worked out a walk.

Collins grounded back to the mound. I hope Erskine saved the ball after they threw it to Hodges for the final out. Gil would be the sort of person to think to save it for Erskine.

Game 4. Ebbets Field. October 4, 1953. The Dodgers must have used a shoehorn to squeeze 36,775 into this bandbox. The official capacity was listed as 32,000. Eddie Stanky, now the Cardinals' manager, attended this game, but in those days access to the field was limited more than it is today and we didn't have a chance to chat. If we had been able to, I am sure some alert photographer would have asked us to pose. The caption on the photo would have read, "Brat Makes Up with Scooter."

This was Whitey Ford's second World Series start. Whitey won, with help from Reynolds, the final game of the 1950 World Series against the Phils. He would face another pitcher from Long Island, Billy Loes. The newspapers called both of the two young pitchers "brash." Jim Turner called it self-confidence. "Best young pitcher I ever saw come up to the Yankees," was what Turner told me and the one thing he liked about Ford was that he only had to be told once. Some of them never caught on, as far as Turner was concerned.

"Brash" Billy Loes struck out leadoff hitter Mantle to open the first inning. Since the day before fourteen of us had done the same, this was a bad way to start. It was worse than bad, it was awful.

Collins and Bauer made outs and we took the field.

Ford gave Gilliam a pitch over the plate and he skied it to right, Bauer misjudged the ball and it bounced into the stands for a ground-rule double. Since the ball was not touched, an error was not charged, but one was committed. Reese grounded Gilliam to third and Jackie drove him in with a single. Hodges forced Robinson at second. With Campanella at the plate, Ford threw a wild pitch, Hodges took second, and Stengel ordered Campy intentionally passed. Duke Snider doubled off the wall and two runs scored. Furillo lined to right but the battle of the brash pitchers read: first inning—Loes, on points.

I was surprised, as I think many of us were, when they took Ford out after the half-inning. It is the sort of move that can damage a young pitcher's self-confidence. Turner, from his home in Nashville, at age ninety, was quick to point out "Ford had an ample supply of self-confidence, so much so that when he came back into the dugout, he went to Stengel and brought up the pitching change." At the time, the Ford–Stengel conversation was private and not obvious, at least to me.

We rode the trains, sat around the hotel and listened and talked baseball. We learned by playing but we also learned a lot by listening. The Yankees gave Joe DiMaggio a roomette on the train and it was the place to gather. I learned more in that room, from Joe and Tommy Henrich, than I learned in any other single place. ⓧ

—*Philip Francis Rizzuto*

I also learned from the chat with Jim Turner that Ford was such a quick study that even if Turner was talking to another pitcher about a particular problem, say holding runners on, that Ford would listen in and learn. "You didn't have to be talking to him for him to learn, you could talk with someone else within earshot and he would learn" were Turner's words. Nice thing to say about a student and a teacher as well.

Whitey came to pitch and he came to learn. I know this sounds like a graybeard talking and when I let mine grow I am one, but when I came into baseball most of us came to learn. Now, with long-term contracts kids say, "I make a million dollars. Why should I listen to a $30,000-a-year coach?"

Holy Cow, it's time to get back to the game.

Berra struck out to open the second. Loes caught him looking. Woodling walked and Martin forced Woodling at second. McDougald did the same to Martin, Reese to Giliam.

Tom Gorman came in to pitch for New York and gave up a double to Gilliam but did not allow any more runs.

The third inning was scoreless.

In the fourth inning the Dodgers added a run while Furillo and Loes and Gilliam combined to push one over. Gorman was getting whacked around. Score 4–zip, Dodgers.

Look back over games you watched or played in and when you are down in the seventh, that is the way it often ends. People like to say that one of the nice things about baseball is that it is not played by the clock and they are right. But the players, especially the ones down, have a clock. It's a clock in their head and it ticks—it ticks and they begin to react. The reaction may cause them to reach a new level or it can work the other way, and things can stay the same or get worse. ⓧ

—*Philip Francis Rizzuto*

Martin, the first hitter in the fifth, banged a triple off the wall in center field and then McDougald hit a two-run home run and we were starting to come back. I flew out to center, and the pinch-hitter, Don Bollweg, batting for pitcher Gorman, was called out on strikes. Mantle took a called third strike and our inning was in the tank.

Johnny Sain came in from the bull pen and the Dodgers didn't score in the last of the fifth. The Yanks failed when Berra managed a two-out single and Woodling grounded to Reese in the top of the sixth.

Then, with Sain pitching in the bottom of the sixth, Snider homered to right. Furillo took a called third strike and after Cox doubled to right, Loes singled. Then Gilliam lined to right and Cox scored. Reese ended the inning with a man on third but they had another run and we just could not get something going.

In the top of the seventh, I singled with two out and pinchhitter Irv Noren, batting for Sain, popped up.

In the Brooklyn half of the seventh, with Art Schallock pitching for the Yankees, Robinson and Hodges made out and then with two out he walked Campanella. Snider doubled and they had another run. Furillo left Snider on second, when he grounded out. Schallock pitched for the Yanks for five years and won 6 and lost 7. I am glad I had a chance to think about him again, we never talked much but he seemed like a nice guy. Glad he got some rings.

In the top of the eighth inning, we got another two-out single, this time from Bauer.

In the last of the eighth, Schallock held Cox, Loes, Gilliam, and Reese in check and it was our last chance.

Don Thompson started the ninth in left. Woodling led off the ninth with a single to left center. Billy Martin singled, Woodling wisely stopped at second. Gil McDougald walked. With the bases loaded, Dressen had seen enough. Clem Labine was called in to pitch. Bollweg had been used as a pinch-hitter so I knew Stengel could not use him but I still wondered as Labine was taking his warmup pitches if I would be called back and told to take a seat. One of the coaches would simply call your name if you were out in the on-deck circle, which is where you should be as you wanted to give the impression you expected to hit. It should be a sort of,

Who me? when you heard your name. As you can imagine, all of
this Will he or won't he? and the Who me?, is not good for your
head. But this time I don't get a chance to say Who me? I got a
chance to bat with the bases loaded. A grand slam, a single. A wild
pitch. Hit by a pitch. Alas, I struck out. Mize, pinch-hitting for
Schallock, lined out to Snider in a shallow center and the runner
held. Mickey Mantle singled to left, Woodling scored, and Billy
Martin challenged Don Thompson's arm and the arm won and Billy
was out at the plate. Game over. 7 to 3. Two hours and forty-six
minutes.

Game 5, October 4. Ebbets Field. 36,775. These numbers never
take into consideration the number of news people, radio and TV
folk, as well as vendors, police and firemen, ushers and ground
crew. A whole lot of people watched part of or all of these games
in Brooklyn. Yesterday's crowd was the largest ever and today's
matched that record.

The weather was clear, no rain to give the pitchers a day off.
So was the decision to pitch Jim McDonald for the Yankees. Jimmie
LeRoy "Hot Rod" McDonald, a five eleven right-hander. This was
only his third year in the big leagues, and his third team—Red Sox,
Browns, and now the Yankees. He won 3 and lost 4 for the Yanks
that year.

He was a "free spirit" sort of guy from the West—Oregon and
California. Turner's feelings today were pretty much what they
were back then: "Our choices were limited, but we made the right
one, at least the way it turned out, it was." Dressen chose young
Johnny Podres, now the pitching coach for the Phillies.

Hot Rod McDonald received an early Christmas gift when
Gene Woodling led off the game with a home run to left. Nothing
like that to give the team a boost, and with the Series tied at two
each we needed one. Collins, Bauer, and Berra made outs and it
was the Dodgers' turn to see what McDonald had.

Bottom of the first. Gilliam singled. Then Reese, Snider, and
Robinson went down quickly.

The Yankees didn't do anything in the top of the second and

McDonald was back on the hot seat.

Campanella singled. Hodges blooped one to center and Hot Rod was in the soup. Furillo hit a double play ball, but my throw to Martin covering second was wild and Campy scored and Hodges took third. The red E flashed on the scoreboard. I knew it would. The back of my neck felt a little hot. Then Cox hit a shot to Woodling in left and Gene threw a strike to Yogi to double up Hodges trying to score. Podres singled but that was the end of the scoring. Tie, 1 to 1.

I walked to open the top of the third. It makes you feel better to get on any way you can after an inning like the last. McDonald bunted me to second. Woodling hit back to the pitcher but I was able to go to third. Collins hit a shot off Hodges's glove for an error and I scored. Podres upset, hit Bauer. Yogi walked. Dressen signaled for Monk Meyer. Before the game you could have guessed the first pitcher to leave would be ours. You would have guessed wrong. Monk came in to face Mickey with the bases loaded and Mantle hit the first pitch for a home run into the upper deck in left. Billy followed with a single and was caught stealing.

6 to 1, Yankees.

McDonald, pumped up, kept the Dodgers at bay in the last of the third and neither team scored in the fourth and fifth.

In the top of the sixth, McDougald tripled, and I walked and stole second. McDonald was called out on strikes. They walked Woodling and I have no idea why. Joe Collins hit a shot to Cox, who forced McDonald at the plate. Cox made a supernatural stop on a Bauer hit and forced Woodling at third. Ouch. We had a chance and Cox stole it.

In the Yankee seventh, Martin hit a two-run home run, Yogi was on base. I singled and Jim McDonald doubled to left and the ball bounced over Jackie's head, allowing me to score.

Belardi pinch-hit for Meyer in the last of the seventh and grounded to short.

Ben Wade opened the Yankee eighth pitching for the Dodgers. Score 9 to 2. With the lights turned on, Joe Collins doubled off the center-field wall. The drive was almost 400 feet from home plate. Bauer sacrificed Collins to third. Yogi hit a drive to deep center and Collins scored 10 to 2. Mantle ended the inning.

Dodger eighth. Collins makes an "Oh Doctor" stop on Snider's smash. One out. Robinson singled. Campanella hit a ball off McDougald's shoulder and the Dodgers had on two runners and the Yankees had a rocky pitcher. Hot Rod struck out Hodges, but then Furillo singled to center for one run. 10 to 3. Cox hit a three-run home to run to left. 10 to 6. Shotgun Shuba was announced as a pinch-hitter for Ben Wade. Hot Rod McDonald was replaced by Bob Kuzava. Shotgun was called back. Instead of Hot Rod and Shotgun, Dressen and Stengel came up with Bob and Dick. Dick Williams pinch-hit for the pinch-hitter. Williams struck out.

Plain Joe Black pitched for the Dodgers in the Yankee ninth. Black struck out Billy Martin and then McDougald came up with the fourth Yankee home run to left. 11 to 6.

Rizzuto popped to second and Black struck out his opposite number, Kuzava, and we needed three outs to go ahead 3 games to 2.

Last of the ninth. All 36,775 fans and some of the vendors and cops and firemen for all I know were on their feet screaming for the Dodgers. It was something I will never forget. Try sinking a six-foot putt with that level of noise. You really can't think straight so you just react.

The first hitter, Jim Gilliam, smacked a home run to left to break a record for most home runs in one game. 11 to 7. Reese flied to left. Snider singled to right center. One on, one out. Stengel took Kuzava out. Allie Reynolds came in from the bull pen. Jackie Robinson was the hitter. Jackie hit into a double play, Martin to Rizzuto to Collins. Game over, 11 to 7. Three hours and two minutes. Winner McDonald, his first and only. Save Reynolds. Left on base: NY 7, Brooklyn 6. Errors: Rizzuto, Hodges.

Game 6. October 5, 1952. Yankee Stadium. 62,370. Whitey Ford set to try again for the Yankees and strikeout king Carl Erskine for the Dodgers.

In the first inning Casey went into a frenzy over a play when

Reese came in hard at second on a double play ball from Jackie Robinson's bat, saying that Reese interfered with Martin's throw to first base. It was not a big play as far as the inning went, they did not score, but it stirred the juices, mostly Casey's.

Woodling walked to open our first. Bauer singled to left. Woodling on second. Yogi hit a ground-rule double, and we had one run and a man on first and third, one out. They walked Mickey. Martin hit a shot off Gilliam at third, it was called an error. I still think it should have been a hit and the Yanks had two runs. McDougald grounded into a double play to end the inning. We were up by two, had scored first and were at home, and most of all, we thought we could win.

In the Dodger second, with one out, Furillo singled down the right-field line but was out on a fine play by Collins at second base, Rizzuto covering. Cox struck out to end the inning.

In the Yankee second, Erskine gave me a pitch I could handle and I singled to open the inning. Then Ford followed with a single to right and I took third. Woodling flied to right and I scored after the catch. 3–zip. We got a big break when Joe Collins tried to check his swing and almost bunted the ball to a surprised Erskine on the mound. Carl hurried his throw to Hodges for an error and the runners moved up. Bauer walked. Yogi was up. When he hit a long fly, Ford tagged up at third but left too soon and was doubled up.

At the end of the fifth inning, the score was the same, 3 to 0, and Bob Milliken had replaced Erskine. Carl had gone four innings, walked four, and given up six hits and three runs.

In the Dodger sixth Jackie Robinson smashed a double, stole third, and when Campy grounded to short, scored 3 to 1.

In the Yankee seventh we had one man on (Berra) when Billy Martin hit into a double play to end the inning.

To start inning number eight, with the score 3 to 1 Yankees, Stengel reached back once again for Allie Reynolds. Allie had been hurt in a team bus wreck in Philadelphia late in the year and simply was not the Super Chief. But Stengel and Turner knew they could ring the bell and Reynolds would respond. The Cleveland team had said Allie didn't have a big heart. When I saw him come in, I could feel *my* heart and it was telling me this game is ours. As a friend of Allie's, I would never have asked him to pitch in this game but I was glad someone else had done so. Ford was great and may have become a better pitcher than almost anyone. Today, I was betting on Allie.

He faced Gilliam, Reese, Robinson, and Campy in the inning and none of them scored.

Nor did we in the last of the eighth. I got a base hit off Labine's glove—he had replaced Milliken—and Allie singled me to third. Woodling hit a bouncer to Reese and he threw me out at the plate. Mize pinch-hit for Collins for his last time as a New York Yankee and grounded to first.

The Yankees opened the ninth with Bollweg at first base and a shortstop with a case of the vapors. Reynolds faced Hodges. Gil flied to center. Allie walked Snider after working the count to 3 and 2 and Carl Furillo came to the plate. Furillo, this year's National League batting champion, took the count again to 3 and 2 and then hit a home run into the right-field stands. Score tied.

Then Allie did something that even makes me proud today. He struck out Cox and Labine.

Last of the ninth. Bauer walked, Yogi lined to right. Mantle beat out a high bounder between third and the mound and was safe as Bauer held second. Billy Martin on the first pitch got his twelfth World Series record hit. When Bauer touched home plate we all went home to get ready to do it all over again next year. Billy was so confident he was probably thinking, "I will get thirteen next year." We all felt good but not complacent. Cro would fry the first guy to smile too broadly.

AFTERWORD

My paperback copy of *The Winds of War*, Herman Wouk's novel of World War II, has pictures of some of the main characters. They are the sort of pictures you might find in a woman's locket and they appear inside the front cover. Seeing what Pug Henry looked like made the book more interesting. At least to me. It shouldn't work that way, but it does for many people. Incidentally, Pug Henry is the only character in the book I remember by name. I do remember the book held my attention and, although I lived through World War II, reading it was like a history lesson.

The dust jacket of *The October Twelve* is an artist's view of what the twelve men looked like when we played the first of the 28 games that took us to a place no other professional team has ever been. Five straight and while it was a new record, every one of us, and the front office, was perhaps even more confident, thought we would do it again in 1954.

However, when the Cleveland Indians, as they did in 1954, win 111 games, just what is a Stengel to do? You can almost hear Stengel and George Weiss. "We didn't win, Casey," says Mr. Weiss to Mr. Stengel. "I feel as bad as you, George, maybe worse, but

1954 was the best year I ever had as a manager, here or anywhere else, for that matter. We won 103 games, more than enough to win other years. We won our season series with the Indians. When I managed the Boston Braves in 1941 and '42, it took me both years to win over 100 games," responds Stengel. Whatever Mr. Weiss said to Mr. Stengel, it worked, because the Yankees returned to World Series play and quickly. While the contribution of the twelve men faded after the high-water mark of 1953, you can probably guess who was the last of the Mohicans—Casey's assistant manager, Yogi Berra.

Joe Collins, Hank Bauer, Yogi, Charlie Silvera, Jerry Coleman, and I were on the Yankee team that played and lost to the Dodgers in the 1955 World Series.

Seventh game. 1955. Alston put Sandy Amoros in to play left for defense. He was playing Yogi wrong, except that it was right and he was able to make the catch, decoy the runner McDougald and kill us with a double play. ⊗

—*Gil McDougald*

Just before the Old Timers' game, early in August 1956 (the Yankees were the first to have one), Casey asked me to come into his office. George Weiss was already there. They both greeted me and told me they would like my help making cuts in the team.

I was pleased to be asked for advice, most of us are. Most years the Yankees of that era began to think about the World Series and this was no exception. Weiss and Stengel were like two shopkeepers taking inventory. We are going to need at least one more of these, but to make room in the window we will have to move this out.

We went down the list and I suggested ideas I felt had merit. For example, a pitcher who had not pitched for a month or catcher in the same boat. In some cases, like Charlie Silvera, I was pointing the gun at players I had known for years.

When the two men you work for ask your advice, you have to be as tough as they are or else they stop asking your advice. After two, maybe three trips down the list, it seemed to me the cat-and-mouse game was over and I was the one with the gun and it was pointed at me and it was loaded.

In any event, I was crushed and even more devastated to learn the player they'd picked up to replace me was even older than I was. Enos Slaughter. Lucky for me that when I went out of the office the first guy I ran into was the late Snuffy Stirnweiss. Snuff was an Old Timer and had played with me in the 1940s. To me he was an angel. He took charge of the patient in shock and not only made me leave my car in the parking lot, he didn't give me time to think for myself.

If you have ever watched a mother cat pick up one of her kittens and carry it across a room, that is what Snuffy did with me. I ended up at home and he told Cora and me to get in the car and find a place to stay in the Catskills. We did as we were told by Dr. Stirnweiss.

After several days I cooled off, the hurt was still hurting but my mind was in control. If I had popped off to the press about the way I felt, a whole lot of things that happened to me after 1956 might never have fallen into place.

In 1957, when we lost to the Braves of Milwaukee, only Coleman, Yogi, Collins, and Hank Bauer were left. When we beat the Braves the next year, 1958, Bauer and Berra were the last two sailors on the SS *Stengel*. Then Yogi went on to play again in 1960 when the Yanks lost to the Pirates and Mazeroski hit the home run over his head in left. Berra's last at-bat for the New York Yankees was on October 5, 1963. He pinch-hit for Jim Bouton and faced Don Drysdale, in Dodger Stadium. Berra lined out to right.

Yogi came back the next year to manage the Yankees to a seven-game finish with the St. Louis Cards. Then the Yankees slipped him the joker, but that's been covered.

What I want to include now you might call the caption under the picture of Pug Henry.

Henry Albert Bauer, born July 31, 1922, East St. Louis, Illinois; Lawrence Peter Berra, born May 12, 1925, St. Louis, Missouri; Robert William Brown, born October 25, 1924, Seattle, Washington; Gerald Francis Coleman, born September 4, 1924, San Jose, California; Joseph Edwards Collins, born December 3, 1922, Scranton, Pennsylvania; Philip Francis Rizzuto, born September 25, 1917, New York, New York; Eugene Richard Woodling, born August 16, 1922, Akron, Ohio; Charles Anthony Ryan Silvera, born October 13, 1924, San Francisco, California; Edmund Walter Lopat, born June 21, 1918, New York, New York; Victor John Angelo Raschi, born March 28, 1919, West Springfield, Massachusetts; Allie Pierce Reynolds, born February 10, 1915, Bethany, Oklahoma; John Robert Mize, born January 13, 1913, Demorest, Georgia.

The Yankee genius didn't work when it came time to say goodbye. Even Weiss and Stengel would learn that hard lesson. ⊗

—*Philip Francis Rizzuto*

E D M U N D   W A L T E R   L O P A T

Born June 21, 1918, New York, New York
Died June 15, 1992, Stamford, Connecticut

One of the twelve to manage a major league team. Lopat managed Kansas City in 1963 and '64. Berra, Bauer, and Coleman also managed in the majors. The refrain, we get too soon old and too late smart, hardly applied to Eddie Lopat. Lopat played the hand he was dealt and while pitching in the rotation with flame-throwers like Raschi and Reynolds, held his own and by example made others on the team think.

His seventh-place tie for the best winning percentage in World Series history made the rest of baseball know what a remarkable pitcher Lopat became after a rocky start.

His record with the White Sox before coming to the Yankees in a deal for three players, Aaron Robinson, Fred Bradley, and Bill Wight, was 50 wins and 49 losses. Two of the wins had come at the expense of the Yanks the year before the trade (1948) and while George Weiss didn't have a computer, he had an excellent memory.

When Lopat was pitching, I didn't need my catcher's mitt. A Kleenex did fine. Some days, if he was throwing well, I would need more than one. ◯)(

—*Yogi Berra*

Five in a row made Lopat savor a sixth even more and he beat the Cleveland Indians five times in 1954, the year they won 111 games to win the American League flag. "Each of us had a little different relationship with Stengel than the next guy, but we all had the same relationship with each other. That's the important issue.

Stengel would tell the press that he was worried about my pitching in certain parks like the Polo Grounds. I would hear about it and I would get mad. He may have figured that, and then again maybe he hadn't. At any rate it worked. I didn't need his help in learning how to pitch, Ted Lyons [on the White Sox] helped me and Jim Turner helped me, that's all the help I needed. I didn't pitch too badly for a guy the Dodgers signed as a first baseman. Counting the screwball and the curve and my fastball and the speeds I used with each, I figure I had eleven pitches. Yogi only counted nine. As long as he was calling the pitches and catching them that was fine with me.''

JOHN   ROBERT   MIZE

Born January 13, 1913, Demorest, Georgia
Died June 2, 1993, Demorest, Georgia

''Hulking Hall of Fame first baseman'' is the way the *New York Times* described Johnny Mize when he died in his sleep on June 2, 1993. The white cottage with a picket fence where Mize was born was his home when he died, just steps from Piedmont College, a private junior college. Mize was one of the better first basemen to play for Piedmont, which lists enrollment as 480 full-time, 80 part-time, a sizable percentage of the thousand or so calling the lovely Georgia hills village home. Driving time on I-85 from Atlanta to the Homer exit is less than an hour. Homer to Demorest? Pack a lunch.

No one is quite sure why Mize took so long to return to his roots, and the only two people with the knowledge, Marjorie and John Mize, make sure a visitor is welcome. However, the welcome is to learn about home runs, pitchers faced, and even Branch Rickey and George Weiss. Mize was private to the end, he had even been so to some teammates, but a man of character, mistrustful with good reason of those he had not learned to trust. By the time Mize reached age seventy the list of individuals he trusted was complete, and making the list was about as hard as it had been for the Big Cat to make it to the Hall of Fame.

Mize lived in several places in Florida, from DeLand to St. Petersburg, but when he came home again the people of Demorest embraced him. The MIZE AVENUE sign is visible from State Highway 365. The only park in Demorest honors Johnny with a large granite plaque.

> He was distrustful of those he didn't know well, especially one wearing a press pass, which contributed no little to the reason the door to the Hall of Fame was slammed in his face so many times. ◍
>
> —*Furman Bisher*, *columnist*, Atlanta Constitution

While Mize was private, his generosity was public. His delayed election to the Hall of Fame in 1981 may have left him bitter, but not without demand. The demand for his autograph took him to baseball card shows across the country, where he would spend several hours sitting at a table signing cards, bats, and balls. Over $40,000 of the autograph income went to local charities. The sponsor of the card show paid the Big Cat's expenses and put him up in good hotels. After spending time playing for Branch Rickey in the St. Louis Cardinals farm system in the days of the "chain gang," Mize was taken with the posh rooms arranged for him.

"Look here, they even give you shampoo and shaving soap in this bathroom," commented Mize. When told that some players felt that playing for Branch Rickey all those years had left scars on Mize, the six-foot-plus "Big Jawn" smiled and said, "They may be right, but this sure is a nice room. We didn't have soap in the bathroom when I played in the minors, the bathroom was down the hall and you took soap with you. Brought it back, too.

Listening to Johnny Mize at age eighty talk about hitting like he would be ready if called on, was one of
my joys as Commissioner ⓧ

—*Fay Vincent, Jr.*

"I knew when I joined the Yankees in August of 1949 I was
going to make the most of it. I knew Stengel, and he knew what I
could do. He liked to kid me about the time the Cincinnati Reds
brought me up on a trial, from the Rochester Cards farm team. He
said it in his 'writer's' voice and it came out 'Them Germans in
Zinncee, didn't know what to make of you, hitting one side and
throwing on the other.' I did throw right and hit left and Stengel
remembering a 'look-see' I had with the Cards was his way of making me feel welcome and it did.

It was a disgrace and a reflection on many of our
brethren. ⓧ

—*Comment by Furman Bisher on the delay in electing Mize to the*
Hall of Fame.

"It was a great way to finish my active life in baseball. You can
hear how good Joe DiMaggio and Rizzuto are, but you don't know
until you see them every day. I think what I did for them helped
keep me in the minds of baseball people and helped me get into
the Hall of Fame. I led the National League fifteen times in some
hitting category and while I was not a Fancy Dan at first, I got the

job done. I led the league four times in home runs, three times in RBIs, and once in triples, yet they said I was slow."

Many of the fans waiting in line for John Mize's autograph were standing in line for something of value. The value was important but the increase in value was the issue. They were making an investment, and hoped it would be worth the time and money spent to acquire the signature. They had no idea of what Mize meant to baseball. Many of them never saw him play. All this was fine with Mize. Working for Mr. Rickey and Mr. Weiss taught him something and it was evident from the soft Southern voice on his answering machine. "This is the Big Cat. Sorry I am not here right now. Leave your name and number and I will call you back. Collect."

V I C T O R   J O H N
A N G E L O   R A S C H I

Born March 28, 1919, West Springfield, Massachusetts
Died October 15, 1988, Conesus, New York

Vic died mowing the lawn. Raschi's lawn stretched for yards, as in a golf course. Sally and Vic built the spectacular home on the failed Cottonwood golf course in 1950. The front of the home faces a lake, over a mile down what was at one time the first fairway. Seemingly all glass, the home is a showplace. Mrs. Sally Raschi can point out her own childhood home down there by the lake.

"We bought that house and one of our daughters lives there now. Our son William is a professor at Bucknell, and our youngest, Mitje, is just starting a new production company and is living at home. Vic owned a liquor store in Geneseo, the home of State University of New York at Geneseo. The college put his name on the baseball field just like Oklahoma State named a ballfield for Allie Reynolds, but Vic would never put his name on his business. The business had to make its own way—if my name has to be on it, it's not a good business is the way he might have put it. Vic was always all business. One year *The Sporting News* said he was the least popular, or maybe it was the least cooperative, player in the big leagues. Seeing him with the kids and how attentive he was to his friends would have been a surprise to anyone voting or writing something like that, but I understood what they meant. When he was getting ready to pitch, he was like a bull fighter—if someone walked up to his locker and took a picture (in those days they had big flash bulbs and it would blind you for a few seconds), it would bother him and he would growl. I didn't blame him then and I don't blame him now.

"Vic made the mistake of getting old and of having a merely 'good' year (13 and 6) and I still have the Western Union wire. 'Your contract has been assigned outright to the St. Louis Cardinal National League Baseball Club. All good wishes for your future success. George Weiss.' And the one from the Cardinals: 'St. Louis Cardinals acquired your contract this date. Please contact me by phone at St. Petersburg 70129 today. Dick Meyer, General Manager.'

Breaking into the Raschi-Reynolds-Lopat pitching rotation was like passing the bar exam. ⓧ

—*The Chairman of the Board, Whitey Ford*

Late in the afternoon during the day of my interview with Sally Raschi, Sally received a phone call from Libby Lopat telling of Ed's death. Within the hour, Bobby Brown, Jerry Coleman, Allie Reynolds, and Yogi Berra all called. ⓧ

—*Tom Horton*

"Some words on faded Western Union paper. My thoughts are perhaps more interesting today than they were when Vic was sold, on February 23, 1954, for $85,000. Bitterness and disappointment are not good emotions to foster clear thinking and that was about what we had to work with, so forget about that. Here is what I think is interesting, the General Manager gave his phone number (that is not his zip code) and was ready to talk. Even though he didn't say welcome to the Cards, he did want to talk.

"George Weiss, and remember a telegram was paid for by the word, used extra ones to say 'all good wishes.' Yet he would not talk to Vic, during what the press was calling 'contract talks.'

"I guess the best way I might sum it up is to ask a question. The *New York Times* obituary started off, 'Vic Raschi, the big right-hander who joined Allie Reynolds and Eddie Lopat in pitching the Yankees to six World Series championships over eight seasons.' Given those words written years later on the occasion of Vic's death, would it not seem reasonable that George Weiss would have called up and suggested dinner?

"Even as I ask the question I know that for him to have called would have been for him to change his nature, so take what I am saying in that vein. That wire should have been the last thing sent, not the first, and I am not one to feel, as some do, that if Vic had been on the team in 1954 they might have won again.

"What I am saying transcends winning. What I am saying is there is a right way and a wrong way of doing just about anything. George Weiss didn't treat Vic well but time heals what reason will not. My memory is a happy one.

"Jim Turner treated his Big Three like they were sons. I cannot tell you how much they cared for each other, then and until Vic died. Allie and Jim Turner know and they are the only ones. Earlene Reynolds is gone and while Libby Lopat and I understand how rare the magic was that the three pitchers and their coach shared, it was a society of four. Whitey Ford was gifted, but by the time he arrived, Allie, Vic, and Ed were looking at the finish line. Whitey was just picking up speed.

"The thing I can understand now even more than I could while my husband and Ed and Allie were winning all those games, is that they were not just pitching to win. They were pitching for the approval of Turner and the other two pitchers. All the million-dollar contracts will never make that magic happen again."

JOSEPH EDWARD COLLINS

Born December 3, 1922 Scranton, Pennsylvania
Died August 30, 1989, Union, New Jersey

A university didn't name a baseball field for Joe Collins but his adopted home of Union, New Jersey, did. Joe Collins Field. It was a point of pride with Collins. Pride and perseverance, two character traits Joe Collins utilized, perhaps more than his native raw talent. Talent, young Collins had in abundance, but like thousands of kids that are the best on their block, as the competition stiffens in the minor leagues, their resolve weakens.

Collins was signed by the Yankees as a teenage first base prospect and was badly hurt in the minor leagues running into a telephone pole. He was sent home and finished high school while on the mend. The damage to his shoulder would dog him the rest of his playing days, and a lesser man would have given up the dream of playing for the Yankees, especially in light of three years in the service during World War II.

Collins spent a total of ten full seasons in the minors, "But once I made it I never went back, and we had some guys on that team that did," Collins said with admiration. "Jim Turner, and for my money he was the best pitching coach any team ever had, spent all the years in the minor leagues and then pitched in the World Series and was sent back down. To do that you have got to be stupid, crazy, or can't do anything else or just love baseball. You know Turner could run a milk business because he did, that's where he got the name, *Jim Milkman Turner*, so you have to bet on love of baseball. Same thing with Woodling. He was sent down. Think about it. You run a business and they tell you you are not good enough and you tend to believe them. Not true with some of those guys.

"Funny thing about my arrival in Yankee Stadium, instead of coming up and watching and waiting for a year, I began playing right away, but always with a bunch of other guys. During many of my years with the Yankees, ten in all, Casey Stengel had names like Tommy Henrich, George McQuinn, Johnny Mize, Bill Skowron, Eddie Robinson, and Harry Simpson to write down under first base. I had as much trouble keeping my job as I did getting it.

"I wouldn't change my years with the Yankees for a bigger role with another team though. My wife felt the same way; we were part of the best. They sold me to the Phillies and I could have reported without even moving my home, but I was a Yankee and that's the way I wanted to end it. When I took off that uniform for the last time, it was not to put on another. Don't get me wrong. I wanted to get paid and would fight with the front office to get more money, but I wanted my checks to say: New York Yankees, American League."

THE HALL OF
FAME

Holy Cow. Over thirty years after he became eligible, the Scooter's long winter of waiting was over. His years of being passed over came to an end when the 1994 votes were counted. Philip Francis Rizzuto received the requisite seventy-five percent and would finally enter baseball's Hall of Fame.

July 31, 1994, was the date. 2:30 P.M., the time.

The place, a stage erected for the occasion on the back side of the Alfred Coring Clark Gymnasium, less than a mile from the Hall of Fame, in Cooperstown, New York, where later the plaque presented to Rizzuto would be bolted to a wall.

The story of Phil Rizzuto, the thirty-eighth Yankee elected to baseball's Hall of Fame (Babe Ruth was the first), rekindled speculation that too many players in Yankee pinstripes had become Hall of Famers, making the inclusion of any others that much more of a long shot. Riding a teammate's coattails might work in the world of politics, but not in the world of baseball: Rizzuto's election reduced the morning line on Allie Reynolds.

The good news of Rizzuto's inclusion reached the seventy-seven-year-old, onetime American League MVP, two-time grandfather by phone. Yogi Berra, a Hall member since 1971, and the twenty-fifth Yankee to be so honored, placed the call. "Phil," he said, "you made it."

"Did Yogi call collect?"

No, baseball paid for the call. Orlando, Florida, where the eighteen-man committee held the meeting, to Hillside, New Jersey, where one man moved around his lovely Tudor home, trying not to watch the phone.

"Yogi knew it was paid when they asked him to make it," Rizzuto said. "My number's been in his phone book so long it still has letters, like Butterfield 8, or Susquehanna 5000. Yogi's number used to be Pilgrim 8." Rizzuto picked up on the first ring. "Yogi knew I would be home."

Detractors whined that the new voters—Berra and Bill White, Rizzuto's announcing buddy, along with Pee Wee Reese—stacked the voting deck. Even Rizzuto told friends, "It meant a lot to me when, in 1984, Pee Wee made the Hall of Fame and said, 'If I am here, Phil should be here.' Now, with Pee Wee, Bill White, and Yogi all voting, I am kind of sorry Pee Wee said it. It puts both of us in an uncomfortable spot." Uncomfortable for the moment, but never awkward. Anyone fortunate enough to see the two men play (Pee Wee was four inches taller and ten pounds heavier than the Scooter), when they dominated their positions in the forties and fifties, would not find the word *awkward* creeping into a description of the two New York City shortfielders.

"People writing and saying the deck was stacked made a tough job harder. Not so tough Phil didn't make it," said Berra.

Selling Rizzuto short was the conventional wisdom when the five-foot-six, Brooklyn-born 150-pound infielder tried out for the hometown Dodgers, managed by Casey Stengel. Bill Terry of the New York Giants also passed on Rizzuto, but without jabs like Stengel's: "Get a shoeshine box, kid."

Rizzuto was short. Rizzuto was not small. The loose-fitting uniforms of the day hid the little shortstop's upper body package.

Viewed from the back, a shirtless Rizzuto would win a Mr. Body contest in a three-man field including Billy Martin and Eddie Stanky. Short legs, large torso, huge heart. Jerry Coleman, a six-foot-tall ex-Marine and former Yankee second baseman, said of Rizzuto, "We wore the same-size shirt. I remember it surprised Pete Sheehy." (Sheehy was a longtime Yank clubhouse doyen. The clubhouse is named in his honor.) "What stays with me when I think back on Rizzuto is his courage. He was fearless when he was the inside man on the double play. Some of those big donkeys, as Casey called them, might have killed Phil. They never got to him. More important, they never got to his mind. Yet put a fishing worm or a mouse into his glove (if we were ahead by nine runs and wanted to have a little fun) and Phil would act like his life was in danger." Rizzuto was in harm's way on the field. Three times during his thirteen years in the big leagues he was carried off the field on a stretcher—on one occasion while his mother watched from her usual seat in the stands.

The 1941 Yankees included Joe DiMaggio, who hit in fifty-six straight games during Scooter's rookie year. Joe knew that Rizzuto was special. It took a special man to replace Frank Crosetti, Rizzuto's popular predecessor. A onetime San Francisco Seal, Crosetti had been a fixture at short for ten years. Cro, at age eighty-four, sitting in the kitchen of his home in Stockton, California, looked back clearly and without any hint of rancor.

"I had my day and I was happy to stay on the team," he said. "I was not replaced by some Humpty-Dumpty. The only regret I have as far as the Yankees are concerned is that I quit in 1964 after cashing twenty-three World Series checks." The 1941 Yankees were still reeling from the loss of their first baseman, Lou Gehrig— the Iron Horse died in June. The Yanks started the 1941 season with Johnny Strum at first, Joe Gordon at second, Rizzuto at short, and Red Rolfe at third. Bill Dickey caught, and DiMaggio, Tommy Henrich, and Charley Keller were the pickets, as the outfielders were sometimes referred to in those days. Red Ruffing, Lefty

Gomez, Spud Chandler, Marius Russo, and Tiny Bonham shared the mound. Fireman Johnny Murphy, a Fordham grad who later served as president of the New York Mets, was the bullpen ace.

Five of the other shortfielders in the Hall of Fame played over 2,000 major-league games, which put Rizzuto's 1,661 games on the light side. Not only did World War II reduce the number of years Rizzuto played for the Yankees, but it also knocked out three of his best years. Rizzuto, however, is not one for regrets.

"I didn't volunteer, but I was proud to serve my country. I played thirteen years. More than a lot of others. All of them with one team, the Yankees," he said with conviction.

If the Baseball Hall of Fame is for winners, Rizzuto's inclusion is overdue. The day after the election, fellow member Bobby Doerr wrote, "Welcome, Scooter, you should have been here years ago." In Scooter's twelve full seasons, before and after World War II, his team won seven World Series and nine American League pennants. Joe DiMaggio, hailed as the best living player, credits Philip Francis as the best shortstop of his time.

The American League voted him MVP in 1950. Some feel Phil should have been named MVP in 1949, but Ted Williams received the honor as the leader of the pennant-bound Red Sox. MVP votes are cast prior to the end of the season. When the Yankees, with Rizzuto at shortstop, beat the Sox two straight to end the 1949 season, the voting had already been completed.

"Had I known the Yanks were going to win, I would have voted for Phil," reported Ed Rumill. The late writer covered the Sox for the *Christian Science Monitor* for over forty years. "I was not alone," Rumill commented, "and I was not alone in hating the Yankees. Many writers—and, after all, they are the ones casting the MVP ballots—hated the Yankees. Writers are much like the general population: When it came to affairs of the heart, the Yankees were hard to like. Love and cherish like the Brooklyn Dodgers or today's Cubs? Not on your tin-type. DiMaggio, Berra, and Rizzuto were hard to dislike, but reaction to Yankee mystique or Yankee arrogance cast a long shadow."

Rizzuto's MVP in the American League in 1950 stands out as one of the few awarded for a glove. Using a cast-off Johnny Mize bat, Rizzuto hit .324 and drove in 66 runs in 1950, but even his most ardent supporters would not confuse Scooter with Slugger. Zoilo Versalles of the Twins and Nelson Fox of the White Sox are two others who earned MVPs largely based on defense. The year Brooks Robinson won the award, 1964, he hit 28 home runs and drove in 118 runners as contrasted with 1950, when Rizzuto hit 7 out to accompany his 66 RBIs. Over his thirteen-year tenure, Rizzuto's contributions to Yankee victories may not have been reflected in box scores, but were understood and endorsed by both writers and players.

Important to the inclusion of Rizzuto and Reese in the Hall of Fame, and significant to poll watchers—the election of both men was accomplished by the Veterans Committee, which was established to rectify the judgments rendered by the writers.

While others worked behind-the-scenes, shilling for his election, Rizzuto did not join in, nor did he approve of the well-intended efforts. When he learned of some drum beating, Phil expressed with chagrin, "If I get in, great. And if I don't, that's OK too. Cooperstown is the place to be if you played, that is for sure, but if I had to take the Hall of Fame and give up the grand things Ted Williams and Joe D said about me, I would take the words of the Yankee Clipper and the Splendid Splinter. As great as those two players were—and they were two of the best ever—well, to have them think I was good . . . What more can you wish for?"

As noted Casey Stengel sent Rizzuto packing when he tried out for the Dodgers. Casey had no trouble with words. His way with words even had a name: Stengelese.

His problem with words was the problem most have. Eating them.

Rizzuto's star didn't shed light on Stengel's rugged features, so it must have been a chore for the old man to describe a play by the Scooter as the "best I ever saw." Don Larsen's perfect game,

Willy's catch off Vic Wert's bat, and both of Allie Reynolds's no-hitters in 1951 were imprinted in Stengel's mind. The squeeze bunt Rizzuto and DiMaggio pulled on Bob Lemon stands behind velvet ropes. The year was 1951.

The Yankees and Cleveland were fighting for the pennant. Score tied, last of the ninth, Joe on third. Rizzuto at bat. Rizzuto took a pitch, and stepped out and gave the sign, running his left hand over the end of the bat. The end of the bat was a lightbulb and the hand served as a semaphore. Rizzuto to DiMaggio, the Clipper cleared for landing. Bob Lemon, the Cleveland pitcher, and later one of the spate of managers to replace and be replaced by Billy Martin, knew that Rizzuto, DiMaggio, and Stengel were cooking some noxious brew. But only the center fielder standing on third and the little shortstop were the straws stirring the drink. Rizzuto called the play without an earphone from the bench. Joe broke for home when Lemon threw a perfect pitch, which flew well behind Rizzuto's head. Scooter, looking more like Harry Houdini extricating his upper body from a straitjacket than a baseball player, dropped a perfect bunt and Joe was safe by a schoolyard mile. Print media from Boston to Washington, D.C., mentioned the feat when writing of Rizzuto's July 31, 1994, induction into the Hall of Fame. The play was older than some of the folks writing about it, and the main source quoted, Stengel, died in 1975. At the time of the feat, Bob Lemon was so angered that he threw his glove into the net behind the backstop. "I threw a ball you can't bunt and he did," Lemon commented.

Several thousand people were close enough when Rizzuto gave his acceptance speech to see his physical size. On seeing him at close range, most people exclaim about Rizzuto's size, even those old enough to remember seeing him play. His size and the size of other players may explain what is considered by many to be the essence of baseball. It is a game of feet and inches—60 and 6 for the pitcher and catcher and 90 for the base runner. Those numbers seemingly set in stone still leave room for a skyscraper like Randy Johnson or a little guy who looks like the best he might do is to shoot a good game of pool every so often, or perhaps bowl a decent line or two.

A writer trying to listen in on a conversation between the late Don Drysdale and Yogi Berra, commented to several other writers trying to do the same, "Pick a game, any game, make one up if you wish. The big guy wins." Later on, the big guy said, "Sure I won and struck him out . . . once." Baseball gives everyone a chance. Even one who a Hall of Fame manager by the name of Charles Dillion Stengel thought should shine shoes. Rizzuto made the most of his chance, and it took him all the way to Cooperstown.

Rizzuto's thirty-eight-minute Hall of Fame acceptance speech was hailed by Ralph Kiner as "the best. I don't recall anyone ever giving a better one in Cooperstown." Yogi Berra held a different view. "That was no speech," commented Berra. Kiner and Berra were both right. Anyone who watched the speech, including the mock departure of Berra and Johnny Bench while Rizzuto moved from mid-rant to the touching ending—complete with a wave to his wife, Cora—will never forget the love directed Rizzuto's way. The emotion that gripped Rizzuto was equally real.

The Hall of Fame golf outing early the day of the induction was marred by the early departure of the 78-year-old "Rookie," Rizzuto. "I need to sit down and be quiet for a bit," Rizzuto told his foursome after playing a few holes. The links were buzzing with what economists call imperfect information. "Rizzuto's taken ill. Heart attack? Nerves?"

"Just a little time, a spot of quiet, that's all I need," said Rizzuto softly.

The Scooter had been quiet long enough. It was time to return the love and affection to the ten thousand people gathered in what had once been a cornfield.

The response from the *New York Post* was a four-inch headline reading: SCOOTER MAKES SUN SHINE IN COOPERSTOWN. And the *New York Times* observed: "Rambling yes it was and everyone understood . . . and laughed between tears or cried between laughter or just stood and cheered. Baseball was never better."

One writer received disturbing news upon calling his office an hour before Rizzuto's speech. "But the instant Phil began to talk, I forgot about the phone call. It was like I was on skis coming down a long trail. The bad news was lost until Rizzuto left the stage, and then, with all the good feeling I had, the news didn't seem so bad after all. To know that this little guy played great shortstop, waited all those years, and was able to hold this crowd in the palm of his tiny hand. It was a benchmark speech by a guy not used to sitting on a bench."

Larry Berra, Jr., Yogi's oldest son and Rizzuto's godson, walked away from the love feast in the cornfield with family and friends. Larry, a serious student of the Civil War and a voracious reader on all manner of disparate topics, leaned down to hear a friend comment, "Larry, I could live to be two hundred years old and never feel the love and affection heaped on your Godfather just now."

"Add a few zeroes to your age, and then add this: You, me and millions and billions of others." When Thoreau said, "Most men live lives of quiet desperation," he didn't have Philip Francis Rizzuto in mind.

Later in the month, on August 9, the Yankees celebrated another day with Rizzuto at Yankee Stadium. Ever thoughtful, Rizzuto counseled friends who had made the trek to Cooperstown to skip the "Day" at the Stadium. "Phil Rizzuto Day" was moved up several days to miss the baseball strike—but the game still drew 50,070. Yankee pitcher Jim Abbott lost to Baltimore, but, after the game, he spoke not of the loss but of the night belonging to Rizzuto. Rizzuto was moved to speak with candor to his friends. "I told you not to come, but I was wrong. Tonight was even more emotion-packed than Cooperstown. This is where I spent the thirteen years that made Cooperstown happen. Holy Cow! This is where I spent much of my life."

Don Mattingly's been a Yankee since 1983. Wade Boggs became a Yankee in 1993. It's a good bet that together the two infielders made more dollars in 1994 than Rizzuto made in all the fifty-plus years working in the Bronx. Given that possibility, it is noteworthy that both men asked Nick Priori, the man in charge of the Yankee clubhouse, "Any chance you can get Phil to sign a few things for me?"

The next day while the Yankees played the last game of the 1994 season, Phil Rizzuto slipped into the clubhouse and signed a few things for Boggs and Mattingly. He didn't have to make the drive from Hillside in northern New Jersey, but it seemed like the right thing to do. Two millionaires asked for the favor, and it might be a long winter.

Thomas M. Horton
Sun Lakes, AZ
November 1994

THE NEW YORK YANKEES—THEN AND NOW

So far this book has featured twelve Yankees center stage. As one of them, Dr. Berra might say, "It started way before any of us. It wasn't over when Babe left or Lou Gehrig died. Joe D retired and Mickey stepped up. Now both of them are gone. Winning 125 games in 1998 is not the end. The Yankees may never be over."

The 1998 baseball season seemed to issue directly from central casting. A line drive into the hands of Steven Spielberg. Mark McGwire and Sammy Sosa developed more interest in baseball than anyone since Babe Ruth. The 1998 Yankees won a record-setting 125 games and swept the San Diego Padres in four games.

Frank Crosetti watched the Yankees and Padres on TV while the second baseman he coached, Jerry Coleman, the voice of the Padres for twenty-five years, saw the games from his old perch in the Yankee press box and his current one in Jack Murphy Stadium.

No one in baseball history saw more Yankees rise, shine, and fade than Frank Crosetti. He played in 1,682 Yankee games, putting him tenth on the all-time Yankee list. He played more games than Rizzuto at shortstop on teams with Ruth, Gehrig, and DiMaggio. Then he coached another twenty, spending in all thirty-seven years

251

in pinstripes. He shook hands with Mickey Mantle when he hit home run number 500 and Maris when he hit 61 in 1961. It would be the only times the low-key coach would do so. "Today the hitter moves a runner, makes an out, and gets high fives from half the dugout."

In 1932, after three years playing infield positions for the San Francisco Seals, twenty-one-year-old Frank Crosetti was sold to the Yankees. After spring training in St. Petersburg, days before the Yankees headed north by train to open the season, Manager Joe McCarthy told coach Art Fletcher the five-foot-ten-inch Crosetti was on the Yankee roster and would start the season at shortstop.

Yankee Stadium was nine years old. The House that Ruth Built would become the most famous venue in the history of sports. On September 28, after the Yanks finished first in the eight-team league, Frank played in the first World Series he ever saw. Crosetti was the youngest man to play in what he then called the Fall Classics. The rookie made four errors.

"They didn't cost a game. We beat the Cubs four straight, but they sure bothered me. Sometimes the harder you try the worse you play."

When California native Crosetti joined the Yankees in St. Petersburg, Florida, it was his first trip east of the state line. Crosetti, the 165-pound lead-off-hitting shortstop along with Lou Gehrig at first, Tony Lazzeri at second, both twenty-nine, and thirty-four-year-old Joe Sewell at third made up the infield. Babe Ruth, Earl Combs, and Ben Chapman were the outfielders.

"Babe was thirty-seven and fading as a player. At least some people, even some players thought," Crosetti observed. "But he hit 41 home runs and drove in 137 runs. And was so popular he never was able to eat in the hotel restaurants with the rest of us. Some fade. The fans worshiped him and he loved the attention."

Bill Dickey caught the balanced pitching staff of right-handed Red Ruffing, Lefty Gomez, left-throwing Herb Pennock, and right-handed George Pipgras. Many of Frank's teammates carried colorful nicknames. Crosetti played without a nickname until Casey Stengel dubbed him Cro in 1949, but he played with Gehrig "The Iron Horse," Lazzeri "Poosh 'Em Up Tony," Combs "The Gray Eagle," Gomez "The Gay Castillion," Babe Ruth "The Sultan of Swat," Dickey "The Arkansas Traveler," and Pennock "The Knight of Kennett Square."

All of them, even the Sultan and the Knight, were assessed a standard uniform allowance.

"I never knew if other teams in the American League did the same. In those days you didn't talk to players on other teams. I know the Yankees charged us. Ed Barrow, the General Manager, probably thought it was a good idea, and Field Manager Joe Mc-Carthy went along with his boss."

Crosetti seldom met Barrow and spoke to McCarthy only when Joe spoke first.

"The first home game of the season they put a voucher in our locker. We signed it and they took thirty dollars out of our pay-checks and then the thirty dollars was added to our last check, at the end of the season. I do not remember anyone complaining. Nor do I recall anyone paying for damage like you might for a rented tux or rental car. Come to think of it, in 1932 I don't think you could rent a car or a tux, so maybe the analogy doesn't fit. The 100 percent wool uniform didn't fit either, but I know they charged us—that is for sure. The thirty dollars did not seem a big deal at the time, and makes these pages because most modern players don't believe it happened. They may not believe grown men were selling apples on street corners in 1932, but they were. Look in your history books. Most of us were just happy to have a job. Playing base-ball for a living was a bird's nest on the ground. I wanted to play baseball for a living when I was in third grade. Before I knew what a living was.

"Most people, even baseball people, are amazed to learn the only three players on my first Yankee team not elected to the Hall of Fame were Ben Chapman, George Pipgras, and Frank Peter Joseph Crosetti."

By the time Joe DiMaggio, Mickey Mantle, Whitey Ford, Yogi Berra, and Phil Rizzuto came along the uniform assessment was long gone.

"With the Yankees some things changed and the thirty-dollar charge only lasted a few years, but one thing stayed. Stuck like a tattoo. Maybe tattoo is not the best choice of words. I never saw a Yankee player with one. When a player entered the clubhouse and found his name over a locker he knew this was a place he wanted to stay. To stay as long as he could.

"Enos Slaughter was forty-three when the Yankees released him in 1959. Enos played over 2,300 games in the big leagues, mostly for the Cardinals. Only a handful wearing a Yankee uniform. When he was released by the team and told by the clubhouse man, it was Pete Previtt I think, Slaughter buried his face in his hands and took off his pinstripes choking back tears. Even some guys on the team, not fans of Slaughter and happy to see him go, had to look away. Enos looked out for himself and signed with the Milwaukee Braves and played in eleven more games that season with Tommy Hawks on his chest. Even Joe D., seldom one to show emotion, knew putting on pinstripes was special. When he died the papers had pictures of Joe putting on his first Yankee uniform. I know he was proud. I never knew anyone so blasé they were not thrilled to be in the clubhouse pulling on Yankee flannels.

"Joe was alone in a group. Even confined in a car with Tony Lazerri and me for eight or nine days driving from San Francisco to Florida for spring training, Joe kept to himself. It was like he didn't want to waste his energy. I miss those drives across the country. Every mile on a two-lane highway. Some of the sunrises and sunsets are still in my mind. Joe was probably thinking what to do with a 3 and 1 fastball from Bobby Feller."

When Joe died *Time* columnist Roger Rosenblat wrote, "Hank Greenberg said if Joe said hello, it was a long conversation, and he wasn't especially lovable, either. He was better than that; he was admirable." Crosetti, like anyone on any team, is proud he played on the same field with Joe and Frank, and was one of a very few to call Joe "Roomy," the term used at the time for a roommate. Today's players have single rooms. Some have suites written as a clause into their contract.

After almost forty years with the Yankees as a player and coach Crosetti has only one regret. "Leaving before they asked me to step down. At age eighty-six I am over it now but I was foolish to walk away from the Yankees for several thousand dollars. Coaching third base for the Seattle Pilots was a long way from the big leagues.

"I thought Ruth was the best, Joe DiMaggio the most graceful, Mantle the most gifted, and Joe McCarthy the greatest manager, and all the while they paid me. On top of regular checks I received twenty-three World Series paychecks. Only Yogi with twenty-one WS checks is close, and he will never catch me. When Yogi won the pennant in '64 and took the World Series to seven games they fired him. I left on my own. I must have been nuts."

Crosetti played with more Hall of Fame members than anyone in the history of baseball, and along the way he was injected with the clubhouse serum, "What you see and hear here stays here." Given an ingrained reluctance to bunt and tell, Crosetti's observations of the fabled Yankee dynasties are always credible.

"Mantle came up in 1951, DiMaggio's last year. Mickey was a shy kid and you had to like him. He had two bad breaks along with his ton of talent. He replaced Joe and endured boos until he and Maris hooked up in the home run derby in 1961 and he played for Stengel. McCarthy did not match Casey Stengel when it came to color. Casey had every hue in the rainbow. His number 37 is still remembered today. McCarthy didn't even wear one.

"But Joe had your number, and the first time Mickey threw his helmet, smashed a water cooler, or came in hungover, Joe McCarthy would have taken Mickey into his office and closed the door. Jim Turner, the Yanks' pitching coach, liked to quote McCarthy: 'One bad apple will in time rot the whole barrel.' Anyone knowing Marse Joe knew he would have been tougher on Mickey than Stengel was."

Cro's fifty years in baseball also commands respect. "Who's to say? Who's to say? I think Mickey would have been a better player for Joe than Casey. On the other hand he did play eighteen years in 2,401 games. More than any other Yankee in history. You can bet Joe D's 56-game streak will be broken before someone breaks Mantle's 2,401 games as a Yankee record.''

Frankie, the name he broke in with and the one he still prefers, saw so many great hitters, from Jimmy Foxx to Nellie Fox, he is wary about pointing out the best hitter he ever saw. "I just know one thing for sure—after hitting 98 home runs in seventeen years it wasn't me.''

Pitching is another matter. "If I had to name a pitcher to win one game I would choose Whitey Ford. He was smart, had the guts of a burglar and more pitches than Yogi had fingers. He was also a fair hitter. His record did not show it, but he could hit.

"In 1936 the Yankees played the New York Giants in the Polo Grounds. Carl Hubbell lost the first game to Red Ruffing. Early in the game I faced the left-hander and Hubbell threw me two balls. Carl had a Hall of Fame screwball and I was sure he would throw me one on the next pitch and I would take it. When he crossed me up and threw a fastball right down the pipe, our third-base coach, Art Fletcher, went nuts.

"He jumped out of the third base box and even some people in the stands could tell he was getting on me. Letting me know I was a fool not to swing at that pitch. We won the game and that was all I could recall except fast-forward to this.

"Years later, I was the third-base coach in the '52 World Series. Whitey Ford was hitting. He took at least two pitches I knew were hittable. I yelled at Whitey (he said I cackled) and he stepped out of the batter's box and looked at me, and mouthed, 'What the hell do you know about hitting?'

"It didn't dawn on me at the time, but the replay of a hitter and a third-base coach with me playing both roles is a memory for the treasure chest. I hit one home run in a World Series. It was off Dizzy Dean. In the 1938 Series with Chicago. I know it happened—it is in the record book. But it doesn't play as well as the irony of an old guy on in the third-base box bugging some kid half his age. So I guess when they say you never forget the little things they are right.

"Coaching from the lines or from the bench has its problems, or so it seems to me. If the manager is calling pitches, how will the pitcher and catcher ever learn how to do so? The same is true of stacking your hitters for right-handed pitchers or left-handed pitchers. How do you learn to hit one or the other if you only see one kind? One time, early in Yogi's storybook career, I happened to be in Stengel's office when he was making out the lineup. Casey was sitting, Yogi was down because of the pitcher. I said, 'Why don't you let him play—I think he can handle this guy.' No one had computers at the time and I was really saying what I believed. You should learn to hit right-handers and southpaws. Casey took my advice and Yogi won the game. Yogi didn't need my help, he was a born hitter, but I like to think the boost that one day helped a little."

Tony Kubek, Yankee shortstop and broadcaster, feels once the game starts, a good third-base coach is as important as the manager. Sending a runner from third or holding him is the key to winning or losing. Kubek, now retired in Wisconsin, would like to see Cro in the Hall of Fame. "He was the best I ever saw. Most coaches last as long as the manager. Cro outlasted the manager."

Dave Anderson, the Pulitzer Prize–winning *New York Times* columnist, described Crosetti's ability to endure by saying, "When the Yankees hire you to manage and you know you already have the best third-base coach in the game, why look further?"

Crosetti, when told of the comments of Kubek and Anderson, reverts to his usual self-effacing "Who's to say? Who's to say? It depends. I know this much—Mickey Mantle had baseball instincts and confidence in his deerlike speed so he knew when he could score or hold up at third as soon as he came around second base. He knew before I did and it was my job to know."

Frank is asked if others on the team knew. "If they did, they didn't know from me," he said with a laugh, "It was not in my best interest to tell all my secrets."

The 1927 Yankees are often called the best baseball team ever. The 1998 record-setters (125 game winners), not yet fabled, are respected by former Yankees. Since 1904, 1,224 men appeared in at least one game for the New Yorkers. Bet the farm every one still living is proud of the association, and symbolically doffs a royal blue hat to the 1998 team.

Bobby Brown, M.D., the American League President for eleven years and a surviving member of the October Twelve, speaks for many. "The men playing before our time in New York were good and so were we."

Looking back has drawbacks. It is instructive to listen to some of the men featured in this book speculate on how the October Twelve might match up with the 1998 team.

We played a different game for different numbers. Huge dollars sullied a lot of games. Football, basketball. Baseball was not immune.

Today's players are spoiled by the money, and if we had been paid those sums the same thing would have happened to us. Human nature is not like the strike zone and the height of the mound. It does not change. Huge windfall dollars do as much harm to many as poverty. I understand the economics of today's game, but I don't understand how smart owners can mess up a great game. Baseball at one time had grace and character.

Maybe Mickey Mantle was right when he said, "When I played we [the players] were stupid. Now the owners are."

"Thinking we would win a series if we played the 1998 Yankees is easy if we are the ones doing the thinking," said several erstwhile Yankees.

Retired surgeons never lose a patient. The minister pensioned off recalls his church full of souls waiting to be saved, most sitting quietly in their pew, giving him their rapt attention. Similarly, Bauer, Berra, Woodling, Silvera, and the rest remember frozen ropes to the gap and runners nipped at second. Two-out singles starting a rally that won the game. Moving the runner with two out. Always hitting the cutoff man.

The late Allie Reynolds would have his own golden memory, knowing that Ted Williams, as a member of the Hall of Fame Veterans committee, expressed one regret, "That I didn't push harder to vote Allie in."

Even in the dim light of advancing years reasonable people must pause to consider that comparing different teams playing different games is at best foolhardy, at worst dangerous. We played with at least two kinds of fear. Since no one wore batting helmets the unspoken fear was serious injury. Rizzuto was one of the few players in the league who felt no fear. "None of the pitchers in the league could hit me unless I wanted them to," Scooter says matter-of-factly. "Stengel used to offer a fifty-dollar bonus to anyone getting hit with the bases loaded if it meant we won the game."

Fear of injury made us different the same way a five-year, million-dollar contract makes you different. Even some modern ballplayers admit that the year after they sign a multiyear contract they let down. There is no question they play more and harder the last year of a long-term contact. The Yankees team running the table five years in a row had varying dollar amounts on the contracts. The dollars varied, but the terms—one year—were constant. The Yankees and the rest of baseball used job insecurity to motivate. At least one Yankee, catcher Berra, turned down several two-year Yankee contract offers. Yogi's flawless instincts in baseball proved just as sound when applied to the heading motivation.

Might the October Twelve have been in the habit of playing harder? Do no-cut, no-trade contracts result in diminished effort?

If the name of the game is pitching, few argue that pitchers Reynolds, Raschi, Lopat, and Whitey Ford made up a foursome minted in gold leaf.

The Yankees of '98 swept the San Diego Padres in four straight, using two catchers, Posada and Girardi. Triple MVP winner Berra ('51, '54, and '55) missed one World Series game in the five straight. If Reynolds, Raschi, Lopat, and Ford were gold, Berra, described by Stengel as "my assistant-manager" was fabricated from space-age goods. The little catcher ranks third right after Gehrig in most Yankee games played. Yogi's 2,116 games is the most of any living Yankee. Little wonder Boss George made peace and continued his attempts to bring the beloved Berra back to Yankee Stadium.

On the other hand, in 1949, the Yankees won on the last day of the season. The next year, it was the last weekend. We never clinched in May. The '98 team seemed like it was over before the season started. The real question in 1998 was not winning but by how many games. We won the flag five times and then the World Series but were never comfortable. Look back on our sweep of the Phillies. That was no cakewalk.

How do you beat the five-man outfield of Woodling, DiMaggio, Bauer, Cliff Mapes, and John Lindell? Ask the departed Yankee historian David Wells whether those five would back him up better than Chad Curtis, Tim Raines, Shane Spence, Paul O'Neill, and Bernie Williams.

Phil Rizzuto was not only fearless at the plate, he also remains sure enough of himself to give Derek Jeter the crown for Best Ever Yankee Shortstop. As the only Yankee short fielder in the Hall of Fame, Phil's judgment is humble and the evaluation final.

Fueling controversy, baseball observers point to the 190 double plays routinely turned in by Rizzuto and Coleman, numbers not seen today by teams with winning records. Jerry Coleman reacts to the observation "They ran slower in those days" with characteristic humor. Chuck Knoblauch, the Yankee second baseman in 1998, batted .265, the lowest average in his eight-year career. If he bounces back to his lifetime .299 the choice might be best made with a coin toss. Coleman, World Series MVP in 1950, would be pleased to see the coin in the air and the results. The classy 1949 Rookie of the Year flew 120 combat missions in World War II and Korea. Jerry has two Distinguished Flying Crosses and thirteen Air Medals and suggests: "We had a great team and winning the league five times will be hard to do. I cannot think with the playoff system they have today anyone will win the World Series five times in a row. But anyone spending too much time trying to figure out if our team could beat your team should think about finding a hobby."

The third base position shines the light on the 125-game winners. Scott Davis Brosius drove in 98 runs, hitting .300 with 19 home runs. Bobby Brown and Billy Johnson had good years (among players with 40 or more World Series at-bats, Dr. Brown's .439 average ranks first all-time) but Brosius, Hillsboro, Oregon's gift to the Bronx, caught the brass ring in 1998.

Neither Brosius nor any American League hitter had to contend with the high strike. The strike zone, like the dollar, grew smaller over the years. Mostly it came down. Reynolds and other power pitchers knew a pitch just under the armpits would be called a strike. They started a hitter off with a fastball four inches above the belt. Strike one. Then they took the hitter up the ladder. Pitch by pitch, inch by inch, pitchers like Reynolds or Raschi could strike out a man on pitches that umpires today would call balls.

Tino Martinez played first base for the 1998 Yankees. He is a fine team player, drove in 123 runs, hit 28 home runs and batted 281.

Johnny Mize and Joe Collins together gave the October Twelve a lock on that position. Mize, another Hall of Fame member, was one of the best and smartest hitters in baseball. Playing for the New York Giants before coming to the Yanks, Big Jawn hit 51 home runs. The next year he hit 40. In fifteen years in the majors he hit 359. By the time he came over the Harlem River and joined the Yankees, he was not able to field his position as he had in his younger days, but he could hit and did. Then with a comfortable lead, Stengel would bring in Joe Collins. Joe had better range than Johnny, and Collins, during his ten years with the Yankees, hit 86 home runs.

Mize and Collins gave Stengel some buttons to push. Casey pushed his buttons like they were on a keyboard, without giving thought to the feelings of the player removed. "If he hates me for taking him out he might play harder to show me up when I put him back in the lineup," would best describe Stengel's thought process. Joe McCarthy wanted to be popular; Casey didn't care as long as he won. That's why he did win in 1949, the start of the Yankee Streak. Joe lost. Stengel won.

About the only thing Casey didn't like was being called a push-button manager. He was, but he was a whole lot more. So were the New York Yankees. They were the toast of the town, but they were one of the last teams to break their own color line. Like much of the nation the team owners found ways to rationalize. Would the black player fit in? Would white fans come to see them? Jackie Robinson changed the world of baseball. A white man, Branch Rickey, for whatever reason, made it possible. Robinson's ability to maintain composure in the storm that followed was truly remarkable.

Less heroic but noteworthy: In March of 1999 the death of Joe DiMaggio rocked his teammates. Joe was that important to those who knew him in the clubhouse—knew him for his enormous gifts and fierce pride.

The importance of DiMaggio is best understood by his teammates; in their golden years, they are proud to look back on their glory years. But listen to how they respond to the question "How long did you play for the Yankees?" Routinely the number of years on the team receive an asterisk: "Nine years, four of them with DiMaggio."

INDEX